Beyond Pleasure

Beyond Pleasure

Cultures of Modern Asceticism

Edited by
Evert Peeters, Leen Van Molle and Kaat Wils

Berghahn Books

New York • Oxford

First published in 2011 by
Berghahn Books
www.berghahnbooks.com

© 2011 Evert Peeters, Leen Van Molle and Kaat Wils

Library of Congress Cataloging-in-Publication Data

Beyond pleasure : cultures of modern asceticism / edited by Evert Peeters,
Leen Van Molle and Kaat Wils.
    p. cm.
  Includes bibliographical references and index.
  ISBN 978-1-84545-773-0 (hardback : alk. paper)
    -- ISBN 978-1-84545-987-1 (ebook)
  1. Asceticism--History. 2. Civilization, Modern. I. Peeters, Evert.
II. Molle, Leen van. III. Wils, Kaat.
  BJ1491.B49 2011
  909.8--dc22

                                        2011000951

British Library Cataloguing in Publication Data
A catalogue record for this book is available from the British Library

Printed in the United States on acid-free paper

ISBN 978-1-84545-773-0 HB
E-ISBN 978-1-84545-987-1

Contents

Part IV: The Lonely Passions of Science

Part V: Discipline in the Age of Affluence

List of Illustrations

Figures on Part pages I–V:
Wilhelm Prager (director) and Nicholas Kaufmann (scriptwriter),
'Wege zu Kraft und Schönheit' (1924).

Acknowledgements

This volume is the outcome of the work of a group of historians involved in the 'Cultural Criticism 1750–2000' Scientific Research Community and engaged in the research projects 'Lebensreform in Belgium 1890–1940' and 'Dwelling Culture in Flanders 1920–1970', all financed by the Research Foundation Flanders. Their reflections regarding the concept of 'modern asceticism' were fleshed out by additional input at the international colloquium in Leuven in October 2005, during which participants further explored the concept and brought it into sharper focus from many different angles. We are particularly grateful to all participants for their contributions and to the research community headed by Hugo Soly for its financial support. Several conference papers also gave rise to articles for this volume. The further development of the volume in terms of concept and content benefited greatly from discussions with Sofie De Caigny, Jo Tollebeek and Geert Vanpaemel. Also of great importance were the many different forms of help received from Hans Cools, Herman De Dijn, Greet Draye, Andreas Stynen, Jens van de Maele and Staf Vos. We would like to express our gratitude to all those involved in the process of creating, producing and finishing this book.

Modern Asceticism:
A Historical Exploration

Evert Peeters, Leen Van Molle and Kaat Wils

Modern civilisation, the famous German film director Wilhelm Prager believed, posed a threat to the physical and mental condition of the German nation. In their hugely popular film *Wege zu Kraft und Schönheit/Ways to Strength and Beauty* (1924), Prager and his script writer, the physician Nicholas Kaufmann, confronted their viewers with a bleak assessment of the state of health of their fellow citizens. The film showed corpulent, bourgeois, chain-smoking youngsters, sickly gymnasium pupils and light-shunning, myopic scholars. The images added up to a diagnosis. Modern Europe, Prager was instructing his public, sat huddled over lifeless ideas. *Wege zu Kraft und Schönheit* showed the European bourgeoisie gaping at the glories of classical antiquity in museums, while in real life the classical ideals of balance and harmony seemed to have been completely lost. In Prager's view, the bourgeoisie paid lip-service to the principle of *mens sana in corpore sano* (a healthy mind in a healthy body), but failed to practise it. Alienated from healthy and 'natural' ways of living, people had wandered astray into book learning and harmful habits. Prager's social critique proved popular, bringing him the biggest success of his career. The strong condemnation, expressed particularly in Catholic circles, of the – often naked – Roman statues and characters appearing in the film merely fanned the flames of popularity and further enhanced the success of Prager's account.

Wege zu Kraft und Schönheit represented more than just an indictment. The film directors also offered a course of therapy. Scene after scene, Prager and Kaufmann demonstrated to their viewers how modern society could get back in touch again with the physical prowess and intellectual peace which

– so the script suggested – had prevailed in antiquity. As their vision of the future, Prager and Kaufmann presented a world of physical and natural beauty. In a Roman bathhouse, they depicted sculpted male bodies, and showed children engaged in martial sports. The film also showed muscular bodies in a contemporary setting. The Roman scenes shifted virtually seamlessly to sequences of modern dancers, runners and champion gymnasts. Physical exercise and dance flowed into one another, such as in the scene in which a female dancer performed the gymnastic exercises of the American gynaecologist Bess Mensendieck before the open, rippling sea. Flowing, rhythmic movements pointed the way to a healthy, full life for German citizens. In the closing scene, the film-makers placed bathing Romans and athletes from the 1920s alongside one another. *Wege zu Kraft und Schönheit* was showing not just an ideal, it was suggested, but also the beginnings of a fundamental change for the better.

In this book, the indictments and promises displayed in *Wege zu Kraft und Schönheit* will be historicised within a broader cultural framework of 'modern asceticism'. Like the makers of *Wege zu Kraft und Schönheit*, proponents of modern asceticism were not just expressing an idealistic dissatisfaction with modernity that was shared at that time by other artists, scientists and politicians. They also seemed to embody this cultural critique in ways which have been insufficiently considered by previous scholars. Strikingly, they combined optimism with a high degree of strictness. In Prager's and Kaufmann's film, this tension revealed itself in various ways. While they used neo-romantic metaphors to illustrate the gap between unspoilt nature and the decadent city, they resorted to scientific diagrams to present the importance of deep chest breathing or correct physical posture. Scene after scene they showed liberated bodies, yet held them captive in a controlled, rhythmical cadence. And although the Christian God was completely absent in *Wege zu Kraft und Schönheit*, Greek temples evoked memories of an organised religiosity. Prager and Kaufmann promised a new freedom, but also employed a discourse of asceticism. Modern emancipation in their view presupposed a high degree of abstinence and control. This tension is the subject of this book.

Even in modernity, we will argue, the complex interplay between freedom and control remains connected to premodern traditions. The use of age-old ascetic forms made *Wege zu Kraft und Schönheit* an emblematic yet confusing film. In Prager and Kaufmann's film, a traditional longing for purity was made to serve modern desires for personal authenticity. In this volume, we will focus on the remarkable ways in which, in the late nineteenth and early twentieth century, premodern ascetic forms came to incorporate modernity. The gendering power of modern asceticism, in the first place, will often take the lead in our analysis. Representations of sobriety and opulence, we will argue, strongly informed the construction of modern masculinity and femininity as they displayed the floating meaning of the self, of authority and submission, of respectability and immorality. In the second place, the making of class was no less informed by the distinctive power of modern asceticism. Sobriety and continence built the bourgeois self-image and propelled working-class opposition against bourgeois hegemony. Thirdly, the rise of modern asceticism also demonstrated the intimate linkage between political and cultural discourses. It contributed as much to the republican rhetoric of the twentieth-century nation-state as it underpinned the quest for artistic purity and scientific truth. In a broader sense, however, the politics of modern asceticism pervaded everyday culture as a whole.

The Polis and the Convent: Gendered Traditions

In a famous essay, Bertrand Russell described asceticism as an 'evil passion', born of the Christian misconception that pleasure can only be found in sensuality, 'and yet, in fact, not only the best pleasures, but also the very worst, are purely mental'.[1] In this way, he expressed the widespread conviction that all asceticism is necessarily centred on mental life, and must therefore be anti-physical; just as it is also directed towards the spiritual and hence should be anti-secular. Asceticism, added Russell, was 'essentially religious'.[2] In parallel, an extensive historical literature links the whole repertoire of ascetic practices with religions and transcendent significance. Asceticism appears inextricably bound up with worship, religious spirituality, piety, contemplation and mysticism, cult prescriptions and monastic rules such as chastity, poverty and obedience.

However, originally the Greek word *askèsis* simply meant 'exercise', primarily the exercising of the body so that it would gain in strength and beauty. Central to the Greek ascetic tradition was not rejection of the body, but in fact the appreciation of it. For example, Socratic philosophy stated that mind and body should be in balance and that both needed maintaining, which in the case of the body involved toughening and abstinence from anything harmful. A life of exercise, abstinence and regularity served the Greek ideal of athletic masculinity. Among modern ascetics, this classical tradition acquired a new lustre. Thinkers such as Nietzsche contended that the Greeks had elevated an ethic of physical control and exercise that differed radically from the Judaeo-Christian form of asceticism, which was hostile to the body. Moreover, this classical asceticism, Nietzsche believed, was only meaningful as an attribute of good citizenship. It could only exist as a republican ideal. For asceticism as physical control was the basic precondition for the polis which, as he commented in *Die Geburt der Tragödie,* 'had to be protected against the elemental life forces'. Only against the background of this control could 'the drama of life play itself out within the citadel, with its civic gods, laws, virtues, sculptures, stories and political philosophies'.[3] Asceticism, so it seemed, was a public affair. Republican discourse was deeply pervaded by its logics.

In the classical polis, this republican asceticism brought along a very masculine imagery. Male citizen-soldiers were supposed to protect the polis against life forces that were defined as feminine. At the games in Olympia, but also in the education at the *Akadèmia*, male citizens performed the reign of asceticism through controlled muscular power. In the army, the same performance was combined with strategies of violence and dominance. In Athens, however, classic asceticism found its highest expression in the democratic ritual of city politics. Here, moderation and virtue were the guarantees of the integrity of elected judges and administrators, but also of the political dedication of the electors themselves. The popular assembly seemed to liberate these citizens, at least for the duration of their deliberations, from their private interests. It was precisely this elevation from the private sphere that further enforced the explicitly masculine character of classical asceticism. The citizen as a political creature rose not just above the concerns of trade and industry, but, more importantly, above the domestic sphere. Greek asceticism as a political condition had no place for women or slaves. In Sparta, the logics of classical asceticism had resulted in military rule instead of democracy, according to a popular reading. Public asceticism took on the form of a military spirit of sacrifice. Not democratic ritual, but military might formed the buffer against Nietzsche's 'elemental life forces'. Even more than in Athens, this militarised asceticism detached the citizen-soldier from the domestic sphere. At the same time, mastery and self-control became an even more central part of the self-image of the polis. Political independence, Herodotos made the Spartan leader Demaratos declare, was impossible without the law. The Spartans' freedom was only possible thanks to the strictest 'control' and 'prudence'. The law was to be feared, and fleeing from battle was regarded as more dishonourable than death. Republican asceticism assumed its most radical form in Sparta. It was a combination of political and military asceticism that would later also be honoured in republican Rome.[4]

The asceticism that Russell described as an 'evil passion' in fact developed in opposition to this classical republican asceticism. During the last centuries of the western Roman empire, Christianity did not invent asceticism, but borrowed it from the Greeks in order to turn it against the pagan polis and against the sinful body. Instead of male athletes, citizens and soldiers, now martyrs and holy virgins, hermits, Syrian stylites and, later on, Carthusians came to the fore. They replaced the polis with the hereafter, the body with the spirit. Individual seekers of Christian purity further radicalised older practices. The quest for truth was already associated by the Greek philosophers with forbearance from bodily pleasures and comfort. The abstinence which fights the desires of the body remained central in Christian asceticism: abstinence from food or drink, such as fasting and not drinking alcohol, temporary sexual abstinence or lifelong celibacy, keeping vigil or abstaining from sleep. Physical discipline could in fact be taken much further, including practices such as not washing, not cutting hair or nails, braving extreme heat or cold, inflicting pain on or mutilating oneself. Christian asceticism also refers to the rejection of personal possessions: the ascetic believes in poverty and material detachment. Moreover, Christian asceticism disengages its practitioners from the society around them, isolates them and throws them back on themselves through self-imposed silence and a retreat into prayer and meditation, through continual roaming – the *peregrinatio* which prevents attachment and enforces an unworldly homelessness – or again, through lengthy, sometimes lifelong, physical separation in caves, deserts and cloister cells, on remote islands or high up on a pillar. The old asceticism had, in other words, been transformed from physical exercise to abstinence and starvation. As the influence of Christianity in the Roman *imperium* grew – and especially when the new faith was elevated to the status of state religion under the emperor Theodosius – this new interpretation also seemed to eradicate the institutional memories of republican asceticism. Elements of the radical asceticism of the martyrs and stylites were passed on to the new monastic lifestyle. This lifestyle paralleled a new 'worldly' order in which monasteries became cultural and economic centres, whereas the previously dominant polis lost much of its importance, for several centuries at least.

Historians emphasise that ascetic suffering, as advocated by Christianity, merely served to establish a spiritual layering of reality, to make the higher prevail over the lower, the soul over the body, the transcendent over the immanent. In this Christian framework, asceticism averts evil and invokes goodness, it combats sin (negative asceticism) and feeds virtue (positive asceticism), with the achievement of transformation as its ultimate goal. For this pivotal moment, too, a rich vocabulary has been developed, with words such as purification, redemption, liberation and rescue. In Christianity, asceticism refers to the way that weak man, burdened with original sin, must go down in order to fulfil the divine purpose. Christian asceticism is pleasing to God, it is fundamentally theocentric. The meaning of suffering on earth lies in the positive prospect of happiness in the hereafter. The detached life of Jesus himself and his twelve apostles serves as a pointer. But the way to heaven is long and strewn with thousands of temptations. The crucifixion bridges the gap between the worldly life and the truly godly life.

In the monastery, the gender relations that had prevailed in the polis were reordered. In the Christian tradition, asceticism became closely connected with both male and female religious authority and respectability. It was not relations in the public forum but a more private, even family-based relationship that was reflected by that authority and respectability. Especially within the monastic orders which developed in the early Middle Ages in both the Eastern and the Western churches, asceticism became a question of surrender – and above all of love. Political mastery was replaced by religious subjugation. Obviously, this change affected the Greek heritage. The private character of Christian asceticism was paralleled by a certain feminisation which took place in the course of the Middle Ages. In theological terms, the achievement of mystical grace and divine election was prepared for through ascetic practices. Monks and nuns practised day in, day out, each for himself or herself, the suppression of worldly desires and yearnings and the instilling of the desired behaviour until it became virtually automatic.

Asceticism, Authenticity and the Rise of the Individual

Yet the triumph of Christian asceticism did not mean the permanent destruction of its republican predecessor and antithesis. Although monastic asceticism was prominent in medieval culture, its civic antithesis seemed to gain a second wind from the late eleventh century on, culminating in the revival of an urban republican ethos at the time of the Renaissance. Particularly in the Italian city-states of the fifteenth and sixteenth centuries, the classical ideal of bodily control was revived. In humanist education, the classical model came to incorporate the spirit of the new republic. In numerous educational tracts, authors such as Vergerio praised the courage and perseverance of the Greeks, as well as their rural way of life, their sober clothing and plain food, their emphasis on physical toughness and their hunting skills.[5] These were qualities which – again – male citizens needed to acquire in order to ensure the independence of the Renaissance cities from the outside world and, not least, against the power of the Church. The independence of the city-state republic was again associated with political or military asceticism, as it had been in classical Greece. While administrators in Venice or Florence presented themselves as new Athenians, democratic in outlook and completely devoted to public affairs, critics such as Machiavelli called for the restoration of a more Spartan or Roman form of government, in order to overcome the political conflicts and impasses which often handicapped the city-states. In these Spartan plans, greater power for the city's nobility and more intense military training went hand in hand. Like Athenian democratic rhetoric, the Spartan current in political discourse pointed above all to a revival of a classical tradition of public asceticism which turned out not to have been completely destroyed by monastic asceticism. Again, the double masculine imagery of the citizen-soldier seemed to triumph over the 'feminine' rhetoric of the Christian ascetics.

In this context of regenerating republicanism, however, Christian asceticism was revolutionised. Whereas medieval Christianity lived on in the cloisters, whose inhabitants found themselves relocated to the margins of urban civilisation once again, the Protestant Reformation founded a new brand of Christian asceticism that started to consume the city from within. Calvinists suspended monastic life and paired religious concern with a new appreciation of worldly profit. Even more than their monastic forbearers, they suppressed worldly desires so as not to divert attention from God or arouse his wrath. The road to sanctification, however, was not confined to the cloister any more. The whole of worldly existence could serve purification, if pursued with the right ascetic attitude and religious goal. As striving for worldly profit gained a religious significance, pleasure for the sake of worldly pleasure alone became even more sinful than before. Only the deep awareness of sin could legitimate worldly profit. Protestantism turned personal profit into a means of purification in an urban context and therefore intensified, not lessened, the individualised asceticism of the medieval hermits and nuns.

Ever since Max Weber's famous thesis,[6] this return of Christian asceticism to the cities of the Renaissance has been discussed as a formative event in the making of modern capitalism. As Henk de Smaele reminds us (this volume), for Weber, asceticism was carried out of monastic cells into everyday life, and began to dominate worldly morality; by doing so it did its part in building the cosmos of the modern economic order. Since material goods were to be piled up for God's glory, they became loaded with a symbolic importance beyond imagination. For Weber, the ascetic work ethic of Protestantism also helped to ensure religious and social order. It guaranteed that private profit led to post-poned consumption and even greater profit, instead of decadence. In comparable terms, John Mandeville and Adam Smith argued that Protestantism guided the private profit principle not to mutual destruction but to greater common profit. Mandeville's *Fable of the Bees* and Smith's *The Wealth of Nations* clearly showed how the invisible hand that held 'private vices' and 'public benefits' in balance was a new tool for an older religious asceticism.[7]

Even if the sources of modern capitalism can be related to a religiously inspired sense of asceticism, they triggered an evolution that in many respects can be called anti-ascetic. The accumulation of wealth that was rendered possible by capitalism gradually opened up the way for a capitalist economy without an ascetic moment. As such, the rise of capitalism did not render traditional religious asceticism obsolete: rather, it was invigorated. That was certainly the case in Catholic countries, where the Weberian link between religious and economic values was less obvious, or at least more complicated. These countries witnessed a return to the ancient monastic ideals as a reaction against the culture of abundance developing in society and in the Church itself. The foundation of the *Ordo Cisterciencis Strictioris Observantiae* at Châtillon in France, and its rapid spread in the seventeenth century, were symptomatic in this respect. The adepts of this order had to refrain from eating meat, and therefore became known as *les abstinents*. In the second half of that century, a new reform of the order began at the monastery of La Trappe, in Normandy, making it even more severe by proscribing an absolute silence and isolation from the world.

If the Christian tradition of asceticism was reinvigorated as a reaction against the development of capitalism, the same holds true for the republican tradition. One of the reasons why Jean-Jacques Rousseau venerated the Spartan tradition was its antipathy to trade and its rejection of individual profit. For Rousseau, most of the material needs by which the materialist society of his time were driven were purely artificial, and therefore deflected man from virtue and from the common good. By creating unnecessary needs, capitalist society threatened the true republic which Rousseau had in mind. That threat was obviously a threat of feminisation. In Rousseau's highly gendered world view, the republic was based on male virtues, whereas consumption was feminine activity.

If the Rousseauist version of republicanism found its way into the idiom of the more radically democratic wing of the French revolutionaries, it did not form the most lasting heritage of the revolutionary wave of the late eighteenth and the early nineteenth centuries. That heritage was monopolised in the first place by the liberal bourgeoisie, who accepted the values of capitalism and tried to exploit them in order to procure as much happiness as possible for as many people as possible. To some extent, the liberal bourgeoisie can be seen as adepts of an 'ascetic' capitalism, opposing the unrestrained accumulation of wealth by the 'idle classes'. Nonetheless, the paradox of ascetic capitalism would even be more striking now than it had been two-and-a-half centuries before. The Industrial Revolution engendered an economic growth which had never been seen before, and created therefore what Thorstein Veblen has famously called 'a leisure class', which could indulge in 'conspicuous consumption', and in the satisfaction of utterly individual needs and wants.[8] The individual self, whose birth historians situate within this context, did not need any external justification, be it in a collectivity or in a supernatural order. When this self was questioned by the last decades of the nineteenth century, it was not so much in the name of some higher entity, but because of the disturbing emergence of the masses as a historical actor. Within this context, loss of the self was seen as a threat rather than as a goal.

For the self-chosen self-denial which is so crucial to asceticism, nineteenth-century European modernity, therefore, was an extremely unwelcoming context. And yet, discourses and practices of asceticism did find their way into modern times. The ancient repertoires of asceticism were reformulated in ways which at one and the same time fitted within the idiom of modernity, and also contained a critique of it. If Rousseau's idea of a democratic republic had turned out not to be a viable political system, a similar kind of self-denying dedication was asked vis-à-vis the nation, which became the central political signifier throughout the nineteenth century. Unlike the republican self-denial, however, 'sacrifice for the nation' had a depoliticising nature. The engagement that was asked from all citizens was not one to construct the polis through deliberating or carrying out offices, but one to glorify or defend the preexisting entity which the nation was supposed to be. Closer to the republican ideal was probably the ideological commitment that was requested of adherents of those well-structured political parties that have developed since the last decades of the nineteenth century. This modern kind of asceticism seems to have been present primarily in those left-wing political movements which explicitly referred to the democratic republicanism of the French revolutionary tradition. Both nation and ideology were often described as systems of belief which had to provide the meaning which could less and less be provided by supernatural beliefs.

The liberal bourgeoisie, however, often experienced this blind dedication to the nation or to ideology as 'self-debasing'. Their critique of the materialist excesses of the dominant culture, therefore, did not result in self-effacement for the sake of some external ideal, but for the sake of a greater personal authenticity. Presumably the most modern form of asceticism was, therefore, what can paradoxically be called the 'self-oriented self-denial'. Through control and abstinence, modern individuals delineated their own space from the crowd. New, 'modern' forms of asceticism were still borrowed from classical sources, but often detached from their public character. They became, as Foucault has called them, technologies of the self.[9] Thus modern city dwellers in the nineteenth century were likewise concerned with a healthy and moderate diet, often cast in the naturalistic terms of classical antiquity. This same focus on self-development dominated the European fascination with the vegetarianism of the Greeks ('pythagoreanism') or the revival of the Ancient Greeks' controlled physicality, which continued without abatement during the nineteenth and twentieth centuries. It was revealed in the revival of Greek bathing in spa culture and the fascination with gymnastics and even fitness. Here too, ascetic discourses and practices primarily served a strictly individualistic goal, although they were borrowed from a republican, 'collective' or a transcendental, religious tradition. From the nineteenth century, modern asceticism became increasingly a vehicle of personal authenticity, embodied in a rich and diverse culture of the self.

Pluralities of Modern Asceticism

In this book, the ambivalent nature of this modern asceticism, with its focus on either self-realisation or ideological dedication, will be considered. The central question in this analysis is to what extent an old repertoire of ascetic practices could have new meanings imparted to it. Light will be shed on the character of modern asceticism itself, but the continuing influence of classical and religious discourses will also be investigated. Through a range of subtopics, this paradox will be further analysed. Thus attention will be paid to the conflicting individualistic and collective characteristics of this modern asceticism, on the processes of cultural distinction and conformism that were at work in this asceticism. Consideration will also be given to the different gender identities which, as in the centuries before the French Revolution, were constructed and experienced with the help of ascetic practices. Finally, the significance of modern asceticism in terms of cultural criticism will be examined. It will become clear that ascetic ideals have been often invoked against the presumed moral and physical degeneration of Western society. At the same time, though, emphasis will be placed on the extent to which modern ascetics themselves helped shape modernity. The quest for a freer, truer rhythm of life, instead of the hollow formalisms and rigid hierarchies of established bourgeois society, was no throwback to tradition, but opened the way to a radically new world. The particularly practical cultural critique, which assumed an almost tangible physical character in *Wege zu Kraft und Schönheit*, will be discussed in this book as a modern discourse.

The fact that this modern, individualistic asceticism seemed to differ in a number of key points from the classical-republican and the Christian traditions did not mean that it constituted a monolithic project in itself. The impression left by *Wege zu Kraft und Schönheit* is not without ambiguity. Modern asceticism is not a uniform cultural trend, and certainly not an organised movement. For this reason, an ideal type will not be presented in this book. Instead, a broad perspective will be opened up. In a number of different fields of cultural and social history, a recurrent dynamic rather than a precisely defined movement will be described. Like the multiplicity of modern cultural expressions with which they became interwoven, the ascetic ideas and practices that form the subject of this book also resist interpretation. Altogether, they constitute the plurality of modern asceticism.

The striking popularity of *Wege zu Kraft und Schönheit*, we have argued, illustrated the continuous lure of plural asceticism in the early decades of the twentieth century. The movie equally displayed, however, prototypical places which sheltered and produced modern asceticism. At these places, discourses of Christian and republican asceticism, carried along and transformed by capitalism and revolution, were most spectacularly appropriated anew. In his contribution, Evert Peeters focuses upon natural therapy, naturism and the German *Lebensreform* ('life reform'). In the midst of the modern capital, these movements heralded the vision of an imaginary natural utopia. The middle-class adherents of *Lebensreform* hoped to flee all too real cities that were perceived to be degenerate and sick. In special centres for nudist recreation and in sanatoria for natural therapy, they tried to make their utopia materialise. At those spots, ascetic practices served in a quest for a 'more genuine' life and a 'more authentic' self, liberated from physical degeneration and alienating mass culture. It will become clear that these prototypical subcultures were European movements which, contrary to what has often been suggested, went far beyond the boundaries of Wilhelmine and Weimar Germany, and fascist Europe. The quest for a more authentic existence, it will be argued, captured the enthusiasm of Western European Catholics, Central European Jews, German conservative *Junkers* and French socialists alike.

The Belgian case, which will be developed in particular by Peeters, illustrates this plurality. It demonstrates to what extent modern asceticism was influenced by very different national traditions. Belgian 'life reform' also sheds some light on the contradictory meanings religion could represent for modern ascetics. Both as a challenge and as a burden, Catholic tradition confronted life reformers with the historicity of their proper practices and ideas. Borrowing from plural sources, Peeters argues, naturopaths and naturists constructed and perceived individual authenticity. The asceticism practised in a group was a tool for the discovery of the true, naked self. Renunciation, Peeters's contribution suggests, was to open the way to a purer pleasure. In this way, the cult places of ascetic authenticity became an antithesis to the modernity which had come in for such criticism.

Incidentally, this did not mean that these places of modern asceticism were not threatened by ambivalence. In a culture typified by excess and consumption, it paradoxically did not always prove easy to define clearly 'correct' pleasure based on ascetic principles from the 'erroneous', alienating enjoyment of modern capitalism, since ascetic projects such as naturopathy and naturism were themselves marketed as modern consumer goods; there was also a danger of asceticism being degraded into a mere means of pleasure. This emerges very clearly in Michael Hau's analysis of German sanatoria and the *Lebensreform* movement, in which the wealthy bourgeoisie, rather than middle-class citizens, are scrutinised. The ascetic naturopathic regime that was offered to patients in expensive sanatoria remained consistent with the broader cultural critique that characterised *Lebensreform*, and thus provided participants with a code of conduct which promised moral superiority. At the same time, however, this regime was constantly 'beleaguered' by notions of pleasure which were external to culture-critical asceticism. If the sanatorium wanted to be attractive, it needed to integrate the burgeoning consumer culture rather than reject it. And nude bathing and walking may have had a hygienic and moral significance, but that did not prevent free physical contact between the sexes from enhancing the sanatorium's attractiveness.

The prototypical places of modern asceticism, so it seemed, were dominated by a specific kind of social regulation that was not only a matter of deliberate individual choices. Being a (non-conventional) part of bourgeois leisure culture, *Lebensreform* practices evidently evoked problems of class identity. Since this leisure culture also included nude culture, it also raised questions of respectability and therefore of social regulation. In the second section of this book, the complex relationship between positive ascetic choices of modern ascetics on the one hand, and the coerced character these 'choices' could take on the other hand, are analysed. What relationship could there be between modern asceticism and modern pleasure? The furore caused by the naked scenes in *Wege zu Kraft und Schönheit* is illustrative in this context. The boundaries between ascetic nakedness and eroticism were unclear; information had to be presented as entertainment in order to reach a large public. The pleasure of asceticism – physical exercise, a natural lifestyle and self-control – that the film advocated was sold using other, non-ascetic means. Nakedness was also erotic, the ascetic images were fast-moving and dynamic, the film's rhythm was captivating. Asceticism was intoxicating. The problematic relationship that existed between message and entertainment, between asceticism and pleasure, also presented the film censors in all Western countries during the interwar period with considerable difficulties. Tom Saunders's contribution to this book examines the inevitable tension which existed between the medium of film and the ideals of asceticism – as well as the political regulation of both kinds of 'pleasure'.

A similar intricate relationship between deliberate abstinence (from pleasure) and coercion is apparent in nineteenth-century and twentieth-century sexual politics. Since the end of the nineteenth century, the interests of the nation were also formulated very clearly in this area. French fears of *dépopulation* after its military defeat at the hands of the Prussians in 1870, German ambitions in Europe, and the British construction of a colonial empire made population growth a political issue of the highest importance in very different contexts. In France after the First World War, policing of the ban on abortion was tightened up and advertising contraceptives was prohibited, while in Germany and Great Britain, eugenics became a new intellectual fashion – in many different forms. Paradoxically, this public concern with reproduction also made the more explicit discussion of personal intimacy possible. Unintentionally, it made it more acceptable to talk about sex, made it possible to discuss individual sexual experiences, and ultimately increased women's right to sexual self-determination.

In the discourse of individual sexual experience that arose in this fashion, abstinence and pleasure with regard to sexuality existed in a complex relationship with one another. Thus Lesley Hall points out in her contribution that participation in sexual relations (or rather the endurance thereof) was an obvious element of self-sacrifice for many women until well into the twentieth century. The feminist critique of the duplicitous morality of marriage was also internalised by a number of men to such an extent that pleasure became a problematic question and abstinence was sometimes opted for. When sexologists began assigning abstinence a role as an exercise in eroticism in the early twentieth century, this provided the impetus for a new framework for the perception of sexuality. Excessive emphasis on asceticism, argued the British sexologist Havelock Ellis in 1910, had placed too much stress on the sexual impulses. Moderation of the former, he suggested to his readers, would be accompanied by moderation of the latter. Sexual abstinence could then be an effective means of regaining control of personal intimacy against the demands of spousal rights or the birth policy of Church and State, although asceticism should not become an end in itself.

Problems of social regulation, however, appeared not only in the fields of mass entertainment and intimate experience. The regulatory power of asceticism also haunted the minds of (late) nineteenth-century intellectuals who tried to conceptualise the link between asceticism and modernity. In his contribution, Henk de Smaele maps out these philosophers' and social theorists' obsession with the persisting reality of asceticism in Western history. He focuses upon the religious motives that haunted these analysts. De Smaele shows that for nineteenth-century theorists such as Max Weber and Emile Durkheim, modern asceticism came down to ascetic capitalism, not republicanism. They convinced their contemporaries that this particular kind of (post-)Protestant asceticism still pervaded modern economy and society. And though this religious asceticism would gradually secularise, it never fully lost its colonising and dominating character. It structured modern power and dominance as much as modern pleasure. And it continues to do so, even today. Indirectly, however, De Smaele also demonstrates how this Weberian account helped to obscure the republican sources of asceticism. Paradoxically, many critics of ascetic capitalism remained imprisoned in the very same tradition.

De Smaele gives ample indices of this imprisonment. The critics of ascetic capitalism's social regulation, so it seems, could hardly think of any (republican or other) regime beyond its scope. For Weber and Durkheim, asceticism became an analytic category which typified and closed modern society as a whole. In other words, asceticism was a concept that enabled the unspoken assumptions of modern society to be laid bare in a new and often surprising way. That society might have abandoned heaven, but not the religious practices that had been associated with the notion of God. Such an analysis was not only popular in the nineteenth century, for it also remains intellectually attractive today. The links that Marx had already drawn in the 1840s between asceticism and the slave morality of capitalism have therefore lost little of their shrewdness. The position defended by later theoreticians –

namely, that asceticism paradoxically represents an essential characteristic of modern consumer culture – also continues to inspire contemporary writers. However, the strength of a general concept of asceticism of this kind also contains a weakness. The concept scarcely had any differentiating power any longer. Consumer urges or thriftiness: both turned out to represent forms of asceticism. In this way, social conformism and anti-capitalist cultural critique, economic success and the rejection of such success, seemed to blend with one another, as related offshoots of a single (Protestant) religious ascetic discourse. In nineteenth-century social theory, the social regulation of ascetic capitalism was no longer something one chose. Rather, it became like the pattern that structured the limited choices of modern individuals.

Rather than consider asceticism as an all-pervading characteristic of modern society as a whole, it seems fruitful to approach it instead as an instrument which enabled individuals and groups to broaden the range of their choices, to search for a distinctive way of life, to construct individual and group identities. The field of aesthetics offers an example of the dynamics of distinction that was implied by asceticism. In the third section of this volume, the focus is in the modernistic visual language that gained currency in the cultural field. More specifically, the ascetic programmes of different groups of modernist architects will be analysed. The divergent target publics of avant-garde architects and of 'functional', standardised construction for the masses will serve as the starting point. A strong element of choice was also apparent in the social and societal ambitions of twentieth-century architecture – aesthetics and distinctiveness were synonymous. Those who opted for asceticism marked themselves out as different. It was based on a belief in the superiority of those who succeeded in voluntarily denying themselves the material perquisites of modern society. Wessel Krul's reading of the early twentieth-century work of Adolf Loos, the 'father' of asceticism in modern architecture, makes this conflict apparent. For Loos, Krul argues, asceticism in architectural aesthetics was very closely bound up with a desire for power, masculinity and order. In Loos's view, that order was needed to provide an antidote to the prevailing culture of externalities and ornament that he associated with decadence and degeneracy.

However, asceticism could equally be aimed at paring back excessive individuality. Austerity played a crucial role in the consolidation of social differences in very different fields, too. This emerges from Sofie De Caigny's contribution about domestic and stylistic advice that was issued during the interwar period by intermediary organisations to working women and farmers' wives. Arguments of a hygienic-scientific and moral nature were employed in the definition of an austere alternative to the model of the nineteenth-century bourgeois dwelling, full of ornament, which was attractive to workers. Modernist architectural ideals of austerity also provided a source of inspiration here. Within modernism, austerity stood for functionality, transparency and social engagement. However, the ascetic traits of modernist architectural theory did not necessarily coincide with a concern for social equality.

The dynamics of cultural distinction that were part of the attractiveness of aesthetic asceticism were equally at work in modern science and philosophy – fields to which the fourth part of this book is devoted. Here too, asceticism served as an element in the construction of modern identities, a subtle and powerful tool in processes of inclusion and exclusion. In the field of science, profound cultural changes occurred from the middle of the nineteenth century. Institutionalisation, professionalisation and internationalisation required a growing application of discipline in behaviour and language on the part of science's practitioners. Just as the national republic became an 'imagined community' with extensive sovereignty during this period, so science also acquired a new kind of autonomy and authority. And just as 'real men' had to be prepared to die for their country, so too one had to be ready to sacrifice oneself for science. The ethics of asceticism that were associated with science in a new way from the late nineteenth century were very much tailored to male concerns. As Kaat Wils indicates in her contribution on Marie Curie, the culture of scientific asceticism and the relative inaccessibility of science to women were intimately bound up with one another. Again, neo-republican masculinity could only prevail against the background of a family-based femininity which it had first invoked itself.

The ascetic character of modern scientific discourse was revealed at an even more fundamental level, however. The desire to rid culture of what was superfluous, superficial, impure or unhealthy did not just introduce new contrasts between the masculine-public and feminine-private spheres. To a certain extent, that desire also placed a strain on classical, controlled masculinity itself. Klaas van Berkel argues in his contribution to this book that Ludwig Wittgenstein's philosophy of language in the *Tractatus* (1922) can be regarded as a constitutive element in the history of modern asceticism. Because language cannot say anything meaningful about religion and ethics, Wittgenstein reasoned, refraining from speech is a precondition for a truly religious or ethical life. The use of language that was so important in the history of philosophy was in Wittgenstein's case an exercise in asceticism – an exercise which, not coincidentally perhaps, was consistent with Wittgenstein's own lifestyle. His philosophy featured not a proud Greek citizen, but a lone eccentric in a barrel. Not a virile soldier but a sickly youth, not the general interest but an intensely private obscurity.

By presenting Van Berkel's interpretation of Wittgenstein, we do not want to suggest, though, that modern asceticism ended in the middle of the twentieth century by silencing itself. It appears, nevertheless, that the Second World War has functioned as a turning point. The postwar world with its unstoppable affluence hence constitutes the theme of the last part of this book. Whereas the search for bodily experienced authenticity became part of mainstream culture, the republican vein of the ascetic tradition lost much of its relevance. In his contribution, Marnix Beyen shows how, in various European countries, the topos of austerity in the reconstruction period following the Second World War primarily served future prospects of growing prosperity of middle-class families and individuals. The moral call for discipline and asceticism was maintained by older elites. They hoped in this way to resurrect both a classical (republican) nation and a traditional (equally republican) masculinity from the rubble of the Second World War. However, it became clear that republican ascetic ideals lost much of their attractiveness with the expansion of affluence and the continual growth of the modern middle classes after the Second World War. Republican asceticism, so it seemed, could not live on without its distinctive quality. It could retain this quality within radical political subcultures, such as European communist parties, but it no longer functioned as a model for the masses of 'ordinary' workers and middle-class people.

Late twentieth-century debates about the postwar welfare state would, however, continue to draw on ascetic maxims. In the United States under Ronald Reagan, the United Kingdom under Margaret Thatcher, and the (socio-)liberal democracies in continental Europe, the conviction grew that social support could also lead to individual laziness. Too many social adjustments to the workings of the market, ran the critique of a number of controversial intellectuals, made the individual urge to perform and the sense of responsibility to society at large crumble away. Neo-liberalism and neo-asceticism could blend together – in such a discourse at any rate – with surprising ease. It remains in other words fruitful to take asceticism into account in analyses of contemporary capitalism.

Such analyses will also take into account the marketing of another, more individual strand of asceticism: the asceticism of contemporary body culture. In the closing chapter, Julia Twigg reflects on the ascetic character of modern body culture by focusing on the culture of dieting, vegetarianism and the pursuit of bodily cleanliness. Individuals are required to monitor and discipline their bodies by means of activities such as conscious abstinence or self-denial, deployed in pursuit of a body ideal which is partly new but equally indebted to ancient aesthetics and ideals of physical beauty. One of the specificities of this contemporary form of asceticism is without doubt its complex interaction with – equally mass-marketed – anti-ascetic hedonism.

Postwar asceticism is, however, not only to be found in radical leftist politics or mainstream body culture. Nostalgic memories of hardship and discipline in the armed forces, youth movements and boarding schools remain as present as the fashionable irritation with presumed modern-day laziness. Even in seemingly autonomous areas such as science, the modern ideal of the ascetic scientist remains surprisingly influential too. Scientific culture continues to be structured by the rhetoric and ethics of asceticism. The highest peaks of contemporary asceticism, however, are reached by modern ecologism. Abandoning one's own comfort zone has to be a project of personal and universal purification. In the most radical variation of that ecological project, the asceticist seems to want to erase their own tracks and, in so doing, themselves. This self-denial remains liable to elicit irritation and ridicule. After all, arrogance is always suspected of hiding behind this asceticism. The distinction indisputably associated with asceticism, however, does not seem to have lost its cultural authority. It remains a source of fear and yet a place of salvation. Is this modern passion ultimately any less evil than its predecessors? Even within academia, it continues to repel as much as it attracts. It is beyond pleasure that the pleasure of asceticism is to be found.

Notes

1. B. Russell, 'Ideas that have harmed Mankind', in B. Russell, *Unpopular Essays* (New York, [1950] reprint 1995), 160.
2. Ibid.
3. F. Nietzsche, *Die Geburt der Tragödie* (1872), quoted in R. Safranski, *Nietzsche. Een biografie van zijn denken*, trans. M. Wildschut (Amsterdam, 2002), 73.
4. E. Rawson, *The Spartan Tradition in European Thought* (Oxford, 1991).
5. 'Mirrors of Princes' and other educational tracts, such as Vergerio, *De ingenuis moribus ac liberalibus studiis* ('On the Manners of a Gentleman and on Liberal Studies') (Venice, 1472).
6. M. Weber, *The Protestant Ethic* (New York, 1958[1905]).
7. J. Mandeville, *Fable of the Bees* (Oxford, 1924 [1723]); A. Smith, *The Wealth of Nations* (London, 1776).
8. T. Veblen, *The Theory of the Leisure Class: An Economic Study of Institutions* (1899).
9. M. Foucault,'Technologies of the Self', in L.M. Martin, H. Gutman and P.H. Hutton (eds), *Technologies of the Self: A Seminar with Michel Foucult* (London, 1988) 16–49.

References

Foucault, M. (1988). 'Technologies of the Self', in L.M. Martin, H. Gutman and P.H. Hutton (eds), *Technologies of the Self: A Seminar with Michel Foucault,* London, pp.16–49.

Mandeville, B. 1924[1723]. *The Fable of the Bees: Or Private Vices, Publick Benefits,* ed. F.B. Kaye, 2 vols, Oxford.

Rawson, E. 1991. *The Spartan Tradition in European Thought,* Oxford.

Russell, B. 1995[1950]. 'Ideas that have harmed Mankind', in B. Russell, *Unpopular Essays*. New York, pp.146–65.

Safranski, R. 2002². *Nietzsche. Een biografie van zijn denken*, trans. M. Wildschut, Amsterdam.

Smith, A. [1776]. *An Inquiry into the Nature and Causes of the Wealth of Nations*, 4 vol., London.

Veblen, T. (1899). *The Theory of the Leisure Class: An Economic Study of Institutions*.

Vergerio, P.P. 1472. *De ingenuis moribus ac liberalibus studiis*, Venice.

Weber, M. 1958[1905]. *The Protestant Ethic and the Spirit of Capitalism*, trans. T. Parsons, New York.

Part I
Cult Places of Authenticity

Wilhelm Prager (director) and Nicholas Kaufmann (scriptwriter) 'Wege zu Kraft und Schönheit' (1924). © Friedrich-Wilhelm-Murnau-Stiftung, Wiesbaden, Germany.

1

The Performance of Redemption: Asceticism and Liberation in Belgian *Lebensreform*

Evert Peeters

Practices of asceticism, it is often assumed, always served a spiritual cause. Medieval monks hoped to elevate themselves above their worldly needs through bodily sacrifice, abstinence and fasting. The body was to be neglected and even hurt in order to obtain entry to the kingdom of heaven. In the twentieth century's culture of the body, one might think, this hierarchy of body and spirit was turned upside down. In such diverse fields as sports, the youth movement, bath culture and health reform, a fascination with nature itself seemed to replace the longing for the supernatural. The body was trained and sculpted, so it is maintained, for the body's sake alone. Since the body itself rose to the level of a new god, the infliction of discomfort on that body became all the more problematic. Traditional discourses of bodily sacrifice and prudery were thus perceived as outdated and irrelevant. In modern body culture, one might believe, premodern restraint was abandoned for the benefit of sensational exuberance and physical pleasure.

Even in this culture of bodily liberation, however, ascetic ambitions were reaffirmed. Although the language of asceticism was refigured, asceticism itself had not completely vanished. In this chapter, I will demonstrate asceticism's surprising persistence in modern body culture, using the example of the *Lebensreform* movement, or 'life reform'. This movement manifested itself in Europe from the late nineteenth century onwards with a vehement criticism of industrial and urban society. In order to redress the balance between modern culture and nature, proponents of natural therapy, vegetarianism and nudist culture propagated a so-called natural lifestyle. Engaging in cold water therapies, eating raw vegetables and exercising naked, they maintained, would help the modern individual keep in touch with their natural origins in the midst of a dangerously degenerate society. First in Germany, but later also in France, Britain and Belgium, these life reformers performed a bodily return to nature. They placed their hopes in 'nature' and 'the body' as a cure for modernity's ills.[1]

In order to cure the perceived dangers of modernity, Belgian life reformers engaged in physical practices which represented an interesting example of non-religious modern asceticism.[2] Even though they propagated a liberation of the body from both a religiously inspired contempt of the body and unhealthy modern lifestyles, they also upheld ascetic beliefs. Life reformers propagated bodily scrutiny and discipline, rather than unlimited bodily pleasure. In their midst, restraint and abstinence made a remarkable comeback. Even though life reformers' ascetic beliefs and practices were made subservient not to a transcendental God but to a mythical Nature, the stringency of the required asceticism did not fade away. Reflecting classical preoccupations with the mythic nature of male beauty, many nudists and life reformers dreamed of a new, naked man who was, at the same time, stronger and purer.[3] Bodily liberation could only be obtained through strenuous exercise and a harsh reform of eating and living habits. In life reform, physical practice and mortification were to open up access not to the Divine, but to Nature. The ascetic character of this physical practice, however, was not diminished at all.

Even for those who no longer accepted God (or the Divine) as the centre of their world-view, ascetic practice retained its attraction. Since this practice was bereft of its religious goal, the underlying asceticism became all the more concrete and visible. Moral edification and physical toughening were the ambitions that replaced the achievement of union with the Divine in this modern asceticism. The sculpted body needed to mirror these ambitions. In that manner, the results of ascetic practices became readable and measurable. In the twentieth century, bodily asceticism became concrete and visible, and it also re-evaluated the importance of the immediate experience. In this paper, I will demonstrate that in modern body culture, it was believed that the benefit of asceticism lay primarily in this concrete experience rather than in the abstract principle on which it was founded. It was (abstract) Nature that was to be repaired, but it was individual experience that was to be reformed and restructured. Feelings of pain and suffering were to be accepted and celebrated, since they helped to reawaken the so-called natural instinct of the degenerate modern individual. The reality of twentieth-century life, which was so much more abundant in objects of desire than medieval Christian asceticism, also presented much more opportunity for conscious abstinence and renunciation. In this secularised age, in which traditional ascetic discourse had lost importance, ascetic experience was continuously reinvented. Even the natural, naked bodies of life reform spoke as much of asceticism as of liberation.

The Chasteness of the Nude

In this chapter, two examples will help to clarify the ascetic experience celebrated within Belgian 'life reform'. I will focus, in the first place, on the radical nudist movement that came into being in the 1920s. This current of life reform was influenced equally by French *naturistes* and by German proponents of the so-called *Freikörperkultur,* or nudist culture. In the second place, this chapter will show how bodily and mental asceticism materialised within the Belgian movement for natural therapy. An equally constitutive part of the movement for life reform, natural therapy was also founded on the French and German examples of *hydrothérapie* (hydropath) and the *natürliche Heilweise* (natural healing). In both currents, modern (bodily) asceticism manifested itself in an equally striking manner.

Belgian nudism, in the first place, was dominated by two different organisations, and these provide the bulk of the evidence about early Belgian nudism. Jozef Geerts founded a group called De Spar ('The Spruce') in March 1928. It operated within the network of what was called the Free Youth Movement, as 'a cultural league for physical culture, ethics, aesthetics and camping sport', according to early literature published by the group, and consisted of around a hundred individuals in Antwerp and Ghent.[4] The group was established by the entrepreneur Oswald Johan de Schampelaere, who put his country estate, Huize Wallaghe, at the disposal of the newly founded society. In his garden, the members of De Spar practised naked gymnastics and swam naked in a so-called 'nudarium'. From 1932 onwards, they also operated on newly acquired grounds in Zoersel, in the Antwerp countryside. They brought along their tents and gas burners, slept on mattresses filled with straw, and devoted themselves to nude swimming and playing volleyball, often spending every summer weekend at the site. A similar group, the Belgian League of Heliophilous Propaganda, but usually called Hélios, was founded by the Antwerp engineer Joseph-Paul Swenne in Ukkel, a small village near Brussels, in 1924. Under the pseudonym Marc Lanval, he combined the direction of the Hélios community with controversial propaganda in favour of 'scientific contraception', the new discipline of sexology, and sexual reform. In one sense, Hélios offered a more acceptable form of nudism, attractive to a bourgeois public with either liberal or leftist leanings. Indeed, in 1934, at the peak of the society's activity, its membership was estimated at around eight thousand by the Belgian nudist magazine *Lumière et Liberté.* Although neither De Spar nor Hélios left precise data about their memberships, fragmentary documents show that most organised nudists in Belgian came from the urban middle classes. Many were teachers, clerks or shopkeepers. This shared background constituted a sort of privilege for nudists. In their own view, their social position protected them against the most extreme circumstances of degeneration that the poor had to endure. Middle-class living conditions, at the same time, allowed the nudists to travel to the countryside at weekends, and even to invest small amounts of money in the embellishment of these vacation spots.[5]

Within these nudist communities, patterns of ritual behaviour derived from two different sources. Nudism was affected, in the first place, by the level of public distrust. The fear of society's disapproval was an active concern in such communities. Both in Hélios and in De Spar, nudity was a joyful event, but it was nevertheless a very complicated undertaking. Huig Hofman, a proponent of folk dancing and one of the leading figures of De Spar, worried about the openly hostile reaction of the group's neighbours in Zoersel. In his correspondence to foreign nudist friends, he wrote at length about the hours spent on the laborious construction of a palisade. Indeed the acquisition of the property had been promptly followed by the construction of an embankment to prevent prying eyes. Only in the summer of 1935, when this bank had reached a satisfactory height, could 'integral nudity' be practised without the fear of outside resentment. Later on, the earthen bank was crowned with a high palisade of timber. Fears about outsiders' hostility were deepened still further by legislation on indecency offences. Article 385 of the Belgian criminal code stipulated that offences against public decency would be punished with a term of imprisonment of between one month and a year, and a considerable fine of up to five-hundred Belgian francs. Perhaps the greatest danger nudists perceived in this respect concerned the role of children. Article 386 of the criminal code doubled fines and prison terms when such a felony had been committed towards children.[6] Therefore, the community of De Spar scrupulously regulated contact between children and nude adults. Certain areas, such as the solarium and the nudarium, were declared off limits to children whenever nude sun bathing was practised, and adult nudity outside these areas was also forbidden.[7]

Indeed, Belgian nudists were preoccupied with preventing offences against public decency as stipulated by the law. Not only did they avoid all contact between adults and children, but they also tried to convince the outside world of the noble purposes of nudist culture by differentiating nudism from eroticism as much as possible. Hélios formulated most clearly the theory of chaste nudity that was advocated by the whole of the nudist community, throughout Belgium and elsewhere in Europe. In *Lumière et Liberté*, the magazine distributed by Hélios, an anonymous writer contemplated the 'impressive spectacle' of naked men and women in the state in which 'God and Nature have created them'. Why, he continued, has 'man made a mystery of his body?' He pleaded for nudism because, 'the view of these bodies, healthy and well proportionate, fills us with admiration and emotion', and because 'this view is the most powerful expression of beauty. We are moved by the grace and the perfection of these shapes, by the harmony of the architecture of the human body'. In this way, he argued, the experience of nudity 'elevated the soul' instead of the senses. 'Pure and edifying sentiments' alone, this anonymous author continued, were at stake here. 'The matter of sexuality' and 'the functioning of the sexual organs' did not have anything to do with this experience, and adversaries who equated nudist culture with 'vice, eroticism and exhibitionism', he concluded, should be left alone with their 'ignorance, vices and miseries'.[8] Because nudism was driven not by sexual desire but by aestheticism, the erotic nude had to make way for 'the chasteness of nudity'. Lanval invited the members of Hélios to admire their own bodies and those of other nudists, but insisted at the same time that sexual intimacy between adults was forbidden at all time while on Hélios property.[9]

Figure 1.1 A Woman and three children at a Belgian nudist camp, 1930s.
© Archive International Naturist Federation, Berchem, Belgium.

Nudists' concerns about the perceived enmity of the legal system were not totally without grounds. Mostly Catholic opponents often deposed complaints against local nudist groups. The Belgian law courts, however, usually acted with greater moderation. Out of more than three hundred complaints deposed by Catholic opponents against nudists in the early 1930s, most were filed by members of the Catholic league Zedenadel ('moral nobility'). This league aimed at a moral purifying of the Gay Twenties' 1920s' leisure culture. The nudist culture movement in Belgium, however their small size and importance, fast became a major target of Catholic protest. Zedenadel members filed complaints at the behest of their leadership, and very often different members filed multiple complaints following one single incident.

The court in Brussels, however, decided to hear only four cases, and in each of these four lawsuits the defendant ended up with conditional penalties, so that the sentence would only be carried out if the offence was repeated.[10] A light sentence was also handed down in a Brussels lawsuit against thirteen members of the nudist club Mieux Vivre ('Better Living'). Not all civil officials were as lenient as these court judges, however, since these thirteen nudists had been surprised by police officers who were watching them with binoculars from a window.[11] Likewise, Belgian subscribers to German nudist magazines such as *Lachendes Leben* found even the delivery of their magazine regularly affected by the censorship of postal officials.[12]

Nudist discourse was, from the very beginning, essentially defensive in tone. Nudist magazines stressed repeatedly the importance of public education and propaganda, and the need to broaden acceptance of their practices. Such pleas, however, were worked out in a rather mechanical manner. While the liberation of the body remained the primary individual quest, such liberation could only ever materialise behind the physical defences of banks and palisades, and – equally important – behind the moral safeguard of an accentuated theory of nude chastity.[13]

Asceticism and Body Culture

The restraints on nudism were put into place then not only by its opponents but also by its practitioners, who conceived an ascetic regime for nudism. As such, they became natural allies with other early twentieth-century proponents of bodily discipline.

The very practicalities of nudism forced certain restrictions. Accustoming oneself to the sun was a demanding enterprise, and nudist behaviour was surrounded by an atmosphere of detailed concern, patience and attention. Hélios warned its new members in *Lumière et Liberté* of 'serious burns', headache, nausea, dizziness, and other complaints related to sunstroke. To avoid such ailments, newcomers were advised to expose their bodies to the sun only between ten o'clock in the morning and three o'clock in the afternoon. The first exposure to the sun should never exceed five minutes, while more experienced beginners were advised to limit their exposure to a maximum of thirty minutes even after one week of practice. Nudism was thus also a gradualist enterprise that needed to be carried out step by step.

Nudism, when properly practised, might promote general health. Lanval asked his followers to combine exposure of the naked body with intensive gymnastics in order to 'breathe more deeply', which would erase every possible tubercular bacillus from the depths of their lungs. Applied in this regulated manner, the sun was thought to be capable of purifying the skin, of strengthening the muscles, of improving the metabolism, and of increasing organic resistance. Furthermore, exposing the nude body to the sun would revive the blood by increasing the amount of red blood corpuscles and the amount of calcium and phosphorus. At the same time, the radiation of the sun would calm the nervous system and increase the appetite, and the ozone inhaled while sunbathing would cleanse the blood by its 'bactericidal' effects. The blessings of the sun could even be extended, Lanval believed, by combining nudism with a more sober diet in which meat consumption was drastically reduced. It is clear that sunbathing was not simply an innocent pastime but – like air and water, 'natural food', healthy movement, and regular rest – constituted an essential 'element of life' that, when adjusted in the right individual doses, was thought capable of regenerating the modern body.[14]

In Belgium, belief in the transformative power of naturism and the outdoors did not originate with Lanval, but had long been part of the doctrine of natural healing. The Antwerp natural therapist Van den Broeck practised natural therapies from the late 1880s. In 1904, he devoted a substantial part of his first systematic study, a booklet entitled *Het levensproblema: De natuurlijke behandeling der zieken* ('The Problem of life: the natural healing of the sick'), to the positive influence of such therapy on health.[15] In the 1920s, the Antwerp natural therapist Aloïs Van Son, himself a devoted student of Van den Broeck, echoed such sentiments in his own writings. Beginning in the era of the First World War, Van Son combined natural hydrotherapy with both a vegetarian diet and nudism, much in the tradition of Sebastian Kneipp, the better-known nineteenth-century Bavarian promoter of natural therapies. In his grand mansion in central Antwerp, Van Son received patients of all different kinds. His therapies – which he recorded and published in the journal *Terug ter Orde*, distributed throughout Flanders – ranged from the regular use of wet shawls, cold baths, and douches, to diets consisting entirely of raw vegetables and fruit.[16] In one edition of his journal, he recommended a clear protocol that sunbathers were required to follow. They were advised to turn over every five minutes while sunbathing. They were to cool down 'fast but stoutly' the exposed parts of their body with cold water every fifteen minutes. Afterwards, they were also advised to cover themselves with a blanket in order to give their bodies an opportunity to 'respond' to the benefits of the sun. The use of this sort of thermal shock therapy was thought to promote great bodily benefits, and Van Son believed that the sequential application of hot and cold left the body stronger. In order 'to re-establish order in all these lives of illness', he said, 'it is necessary the body undergoes a series of treatments, that all aim at supporting the enduring activity of the body, in hope that the forces God had put into this body … will recover and bring new life to organs that have become ill and weak'.[17]

In searching for an explanatory mechanism for the bodily regeneration they hoped for, natural healers and naturists elaborated the notion of 'natural human instinct'. This quasi-mystical concept appears repeatedly as a core principle in nudist writings. As Van den Broeck proposed in his 1904 booklet, the 'natural regulation of life' formed part of the spontaneous demands and inclinations of the human organism. While the body responded to the stream of information the senses generated, it also reacted to the impulses produced by this instinct, located in every single cell. Human behaviour, therefore, resulted from the brain's handling of this double signal. As Van den Broeck also argued, however, this duality had been upset in the modern individual. Modern social behaviour, with its counterintuitive understandings and regimented activities, had distorted these 'natural instincts'. The modern body had, in short, been 'coded wrongly' and even 'corrupted'. At best, this distortion resulted in a slight overdependence on 'things or acts' that were useless but ultimately harmless. At worst, however, such distortion brought with it a serious physical mutation. The individual cells lost their 'original composition' and the signal they sent to the brain was distorted, with the result that the organism became completely dependent upon 'false needs'. This cellular 'degeneration' explained why so many individuals in modern urban society had become sick. Without their realising it, those living within modern society were clinging to a lifestyle that was gradually killing them.[18] It was because of this mutation that modern individuals needed to re-establish the link with their inner and natural self. A Luxembourg clergyman of the late nineteenth and early twentieth century, Nicolas Neuens, who had been a great inspiration to Van den Broeck, concluded that 'man has to stick to his instinct' as well as 'to his good sentiments, to moderation, and to the law of morality'. Only once the individual had learned the rhythm of natural behaviour would such instincts once again acquire their silent certainty. 'Life is labour', Neuens stated firmly, 'a continuous, intelligent and reasonable undertaking and a struggle one has to keep up with perseverance'.[19]

Borrowing from the beliefs of these early natural therapists, many naturists at De Spar and Hélios also believed in an abstract force within the person's physical being. Yet if natural therapists had identified this elusive, mysterious force with life itself, with a 'universal energy' or with the 'forces of nature', nudists often attributed similar qualities to the sun. In this new and heliocentric discourse, the sun controlled the solar system, bringing life to the earth and to its inhabitants. The full benefits of this life force had been corrupted, so the theory continued, by too rigorous an adherence to conventional behaviour. Nudism, however, could remove the stultifying accretions of modern life. It was capable, Geerts wrote, of 'restoring the broken unity' and of bringing modern man back 'to the natural order'. This reconciliation between the being and its intrinsic essence would elicit from the modern individual 'the cry of jubilation, of the genuine joy of life'. It would allow people once again 'to feel oneself both materially and spiritually at one with flowers and birds, to look for the rejuvenating contact with water, air and light, to tread the ground with nude foot in order that the earth would feed one with its magnetic forces'. Nudism was not simply a therapy but a panacea: it was necessary 'in order to be beautiful and strong, in order to grow old and happy, and to preserve the future of the race and the prosperity of our country'.[20]

Spiritual renewal through physical engagement with the inner self lay at the heart of Belgian nudism during the interwar period. Yet if some nudists sought renewed vitality solely through physical engagement, many more aimed at a reframing of the human mind in tandem with the body. Their self-discipline was thus extended from the world of external performance to the sphere of inner thought and imagination, and the scope of the ascetic programme of naturism was considerably expanded.

Asceticism and Mental Exercise

Like nudists, natural healers and vegetarians had also sought to encompass both the human body and the human mind alike in a unified experience of nature. Before the First World War, Belgian natural therapists had indeed focused on physical therapies such as hydrotherapy and dietary reform, but by the interwar period the ambitions of the movement for life reform had expanded to the reframing of the mind, too. Most life reformers believed that the mind itself possessed a hidden order like both organic tissue and the instincts of the body. The sick mind was to be healed by life reformers through psychoanalysis, psychognomy and other mental therapies. Most strikingly, however, the ascetic regime of the mind which life reformers stood for unfolded itself through the art of self-suggestion. The goal remained an authentic and natural lifestyle and the agenda of the life reformers continued to be tied to the dynamics of performance.[21]

It was the Brussels vegetarian and nudist Paul Nyssens who published most extensively about auto-suggestion. Within the Franco-Belgian vegetarian circles around the periodical *La Réforme Alimentaire*, the therapy of auto-suggestion was first advocated and employed by the Parisian therapist Victor Pascault.[22] Modern humans, Pascault argued, simply bothered too much about their physical condition. In his mind, the age of neurasthenia turned out to be the age of hypochondria. 'It's not natural', he said, 'that every sensation had become linked up with pain'. Neither did it seem reasonable to him that the 'oversensitive man … almost all of us have become' fitted into the natural scheme of things. Pascault linked this mental malaise to the rise of modern life and the consequent loss of 'primitive rustic life'. The solution, he continued, lay in the practice of auto-suggestion. Modern humans needed to relearn what 'primitive man' had been capable of doing by instinct. 'Primitive man', Pascault wrote, 'bears, not stoically but passively, many tortures that seem horrible to us'. If modern individuals aimed at re-establishing this innate human ability, they needed only to strengthen their will. Their act of the will aimed at a reframing of their experience though logical appraisal. Neurasthenics, for example, 'should tell themselves not to exaggerate the pains they felt'. 'Let us think differently', he continued, 'or better, let us not think at all'. Patients were encouraged to reject all negativity from their minds, and even to surrender to sickness and pain, in order to permit natural 'courage, patience and resignation' to wake again inside themselves.[23]

Pascault's exhortation 'not to think' in fact meant to think differently, to control the mind's thoughts in particular directions. It was a challenge avidly taken up by Belgian natural therapists and, paradoxically, the quest to free oneself meant disciplining oneself to adopt an extremely regimented manner of thinking. The idea found its fullest treatment in the writings of the Brussels natural healer Léon Neuens, the nephew of Nicolas Neuens and a devoted contributor to *La Réforme Alimentaire*. He opened an office in Brussels shortly before the First World War. In his book *Malades, guérissez-vous par les moyens naturels* ('Sick persons, heal yourselves by natural means'), published in 1912 and applauded by Nyssens, he urged his patients to accept all the experiences of life, including both sickness and health, regardless of their impact. Being immobilised himself by a mysterious illness, and writing and seeing clients from his own sickbed, he suggested that the simple wish to become happy would materialise itself in true happiness.[24] In the closing remarks of his book, Léon Neuens concluded that through 'positive auto-suggestion' one could both hasten healing if sick and perpetuate that condition if one was in good health. He urged the following: 'Let us survey constantly our mental attitude, let us be optimistic, let us always believe in the existence of a better destiny'. The conscious control of mental well-being and the exercise of a strong and independent will could help the modern individual to 'be happy with his fate'. This mental discipline also implied the disciplining of one's sexual desire. Neuens urged his readers to realign their sexuality with the 'universal energy'. Sex without the purpose of procreation was discouraged, for example, because it ignored the natural inclination towards the perpetuation of the species. More generally, Neuens asked his patients to 'perfect their bodies and desires'. In this respect, Neuens did not perceive sexuality as being dangerous in itself, though he advised lifting up the sexual act towards its 'purification', and away from its 'bestial origins'.[25]

Life reform's auto-suggestion relocated the asceticism of naturists from the physical to the mental level. In a book published in 1930, *Pensée féconde* ('Fertile thinking'), Nyssens linked up his older phrenological beliefs with the mental therapeutics of auto-suggestion. In it, he argued that one might overcome phrenological weaknesses by means of a relentless effort to eradicate the deficiencies of one's 'degenerated' mind.[26] He no longer described his enterprise as an undertaking to transform the 'involuntary mind', but rather to reframe the 'subconscious'. This subconscious did not refer to the dark and unattainable set of complexes of the Freudian id. Instead, Nyssens's 'subconscious' turned out to be a layer of pre-reflexive behaviour that could be turned into conscious behaviour through discipline and drill.[27] 'The subconscious', Nyssens wrote, 'is an organic tissue of habits', and Nyssens aimed at reinforcing 'favourable impressions' every moment of the day. The recording of diary notes at the beginning of every day played a crucial role, since in this way the crucial self-transformation could be closely monitored. It all implied a serious investment in personal self-control and moral discipline.[28]

The subconscious was, in Nyssens's words, 'a real person, a human being'. It was a person, however, who needed strict and regular discipline. Nyssens even suggested that his readers talk to their subconscious, pronouncing sentences aloud like 'I'm here!' to show that 'my consciousness is there, awake, in full control of the situation'. For Nyssens and the other practitioners of auto-suggestion, the ascetic practices of the nude body meant to enforce its purity and wholeness found their counterpart in such techniques of the mind.[29] Of course, mental discipline and physical asceticism reinforced each other. On the one hand, nudists provided the 'real life' image of perfect health and beauty that the practitioners of autosuggestion hoped to achieve. On the other hand, Nyssens' mental techniques helped the practitioners of nudism to perform nude culture without their ideal being disturbed by sexual arousal. The influence was not only conceptual. Indeed, the commonplace integration of the vegetarian and nudist movements in the Belgian interwar period facilitated the exchange of behaviours and ideas among its members. The ideal of chaste nudity became an umbrella under which both mental and bodily reform could take shelter.[30]

Asceticism and Social Change

Nudists placed great importance on the concepts of 'Freedom' and 'Nature'. They loaded these terms with assumptions and inflated expectations. The ideas behind the terms were thought to be stronger than any degenerative influence, more powerful than the contradictory realities of modern life, and mightier than the social disorders perceived to be around them. Nudists hoped not only to find personal self-fulfilment by living out these concepts, but also worked towards a utopian society built on them.

The power of the nudist experience was believed not only to change the individual but could also help to change society as a whole. One might even say that nudist experience became the choreography of personal redemption.

Being naked in a group, members of De Spar maintained, was 'a pedagogic undertaking'. Through an 'intimate feeling of being one with nature', it helped one to develop 'a sense of community' and to eradicate antisocial sentiments like the egoism that was cultivated in the midst of the 'harsh struggle for life'.[31] Geerts expressed the same idea in a more poetic manner. 'When the stream of life is obstructed by rigidity', he wrote, 'contemplation and repentance do appear'. He continued: 'With rhythmic steadiness we are led back to the heart of life. Then the cry for renewal and liberation rises again. Then the fortress of old traditions and conventions will be demolished and out of the rubble the fundamentals of a new world will rise'. He considered his brothers and sisters to be able to demolish 'the personality of power' and to establish 'unity and brotherhood'.[32]

The transformation of society was not represented as a social struggle, nor even as the rise of a new ideology. Life reformers imagined their revolution as a discourse incorporated into human flesh. 'Let us be proud', the Hélios leader Lanval said, 'to be part of an elite of bronzed skin, that is growing stronger every day!'[33] The members of this elite needed no external uniform nor any symbol. A bronzed skin alone would serve as their membership card. Nudists believed they had made contact with a deeper truth that all were desperately wishing to achieve. This truth was too important and too essential to be shared in an academic manner: one could not lecture about it; rather, one needed to embody it. Those who reunited themselves with nature, naturists believed, developed a more organic mode of understanding. Instead of spiritual reflection, naturists submerged themselves in the spectacle of nudism itself and became at one with nature. In this bodily experience, they hoped, the secret powers of life would reveal their answers without words, and nudists could rediscover the serenity that was increasingly absent from modern society. Once again, nature would take possession of humanity. According to this view, even the healing of modern diseases came not from a complicated quest but by means of a simple choice: giving up an allegedly artificial distance between the human mind and the natural body.[34] The Dutch writer Yge Foppema, who lived at Van Son's institute for short periods between 1924 and 1930, made the same point by paraphrasing Plato's allegory of the cave in Van Son's journal, *Terug ter Orde*. In a little story about 'delusion and the essence of things', he compared the modern individual with a 'blind fool' in a country far away, sitting in front of a wall. That fool scrupulously studied the shadows on the wall instead of living the life that went on behind their back. If the modern individual wanted to escape artificial modernity, Foppema argued, they only had to turn around to 'look with blinking eyes into the laughing landscape before him'.[35]

Indeed, this 'reunification with nature' proved to be a highly apolitical approach of societal reform. In nudist communities from the 1920s onwards, it became clear that the conception of a natural revolution implied a depoliticisation of reform (just as the idea of chaste nudity implied a desexualisation of the body). All Belgian nudist communities stated clearly in their articles of association that divisiveness should be avoided. In the rules of De Spar, the phrasing ran that 'in matters of religion, politics, parlance [of the French or Dutch languages] and whatever philosophical considerations', the association would 'adopt a strict neutrality'.[36] Nudists referred to the kind of community that they wished to establish in terms of a general camaraderie. They constituted first and foremost a circle of friends: friends who, for example, often sent each other cards on special occasions.[37] Members who could not distance themselves from their political sentiments were often heavily reprimanded. And yet, such requirements undeniably displayed a growing tension beneath the surface. Indeed, while the political polarisation of the outside world continued, nudists experienced more and more problems in keeping external debates outside the nudist community. The growth of the far Right and Left was reflected in the results of the 1936 Belgian elections, when these extremist parties together received one third of the votes cast. Even before that date, however, these and other ideological influences made themselves felt at meetings of Belgian nudists. Hofman wrote to a prospective member of De Spar that he would have no chance of becoming a full member as long as he did not accept political neutrality. He had to understand for once and for all that 'our tendency is not German nor Aryan nor socialist'.[38] Another aspiring member was firmly assured that his fears about finding 'only leftist people' within De Spar were unfounded.[39] A third was warned severely that De Spar would not grant membership to 'combative socialists nor fascists'.[40] These quarrels nonetheless reflect the growing presence of the political factionalism of the period.

The temptation towards political radicalism grew stronger with time. A small minority took up such issues outside the confines of the nudist movement proper and became more politically engaged. If they were not allowed to express their opinions within the nudist community, a few dozen were quite prepared to articulate a philosophy of political engagement outside the walled enclaves of nudism. In radical youth movements such as the right-wing club called the Vlaamsche Kampeer Gemeenschap (Flemish Camping Community), where nudism was practised, the mythical conception of an apolitical community of good intentions was transformed into a totalitarian utopia where individual authenticity was joined to notions of racial regeneration. In nudist magazines, some of the similarities between these extremist groups and older nudist groups were met with alarm. The members of De Spar could read in an internal communication that neither Nazism nor communism would serve the nudist cause. Only individual education against the prejudices of the masses could bring true benefit to humanity.[41] But nudist sympathisers within the radical free youth movement to which Geerts and others belonged often judged these political risks differently. They blended a host of contradictory concepts and ideas together: a rabid anti-parliamentary discourse with vegetarianism, nudist imagery with Flemish nationalist slogans, and even an interest in camping and environmentalism with the symbolism of swastikas. Mostly based in Antwerp, these right-wing youth cells formed a wayward fringe of the Flemish nationalist movement in that city.[42] From 1932 onwards, *Naar Bosch en Hei*, the journal of the Flemish Camping Community, provides clear evidence of vehement protests by a leftist minority against the rising nationalist tendencies of most members. This minority was eventually driven out, and joined with other groups, like the free youth movement called Mane-sching (Moonlight), based in Aalst, which combined the ideal of life reform and the hope for a natural community with a programme of revolutionary social demands. Members of Manesching put on radical theatrical works in urban neighbourhoods across Belgium, calling for communist revolution while maintaining a rigorous lifestyle in which 'fashion slavery', the use of alcohol, tobacco, and even sweets was strictly prohibited. At the same time, they experimented with vegetarian cooking and practised nudist culture in the garden of their club house, De Vlam ('The flame').[43]

The silent majority of nudists did not seem to share these ideas – only a dozen of them seemed to have expressed extremist political views – but, with rare exceptions, neither did they counter them.[44] When Hitler rose to power in Germany, Lanval harshly condemned his regime. He even seemed to fear the collusion unfolding in Germany between some elements of the German nudist movement and the Nazi regime.[45] Instead, Lanval argued that German National Socialism was fuelled by 'a homosexual psyche'. It was a violent dictatorship, in which the rights of women were heavily circumscribed, and in which men were atomised within an anonymous mass and at the service of an elite that sought 'sexual satisfaction' in humiliation and terror. The Nazis's rally in Nuremberg in 1936 testified to their adoration of male force and brutality. The Nazi ideal could not regenerate the human race, Lanval continued, as it was itself a phenomenon of degeneration and a reflection of the unequal position women still held within European society. In order to overturn the excesses of totalitarianism, Lanval concluded, the world needed to promote individual thought, free initiative, women's emancipation, and political democracy.[46]

Asceticism and the Language of the Body

Could a vision of a new world also be developed using physical and mental asceticism? And did nudist culture really propagate a social message? When German troops invaded Belgium in May 1940, the life reform movement was conspicuous by its silence. The individual, physical asceticism that naturists practised, for example, had little resistance to offer against the totalitarian logic of extreme Left and extreme Right, or against the harsh reality of the war. The publication of the Hélios magazine *Lumière et liberté* had to be suspended, the naturist associations were abandoned, and De Spar's grounds in Zoersel were destroyed by vandals. If bodies really could talk, what did they have to say in such troubled times?

Life reformers believed in life, not politics. But 'life' proved unequal to the task of defending itself against the (geo-)political disasters that afflicted Europe. Life did not tell people how to make political judgements, or help heal the new, violent conflicts that were generated by the coming of the Nazis and the collaborationist policies of Belgium's far Right. Asceticism offered access to a physical experience but did not provide intellectual understanding. On the contrary, it had always been a form of escape, escape from what were perceived as the degenerate cultural norms of the bourgeoisie and from the conflicts that the modernisation of society brought with it. That escape made life reform attractive, but also rendered it powerless and naïve. Could utopian liberation be found in such an escape? Life reformers had no clear answer to that question. Nature and the body may have held out the better promises, but they offered no tangible answers.

Belgian life reformers – nudists as well as natural therapists – had placed their hopes in an ascetic experience that could be shared, but not communicated. In the nudist community or in naturopathic practice, life reformers hoped to demonstrate a natural harmony that was impossible to describe. They believed in showing rather than in saying. The modern asceticism they engaged in could be fully experienced, but not expressed. In ascetic body culture, so it seemed, experience and intelligibility were mutually exclusive. The promises of asceticism did not unveil their source.

Notes

Parts of this chapter have been published as 'Authenticity and Asceticism: Discourse and Performance in Nude Culture and Health Reform in Belgium, 1920–1940', *Journal of the History of Sexuality*, 2006. My thanks to the University of Texas Press for permission to reproduce them here.

1. For an overview of the relation between nudism and contemporary discourse on racial degeneration, see M. Hau, *The Cult of Health and Beauty in Germany: A Social History 1890–1930* (Chicago, 2003), 82–100, 150–75; and C. Ross, *Naked Germany: Health, Race and the Nation* (Oxford, 2005), 1–15, 135–60. For an extensive discussion of asceticism and nudity, see A. Labrie, 'Het verlangen naar zuiverheid: Een essay over Duitsland', in R. van der Laarse, A. Labrie and W. Melching (eds), *De hang naar zuiverheid: De cultuur van het moderne Europa* (Amsterdam, 1998), 15–50; and A. Labrie, 'De "Kultur- und

Lebensreformbewegung"', in *Zuiverheid en decadentie: Over de grenzen van burgerlijke cultuur in West-Europa, 1870–1914* (Amsterdam, 2001), 144–54.

2. On the mythical implications of nudism, see M. Möhring, 'Performanz und historische Mimesis: Die Nachnahmung antiker Statuen in der deutschen Nacktkultur,
1890–930', in J. Martschukat and S. Patzold (eds), *Geschichtswissenschaft und
'Performative Turn': Ritual, Inszenierung und Performanz vom Mittelalter bis zur
Neuzeit* (Cologne, 2003), 255–85.

3. In the study of *Lebensreform* in general, this ascetic experience has similarly
been neglected in favour of a discursive perspective. This discursive approach
has been marked deeply by a prolonged debate on the 'modern' versus 'antimodern' nature of life-reform ideology. Antimodern characterisations can be
found in: J. Frecot, J.F. Geist and D. Kerbs, *Fidus 1868–1948: Zur ästhetischen Praxis bürgerlicher Fluchtbewegungen* (Munich, 1972), 9–12, 15–24;
J. Frecot, 'Die Lebensreformbewegung', in K. Vondung (ed.), *Das wilhelminische
Bildungsbürgertum: Zur Sozialgeschichte seiner Ideen* (Göttingen, 1976), 138–52;
and W.R. Krabbe, *Gesellschaftsveränderung durch Lebensreform: Strukturmerkmale
einer sozialreformerischen Bewegung im Deutschland der Industrialisierungsperiode*
(Göttingen, 1974), 27–47, 48–111. More recent studies mostly overlook the antimodern thesis, though some contributions show that it has not faded completely:
e.g., T. Faltin, *Heil und Heilung: Geschichte der Laienheilkundigen und Struktur
antimodernistischer Weltanschauungen in Kaiserreich und Weimarer Republik am
Beispiel von Eugen Wenz (1856–1945)* (Stuttgart, 2000), esp. 143–83, 389–402.
More open approaches, acknowledging the possible modernity of life reform
though remaining within a predominantly discursive perspective, can be found
in: E. Barlösius, *Naturgemässe Lebensführung: Zur Geschichte der Lebensreform um
die Jahrhundertwende* (Frankfurt, 1997); T. Rohkrämer, *Eine andere Moderne?
Zivilisationskritik, Natur und Technik in Deutschland, 1880–1933* (Paderborn,
1999); and Hau, *The Cult of Health and Beauty*.

4. On the radical free youth movements in the Belgian interwar period, see
M. Van Doorselaer, 'Vrije jeugbeweging: Volksdansbeweging en jeugdherbergen in
Vlaanderen, 1918–1940' (University of Gent, 1980), 33–38; M. Van Doorselaer
and P. Vandermeersch, 'Alternatief jeugdleven in Vlaanderen (1918–1940)',
Spieghel Historiael 21 (1986), 192–98; A. Labrie, 'Het verlangen naar zuiverheid:
Een essay over Duitsland', 15–50; and L. Vos, *Bloei en ondergang van het AKVS:
Geschiedenis van de katholieke Vlaamse Studentenbeweging 1914–1935*, 2 vols.
(Leuven, 1982), 1: 207–27. For membership numbers, see the interview with
M. Vreugde in R. Caers, 'Naturisme in het interbellum: een verkenning'
(University of Gent, 1996), 118. On the origins of De Spar, see Internal bulletin,
2 August 1931– Archive Athena 'De Spar', Antwerp (AADS/A).

5. 'Un ordre du jour', *Lumière et Liberté* 3,19 (1934), 1. Also Caers, 'Naturisme in
het interbellum', 31–34, 34–37. On the pseudonym of Paul-Jozef Swenne, see
Caers, 'Naturisme in het interbellum', 101.

6. J. Simon, *Belgische strafwetten: Strafwetboek, wetboek van strafvordering en bij-
komende wetten* (Brussels, 1938), 104–7. Also M. Lanval, *Les peaux de bronze:
Nudisme, naturisme, libre-culture, héliothérapie et eugénique* (Paris, 1931), 124–27.
Lanval's study also appeared in a Dutch version: *Het Naakte Leven: Lucht, licht-*

en zonnebaden, vrije lichaamscultuur, enz. Hoe? Waarom? Wanneer? Geïllustreerde uitgave (Antwerp, 1931).

7. Circular letter, April 1934 – AADS/A.

8. 'Pourquoi nudisme intégral?', *Lumière et Liberté* 1,1 (1932), 4.

9. Lanval, *Les peaux de bronze*, 70, 69, 73.

10. Evidence of multiple complaints filed by Zedenadel members relating to a single offense can be found in: 'Wat kan ieder persoonlijk doen?', *Zedenadel* 1,1 (1933/34), 12; and in: 'Wat onze leden kunnen', *Zedenadel* 2,4 (1934/35), 67. Most were dismissed, since those lodging the complaints were not witnesses to the offense.

11. *Le rouge et le noir: Tribune libre de Bruxelles*, 12 July 1933, 5. See also Caers, 'Naturisme in het interbellum', 91–93.

12. Caers, 'Naturisme in het interbellum', 93.

13. Circular letter, April 1948 – AADS/A.

14. C. De Smeth, 'La cure de soleil', *Lumière et Liberté* 1,1 (1932), 2; Lanval, *Les peaux de bronze*, 18–19, 28–29, 32.

15. F.J. Van den Broeck, *Het levensproblema: De natuurlijke behandeling der zieken* (Brecht, 1904). A French version of the same brochure was also later published as: *Le problème de la vie et le traitement hygiénique des malades* (Brecht, 1907). A biographical survey of Van den Broeck can be found in a series of essays written without attribution by A. Van Son et al., entitled 'Beknopte levensschets van F. J. Van den Broeck', *Maandschrift van het Hygiënisch Gesticht Van den Broeck* 1,10 (1923/24), 149–59; ibid. 1,11 (1923/24), 165–70; ibid. 1,12 (1923/24), 191–94; and *Terug ter Orde* 2,1 (1924/25), 207–11; ibid. 2,2 (1924/25), 219–22; and ibid. 2,5 (1924/25), 265–70. On Van den Broeck's admiration for Rikli en Priessnitz, see [A. Van Son], 'Sebastiaan Kneipp bij Paus Leo XIII', *Terug ter Orde* 5,1 (1928), 877–91.

16. For biographical details about Van Son, see M. Gijsen, *De leerjaren van Jan-Albert Goris* (Brussels and The Hague, 1975), 65–69; J.G. van Schaik-Willing, *Dwaaltocht: Een stukje eigen leven* (Rotterdam, 1977), 55–114; Y. Foppema, 'Alwyn Van Son mistekend door zijn bruid', *Juffrouw Ida* 11,1 (1985), 22–25; and L. Simons, 'Het derde leven van Stijn Streuvels', in K. Wauters (ed.), *Verhalen voor Vlaanderen: Aspecten van het Vlaamse fictioneel proza tot aan de Tweede Wereldoorlog* (Kapellen, 1997), 154.

17. [A. Van Son], 'Het Zonbad', *Terug ter Orde* 3,5/6 (1925/26), 493; [A. Van Son], 'Kuischheid en Naaktheid', *Terug ter Orde* 3,1/2 (1925/26), 401.

18. Van den Broeck, *Het Levensproblema*, 23, 25, 43, 22.

19. N. Neuens, *Le naturisme intégral: Cent vingt conférences* (Gembloux, 1923), 325–26. On the career of Nicolas Neuens, see E. Welter, 'Ein Einblick in das Leben und Wirken von Pfarrer Nicolas Neuens', in E. Welter (ed.), *Abbé Nicolas Neuens, sein Leben, sein Lebenswerk: Gründer des integralen Naturismus, 1845–1925* (Luembourg, 1967), 21–28.

20. J. Geerts, 'Nudisme en levenshervorming', *Naar Bosch en Hei* 2,6 (1931), 6; Lanval, *Les peaux de bronze*, 3, 24, 45.

21. On the logical coherence of naturopathic practice, see W.R. Krabbe, 'Naturheilkunde', in D. Kerbs and J. Reulecke (eds), *Handbuch der deutschen Reformbewegungen* (Wuppertal, 1998), 80.

22. On the emergence of self-suggestion within the Franco-Belgian vegetarian movement, see A. Baubérot, *Histoire du naturisme: Le mythe de retour à la nature* (Rennes, 2003), 152–57.

23. V. Pascault, 'Moral et maladie', *La Réforme Alimentaire* 12,1 (1908), 5–7.

24. Some biographical remarks on Léon Neuens can be found in J. Magnus, 'Ter nagedachtenis', *Het Voorlichtingsblad* 1,6 (1936/37), 81–82.

25. L. Neuens, *Malades, guérissez-vous par les moyens naturels* (Brussels, 1912), 107, 112, 116.

26. P. Nyssens, *Pensée féconde: Entrainement intensif à l'autosuggestion* (Brussels, 1930), 5.

27. Ibid., 28.

28. Ibid.

29. Ibid., 10–11, 28.

30. E. Peeters, 'Degeneratie en dressuur. Natuurgeneeswijze, vegetarisme en naturisme als ontwerpen van een moderne samenleving, 1890–1950', *Bijdragen en Mededelingen op het gebied van de Geschiedenis der Nederlanden*, 119,3 (2004), 329–57.

31. Letter from Huig Hofman to A. de Deckère, 8 August 1934 – AADS/A.

32. Geerts, 'Nudisme en levenshervorming', 6–7.

33. Lanval, *Les peaux de bronze*, 54.

34. Ibid.

35. Y. Foppema, 'Het sprookje van waan en wezen', *Terug ter Orde* 3,5/6 (1925/26), 469–71.

36. 'Uittreksel van de bijlage van het staatsblad van 12 december 1931, n° 1385' (extract of the appendix of the Belgian Bulletin of Acts, Orders and Decrees, 12 December 1931, n° 1385); and 'Standregelen De Spar' (Standing Orders of De Spar) – from the private archive of Jan Vroman of Mortsel, Belgium (JV/M).

37. Letter from H. Hofman to the family De Rache-Vanrintel, 15 November 1938; interview with J. Vroman at Mortsel, 8 September 2004 – AADS/A.

38. Letter from H. Hofman to H. de Ryck, 10 July 1934 – AADS/A.

39. Memo by H. Hofman, 23 July 1933 – AADS/A.

40. Letter from H. Hofman to A. Janssens, 2 November 1934 – AADS/A.

41. Internal communication, n.d. – AADS/A.

42. R. Hemmerijckx, 'Bert van Hoorick: van flamigantisme naar communisme. Deel I', *Wetenschappelijke Tijdingen op het Gebied van de Geschiedenis van de Vlaamse Beweging* 62,2 (2003), 107.

43. B. Van Hoorick, 'Levenshervorming', *Noodhoorn* 3,1 (1932/33), 25, quoted in K. Humbeeck, 'Dat donkere ding, de massa: Omtrent Louis Paul Boon en de jonge generatie in de jaren dertig', in L.P. Boon, *Boontjes 1966*, ed. J. Weverbergh (Antwerp, 2001), 361. 'Verslag van de bestuursvergadering van A.V.S. op 18-2-33', *Opkomst* 6,3 (1932/33), 100, quoted in Humbeeck, 'Dat donkere ding', 370. On Van Hoorick's vegetarianism, see Hemmerijckx, 'Bert van Hoorick', 110; also Hemmerijckx, 'Bert van Hoorick: van flamigantisme

naar communisme. Deel II', *Wetenschappelijke Tijdingen op het Gebied van de Geschiedenis van de Vlaamse Beweging* 62,3 (2003), 163–76.

44. For one Nazi sympathiser's comments, see E. Nillsen, 'L'Allemagne actuelle', *Lumière et Liberté* 3,22 (1934), 3.

45. On the connections between *Lebensreform* and Nazi ideology in Germany, see, e.g., the role of Hans Surén: G. Spitzer, 'Gymnastik oder Parademarsch? Die Rolle Hans Suréns für die Einführung der Leibesübungen in des Nationalsozialistischen Arbeitsdienstes', in G. Spitzer and D. Schmidt (eds), *Sport zwischen Eigenständigkeit und Fremdbestimmung* (Bonn, 1986), 193–212.

46. M. Lanval, 'Le phénomène hitlérien devant la sexologie', *Lumière et Liberté* 5,43 (1936), 1, 4.

References

Published Sources

Barlösius, E. 1997. *Naturgemässe Lebensführung: Zur Geschichte der Lebensreform um die Jahrhundertwende*, Frankfurt.

Baubérot, A. 2003. *Histoire du naturisme: Le mythe du retour à la nature*, Rennes.

Caers, R. 1996. 'Naturisme in het interbellum: een verkenning', Master's thesis, University of Gent.

Faltin, T. 2000. *Heil und Heilung: Geschichte der Laienheilkundigen und Struktur antimodernistischer Weltanschauungen in Kaiserreich und Weimarer Republik am Beispiel von Eugen Wenz (1856–1945)*, Stuttgart.

Foppema, Y. 1985. 'Alwyn Van Son mistekend door zijn bruid', *Juffrouw Ida: Nederlands Letterkundig Museum en Documentatiecentrum* 11(1): 22–25.

Frecot, J. 1976. 'Die Lebensreformbewegung', in K. Vondung (ed.), *Das wilhelminische Bildungsbürgertum: Zur Sozialgeschichte seiner Ideen*, Göttingen, pp.138–52.

Frecot, J., J.F. Geist and D. Kerbs. 1972. *Fidus 1868–1948: Zur ästhetischen Praxis bürgerlicher Fluchtbewegungen*, Munich.

Geerts, J. 1931. 'Nudisme en levenshervorming', *Naar Bosch en Hei: Maandblad van de Vlaamsche Kampeergemeenschap* 2(6): 6–7.

Gijsen, M. 1975. *De leerjaren van Jan-Albert Goris*, Brussels and The Hague.

Hau, M. 2003. *The Cult of Health and Beauty in Germany: A Social History 1890–1930*, Chicago.

Hemmerijckx, R. 2003. 'Bert van Hoorick: van flamigantisme naar communisme. Deel 1', *Wetenschappelijke Tijdingen op het Gebied van de Geschiedenis van de Vlaamse Beweging* 62(2): 98–111.

———— 2003. 'Bert van Hoorick: van flamigantisme naar communisme. Deel 2', *Wetenschappelijke Tijdingen op het Gebied van de Geschiedenis van de Vlaamse Beweging* 62(3): 163–76.

Humbeeck, K. 2001. 'Dat donkere ding, de massa: Omtrent Louis Paul Boon en de jonge generatie in de jaren dertig', in L.P. Boon, *Boontjes 1966*, ed. J. Weverbergh, Antwerp, pp.297–420.

Krabbe, W.R. 1974. *Gesellschaftsveränderung durch Lebensreform: Strukturmerkmale einer sozialreformerischen Bewegung im Deutschland der Industrialisierungsperiode*, Göttingen.

——— 1998. 'Naturheilkunde', in D. Kerbs and J. Reulecke (eds), *Handbuch der deutschen Reformbewegungen, 1880–1933*, Wuppertal, pp.77

Labrie, A. 1998. 'Het verlangen naar zuiverheid: Een essay over Duitsland', in R. van der Laarse, A. Labrie and W. Melching (eds), *De hang naar zuiverheid: De cultuur van het moderne Europa*, Amsterdam, pp.15–50.

——— 2001. *Zuiverheid en decadentie: Over de grenzen van burgerlijke cultuur in West-Europa, 1870–1914*, Amsterdam.

Lanval, M. 1931. *Les peaux de bronze: Nudisme, naturisme, libre-culture, héliothérapie et eugénique*, Paris.

Magnus, J. 1936/37. 'Ter nagedachtenis', *Het Voorlichtingsblad: Gezondheid en hygiene voor allen* 1(6): 81–82.

Möhring, M. 2003. 'Performanz und historische Mimesis: Die Nachnahmung antiker Statuen in der deutschen Nacktkultur, 1890–1930', in J. Martschukat and S. Patzold (eds), *Geschichtswissenschaft und 'Performative Turn': Ritual, Inszenierung und Performanz vom Mittelalter bis zur Neuzeit*, Cologne, pp.255–85.

Neuens, L. 1912. *Malades, guérissez-vous par les moyens naturels*, Brussels.

Neuens, N. 1923. *Le naturisme intégral: Cent vingt conférences*, Gembloux.

Nyssens, P. 1930. *Pensée féconde: Entrainement intensif à l'autosuggestion*, Brussels.

Pascault, V. 1908. 'Moral et maladie', *La Réforme Alimentaire* 12(1): 5–7.

Peeters, E. 2004. 'Degeneratie en dressuur: Natuurgeneeswijze, vegetarisme en naturisme als ontwerpen voor een moderne samenleving, 1890–1950', *Bijdragen en Mededelingen op het Gebied van de Geschiedenis der Nederlanden* 119(3): 329–57.

Rohkrämer, T. 1999. *Eine andere Moderne? Zivilisationskritik, Natur und Technik in Deutschland, 1880–1933*, Paderborn.

Ross, C. 2005. *Naked Germany: Health, Race and the Nation*, Oxford.

Simon, J. 1938. *Belgische strafwetten: Strafwetboek, wetboek van strafvordering en bijkomende wetten*, Brussels.

Simons, L. 1997. 'Het derde leven van Stijn Streuvels', in K. Wauters (ed.), *Verhalen voor Vlaanderen: Aspecten van het Vlaamse fictioneel proza tot aan de Tweede Wereldoorlog*, Kapellen, pp.153–177.

Spitzer, G. 1986. 'Gymnastik oder Parademarsch? Die Rolle Hans Suréns für die Einführung der Leibesübungen in des Nationalsozialistischen Arbeitsdienstes', in G. Spitzer and D. Schmidt (eds), *Sport zwischen Eigenständigkeit und Fremdbestimmung*, Bonn, pp.193–212.

Van den Broeck, F.J. 1904. *Het levensproblema: De natuurlijke behandeling der zieken*, Brecht.

Van Doorselaer, M. 1980. 'Vrije jeugdbeweging: Volksdansbeweging en jeugdherbergen in Vlaanderen, 1918–1940', Master's thesis, University of Gent.

Van Doorselaer, M. and P. Vandermeersch. 1986. 'Alternatief jeugdleven in Vlaanderen (1918–1940)', *Spieghel Historiael* 21: 192–98.

Van Hoorick, B. 1932/33. 'Levenshervorming', *Noodhoorn* 3(1): 25.

van Schaik-Willing, J.G. 1977. *Dwaaltocht: Een stukje eigen leven*, Rotterdam.

Vos, L. 1982. *Bloei en ondergang van het AKVS: Geschiedenis van de katholieke Vlaamse Studentenbeweging 1914–1935*, 2 vols., Leuven.

Welter, E. 1967. 'Ein Einblick in das Leben und Wirken von Pfarrer Nicolas Neuens', in E. Welter (ed.), *Abbé Nicolas Neuens, sein Leben, sein Lebenswerk: Gründer des integralen Naturismus, 1845–1925*, Luxembourg, pp.21–22.

Periodicals

Le rouge et le noir: Tribune libre de Bruxelles.

Lumière et Liberté: Organe officiel de Hélios, Ligue belge de propagande héliophile, 1932–1936.

Maandschrift van het Hygiënisch Gesticht Van den Broeck: Natuurgeneeskundig Tijdschrift: Fides-Caritas-Ratio, 1923–1924.

Terug ter Orde: Fides-Caritas-Ratio: Natuurgeneeskundig Tijdschrift van het Hygiënisch Gesticht Van den Broeck, 1924–1928.

Zedenadel: Driemaandelijksch Orgaan van den Bond voor Openbare Zedelijkheid, 1933–1935.

Archives

AADS/A – Archive Athena 'De Spar', Antwerp.

JV/M – Private archive of Jan Vroman, Mortsel, Belgium.

2

Asceticism and Pleasure in German Health Reform: Patients as Clients in Wilhelmine Sanatoria

Michael Hau

The history of German health reform is a particularly rewarding field for the exploration of modern ascetic practices since so much of health reform is about abstinence, denial and self-discipline. In the late nineteenth and early twentieth centuries, reformers castigated the indulgences and debauchery that in their view characterised modern civilisation, and blamed it for the ill health, degeneration and misfortunes of modern mankind. As remedies they advocated a way of life involving the rejection of the pleasures of consumption and comfort. Vegetarians denounced the consumption of meat, advocates of natural therapies conjured up the dangers of alcohol abuse, while promoters of physical culture and nudism exhorted people to exercise and overcome the debilitating effects of physical idleness.[1]

In early twentieth-century Germany, these various health reform concerns became known as 'life reform' (*Lebensreform*) – a socially and politically heterogeneous movement. Its supporters were socialists, liberals, conservatives, feminists and anti-feminists. While life reform was mostly an urban phenomenon, health reform advocates came from different social classes. Therefore life reform meant quite different things to different people. I have argued elsewhere that lower-middle-class physical culturists found the ascetic aspects of life reform quite attractive, because it enabled them to develop a sense of moral superiority in relation to wealthy and cultivated people with *Bildung* (in the sense of formal higher education), who enjoyed many privileges from which the lower middle classes were excluded. In other words, life reform provided them with a language and symbolic practices (such as physical culture) that allowed them to denounce wealthy and cultivated people as immoral and degenerate 'beer philistines' with fat bellies. Ascetic discipline enabled physical culturists to give free rein to their passions and engage in symbolic aggression against their social superiors.[2] In this way, asceticism became a source of pleasure. This makes us question assumptions about the contradictory nature of pleasure and ascetic practices, and ask in what ways individuals might have experienced body discipline and health reform as pleasure.

German health reform may even have been one of the prototypical settings of this intriguing dynamic between pleasure and asceticism. In keeping with traditional dietetic prescriptions for moderation in all areas of life, some life reformers rejected excessive sexual activity as well as the consumption of food, alcohol and other luxuries, such as white bread and feather beds. For them, only a life lived in moderation was a healthy and wholesome life. However, the historian cannot help but notice that the discourse of moderation and the rejection of luxuries also validated alternative forms of consumerism that undermined such notions of the simple ascetic life. A good example for this alternative consumerism is what one could call the 'wellness industry' of Wilhelmine Germany (1890–1914), in particular the catering for the needs of wealthy patients in expensive health resorts. On the one hand, these patients looked for relief for their personal ailments even if that meant forgoing, at least temporarily, some of their customary luxuries. In this respect they were patients who hoped for therapeutic relief in an environment set apart from their daily routine at home. On the other hand, these patients were also paying customers who expected the comparatively harsh ascetic experience of their cures to be framed by an experience that lived up to their expectations of comfort and standards of consumption. These contradictory expectations of sanatorium visitors – as patients and clients – were reflected in the ways in which the owners and managers of Wilhelmine health resorts promoted their institutions. They promised harsh treatment for what many patients experienced as serious afflictions, but they also indicated that the harsh treatment was framed by a package of socially exclusive consumption that provided great pleasure. The 'pain' of the cure made the pleasure of luxurious consumption all the more pleasurable. Apart from the ascetic radicalism practised by other life reformers, the proponents of this wellness industry offered a different version of early twentieth-century 'asceticism'. In this chapter, the German wellness industry of that era will be studied as yet another arena of modern asceticism.

As I will show, Wilhelmine sanatoria tailored their services and ascetic health regimens to the expectations of their wealthy clientele. High fees and explicit regulations of good behaviour guaranteed the bourgeois respectability of these institutions. At the same time, the joys of asceticism also contributed to the self-image of the alleged moderate and disciplined bourgeois classes. At the beginning of the twentieth century, wealthy individuals easily reappropriated the Rousseauian language of bourgeois senses and sensibilities. They tended to believe that their cultivation and refinement made them both more vulnerable to physical and psychic illnesses and more capable of achieving perfection.

Within the bourgeois wellness industry, the cures and hygienic practices in German health resorts serve as the basis for my examination of the relationship between asceticism and pleasure. I first discuss the ways in which one could consider the cures in these sanatoria as ascetic practices. I then show how sanatoria operators tried to reassure their wealthy clientele that their ascetic health regimen would not interfere unduly with their individual needs and desires. I also demonstrate how Wilhelmine health sanatoria framed their therapies and leisure activities as part of an exclusive consumer experience. As I argue, the offerings of Wilhelmine sanatoria were attractive for people because they promised the fulfilment of individual self-realisation through consumption. In other words, the ascetic – and at times painful – aspects of healthy living were part of a wellness experience of luxury consumption. Wilhelmine sanatoria were sites of a bourgeois culture of leisure, indulgence and entertainment that replaced the aristocratic social ostentation of the expensive spas of eighteenth- and nineteenth-century Europe and Germany.[3] The owners and promoters of their modern, bourgeois counterparts in the early twentieth century invoked bourgeois values such as moderation, self-discipline and self-denial for patients who willingly submitted to ascetic health regimens, but that asceticism was at least in part for pleasure. It was a recreational experience for people who found fulfilment in choosing aspects of healthy living as part of a lifestyle of expensive travel and luxury consumption.

Ascetic Practices in German Life Reform and Natural-Therapy Sanatoria

Late nineteenth-century life reform discourse about illness was based on moral assumptions about health and disease. For many life reformers, a simple life without luxuries was the basis for individual health and well-being. In their view, people could prevent physical sickness and psychological troubles by following prescriptions for an ascetic life in accordance with human nature. At the same time, the realities of a highly industrialised and urbanised society made it difficult for many people to lead such wholesome lives as a matter of course. Life reformers claimed that the consumption of expensive foods, alcohol and other luxuries contributed to a deplorable state of health among upper and middle-class Germans, as did the sedentary occupations of many city dwellers, who did not get enough exercise. Health reformers, therefore, rejected the luxuries of modern consumerism and demanded that people practised moderation in all aspects of their lives. This was in accordance with early nineteenth-century bourgeois virtues of moderation and self-restraint that distinguished the bourgeois middle classes from the debauchery and luxury consumption of the aristocratic upper classes.[4]

Contemporary views of what exactly a hygienic, moral and 'natural' way of life entailed varied. Hard core life reformers, such as many vegetarians, demanded that people reject all luxuries and irritants that stimulated the appetite. They demanded that people abstain from the consumption of meat, alcohol, tea and coffee, exercise regularly, and abstain from sexual excess. In their view, an individual's health was the result of moral restraint and hard work, and their asceticism gave them a sense of moral superiority over those who lacked moral restraint and self-discipline, and as a result became ill. The vegetarian physician Gustav Selss, for example, went so far as to claim that people who became sick did not deserve much pity because they were themselves responsible for their fate. They simply lacked the moral fibre to live a healthy and ascetic life.[5]

The most successful propagators of health, however, lacked such radical moral absolutism and offered people pragmatic help in their efforts to live healthier lives. They also insisted that a simpler life involving dieting, exercise and sexual moderation was the precondition for health and happiness. Instead of demanding total abstinence from alcohol and meat, and other stimulants like tea and coffee, they advocated moderation. Some, like the popular health entrepreneur Friedrich Eduard Bilz, emphasised that a reformed lifestyle could be fun. In his view, healthy eating could still be delicious, and exercise in fresh air gave people joy because it satisfied their natural needs.[6] Bilz was one of the most successful advocates of natural living and therapy in late nineteenth and early twentieth-century Germany. His health advice book for self-guided therapies not only sold millions of copies; he also ran a commercial natural-therapy sanatorium in Radebeul, near Dresden.[7] Bilz became wealthy by selling people the pleasures of a healthy life. One of the most popular consumer items of the Wilhelmine health industry was a lemonade which he marketed first under the name Bilz-Brause and then as Sinalco. Its popularity attested to the dialectical relationship between the ascetic and hedonistic impulses of health reform. Sinalco (derived from the Latin *sine alcohole*, 'without alcohol') became a symbol for abstinence from alcohol and the sweetness of consumption at the same time.[8]

Bilz still emphasised the ascetic aspects of life reform. One of the first articles of his popular turn-of-the-century guide to natural therapies dealt with what the Germans call *Abhärtung*, literally 'hardening' of the body. *Abhärtung* was a process aimed at fortifying the body against all kinds of diseases through a health regimen that emphasised physical exercise, diet, moderation in alcohol consumption, and cold water therapies. According to Bilz, *Abhärtung* aimed at reversing the process of the 'softening' (*Verweichlichung*) of bodies that had come about through modern civilisation. In earlier times, he claimed, ascetic practices of 'hardening' were unnecessary because people's living conditions were harsh and wholesome. There were no steamships and trains, which meant that women, children and men had to walk in all kinds of weather. Whether people lived in villages or cities, they were accustomed to long hikes. Artisans had to work in workshops without heat and double glazing, while servants and many others had to sleep in ice-cold attics. Even in wealthier circles, housework was physically exhausting, which led to the 'hardening' of girls. In these good old days, Bilz maintained, doctors had an easy prescription for the prevention and cure of chlorosis and weakness in girls: physical work at home and exercise in fresh air.[9]

Bilz endorsed Sebastian Kneipp's cold baths and recommended that people dip their arms and feet into cold water for about one minute as a means to safeguarding their health. While Bilz stressed the ascetic and even painful aspects of his natural health regimen, he also pointed to the liberating effects of healthy living. Walking barefoot was in his view one of the most simple and natural ways of fortifying people against ill health. The rural poor would never envy the inhabitants of cities for their fashionable shoes that distorted their feet. Small children, therefore, should never be forced to wear shoes. Liberated from tight stockings and confining shoes, young children should be allowed to romp about freely and happily. In this respect the 'children of the poor' were rarely disturbed in their pleasures. Less favoured by luck were the children of the rich.[10] Along with other advocates of natural therapies and life reform, Bilz tried to convince people that there were rewards for the ascetic in terms of health, happiness and even pleasure.

Bilz, and other health entrepreneurs like Heinrich Lahmann, tried to convince people to either change their entire way of living or visit expensive sanatoria in order to live – at least for a couple of weeks or months – a life that promised to replace their customary comforts with a healthier regimen that denied them some of their usual luxuries. One of their marketing tools was the presentation of patient testimonials that attested to the success of their cures. In Bilz's health advice book, one can find numerous stories about the miraculous recovery of patients.[11] In addition, health entrepreneurs presented themselves as models for their patients. The health entrepreneur Louis Kuhne, for example, recounted his own life story in order to convince his clients that they too could achieve health and happiness by turning to life reform and natural therapies.[12] Bilz presented himself as an ascetic who rejected warm underwear and stockings, walked barefoot whenever he could, and even in winter slept on the balcony of his house in order to fortify his body against illness.[13] The entire Bilz family vouched for the effectiveness of the Bilz system by living and eating with their patients, as well as using the same therapeutic applications.[14] At the same time, Bilz and others affirmed that living in accordance with the laws of human nature would make it possible for everyone to achieve and maintain health into old age. That there were prominent examples to the contrary – the prominent life reform physician and sanatorium operator Heinrich Lahmann died early, aged 45, in 1905 – did not seem to dent the popularity of life-reform sanatoria whose client numbers rose steadily in the years prior to the First World War.[15]

The success of sanatoria might be taken as an indication that health reform asceticism provided real relief for patients. The pleasure associated with therapeutic relief was one of the main reasons why many people were prepared to submit to ascetic health regimens in the first place. This was true not only for those who could afford to attend expensive sanatoria. A large number of the less affluent who were members of natural-therapy associations went to natural therapists for cures, or merely purchased therapy manuals or healthcare products for self-administered cold water therapies. Healthy ascetic living promised personal agency and self-mastery (*Selbstbeherrschung*). For those who turned to life reform because of psychological conditions like neurasthenia, hysteria, or hypochondria, an ascetic health regimen promised relief. Health reformers described their regimes in terms of hard work on their selves that eventually would be rewarded.[16] By strengthening their bodies, they would overcome their own inner weakness and softness and harden not only their bodies but also their will.

Overcoming one's own physical and psychological ailments through one's own hard work validated the bourgeois work ethic and became a source of pleasure. This was the rationale behind different forms of work therapies in health sanatoria. In Dr von Ehrenwall's sanatorium for people with nervous and emotional disorders, patients were encouraged to participate actively in their recovery. Under the supervision of physicians, they could develop their own individual workout programmes on so-called *Zanderapparaten*, exercise machines that targeted and trained individual muscle groups, and on rowing machines and free weights (see Figure 2.1).

Figure 2.1 Exercise room in Dr. Ehrenwall's sanatorium, 1907. © Staatsbibliothek zu Berlin, Berlin, Germany / Bildarchiv Preussischer Kulturbesitz, Berlin, Germany.

Dr von Ehrenwall's wealthy patients were also offered the opportunity to engage in manual work in the sanatorium workshop. Wood carving, pottery, leather work and photography helped people develop their own creativity and work on their own recovery.[18] In other sanatoria, people sawed and chopped wood (see Figure 2.2), and engaged in forms of manual labour which they did not have to confront during their normal bourgeois existence.[19]

Figure 2.2 Chilling, chopping and sawing: leisure and occupational therapy in the Sanatorium Rumburg, 1912. © Staatsbibliothek zu Berlin, Berlin, Germany / Bildarchiv Preussischer Kulturbesitz, Berlin, Germany.

Von Ehrenwall's sanatorium also promoted physical labour in the open air. The extensive gardens of the sanatorium provided men from the 'most varied social classes' with the experience of 'joy and interest in garden work'.[21] The promotional material for the sanatorium, however, indirectly acknowledged tensions between the sanatorium's ascetic health regimen and the consumer orientation of its clients. The advertising booklet recommended gardening in the extensive orchards and vegetable gardens of the sanatorium as an excellent therapy, but the promoters had to concede that this form of physical occupational therapy in the open air was not taken up enthusiastically. While such work was 'for the entire metabolism of the greatest importance', the operators of the sanatorium had to admit that they were not very successful in keeping 'cultivated patients' (*gebildete Patienten*) interested in such activities.[22] This admission also points to different levels of enthusiasm among patients for the ascetic aspects of the natural health regimen. While some might have taken up physical activity eagerly, others, like the painter George Grosz, had doubts about the genuineness of people's commitment to health reform. For Grosz, who spent some time at one of the health reform sanatoriums in Dresden, most of the patients were simply wealthy neurotics with imaginary ailments.[23]

While wealthy patients in expensive sanatoria were encouraged to take up offers of work therapy in order to participate voluntarily in their recovery, the situation was different for patients in therapeutic institutions funded by Germany's growing health insurance system.[24] After Bismarck's introduction of health, accident, invalidity and pension insurance in the early 1880s, charitable foundations and the German state built large therapeutic institutions for people who suffered from work-related injuries and nervousness. The goal of large *Heilstätten* complexes, such as Beelitz near Berlin, was to reintegrate insured patients as quickly as possible back into the work force in order to keep down health-insurance costs. As in private sanatoria, the treatments combined aspects of natural therapy such as hydrotherapy with modern forms of technological therapies such as electrotherapy. Compared to private natural-therapy sanatoria, occupational therapies were significantly harsher, sometimes to the point of being punitive. Some critics, therefore, talked about 'forced labour' (*Arbeitszwang*). The asceticism of these institutions was not voluntary. Work therapy in particular aimed to prevent people from malingering at the expense of the social insurance system by compelling them to work.[25] In contrast to expensive private sanatoria, these institutions emphasised a stern asceticism and tried to counter public suspicions that they also were places of leisure and frivolous consumption.

Wealthy Clients and Asceticism: Individualised Therapies for the Bourgeois Individual

Occasionally the advertisements and promotional literature for private natural-therapy sanatoria claimed that clients came from different social classes. This should be taken with a pinch of salt. To some extent it is true that natural-therapy spas and sanatoria offered services that could be afforded by people from different social backgrounds. The industrialist and benefactor Johann von Zimmermann founded a natural-therapy sanatorium in Chemnitz, and supported it with an endowment for 'people with lesser means'.[26] Friedrich Bilz's sanatorium treated people with lesser means as out-patients and his staff also treated people by correspondence. But staying at these sanatoria was usually very expensive, and their clientele was therefore rather exclusive. That these sanatoria were mostly intended for wealthier clients is evident from the prices they charged for cures and accommodation. In 1894, Bilz's sanatorium charged its patients between 150 and 300 marks per month, depending on the size and comfort of their accommodation.[27] By the early 1900s, a stay at the sanatorium cost between 7 and 13 marks per day.[28] Other sanatoria charged even more. Dr Ziegelroth's natural-therapy sanatorium in Zehlendorf near Berlin charged between 10 and 16 marks or about 300 to almost 500 marks per month (see Figure 8.3).[29]

Figure 2.3 The Ladies' Bath in Dr. Ziegelroth's sanatorium: room with bathing tubs, electrical therapy device, and central heating, 1906. © Staatsbibliothek zu Berlin, Berlin, Germany / Bildarchiv Preussischer Kulturbesitz, Berlin, Germany.

In 1907, Dr von Ehrenwall's sanatorium charged 240 to 260 marks for a small room, 280 to 350 marks for a bigger room, and a salon with a small side room cost between 400 and 600 marks per month.[31] Even the cheaper rooms were still quite expensive. Many patients stayed at these sanatoria for more than a month and, depending on the kind of cure they undertook, sometimes several months, which means that they possessed considerable means. If one takes into account that in 1912, 52 per cent of all Prussian taxpayers had an annual income of less than 900 marks, one realises that only wealthier people could afford to participate in the wellness experience of most private Wilhelmine sanatoria.[32] In contrast to social-insurance-funded *Heilstätten*, the working classes and the lower middle classes were not part of their usual clientele.

In March 1902, the Prussian Prince Woldemar visited Heinrich Lahmann's sanatorium Weisser Hirsch near Dresden, which was seen by supporters of alternative therapies as an endorsement of natural therapy by members of the imperial household.[33] For wealthy bourgeois clients the visit by the Prussian prince must have endorsed their sense of social exclusivity. Given the comfort to which people from such elevated social backgrounds were accustomed to, we have to ask how ascetic was the life in such sanatoria in reality? If one looks at some of the promotional literature, one is struck by how the ascetic aspects of a stay in a sanatorium were carefully framed by the promises of luxury and consumption. This was all the more important because the sanatoria had to negotiate between the somewhat contradictory expectations and desires of their clients. On the one hand, patients expected that they had to live according to some of the life-reform prescriptions of the ascetic life: diet, exercise, even painful therapies such as electro-shock treatments, and alternative therapies such as Sebastian Kneipp's cold-water therapy or the 'Schroth cure' were aspects of a health regimen that seemed to deny promises of luxury, consumption and comfort. On the other hand, patients also went to these sanatoria for pleasure and relaxation as a study of the Swiss sanatorium Monte Veritá has recently emphasised.[34] When Thomas Mann, for example, attended Dr Lahmann's sanatorium, he wanted to 'take care of himself a little bit' and hoped that he would be inspired by some of the 'applications'.[35] The hedonistic aspects of the early twentieth-century sanatoria were of course carefully noted by Mann, who left us with an extensive literary treatment of the luxurious social life in an exclusive tuberculosis sanatorium in Davos.[36]

While Wilhelmine sanatoria sometimes advertised harsh and painful cures, they also tended to play down some of the more ascetic aspects of their offerings. Bilz's natural-therapy sanatorium, for example, offered its clients the full treatment according to Sebastian Kneipp's 'water cure' in order to fortify people against illness. The cure involved walking barefoot on wet grass, rocks and snow. Cold water applications were supposed to improve the circulation of the blood by distributing the blood throughout the entire body more evenly. According to Bilz, partial showers of the knees (*Kniegüsse*) and standing or walking in cold water would improve blood circulation in the feet and reduce blood pressure in other body parts affected by 'inflammations'.[37] Since Kneipp thought that water applications were more effective the colder they were, they were probably not all pleasure for most people. The operators of health sanatoria realised that people used to the comforts of civilisation might be somewhat unwilling to undergo such treatments, which is why they were careful to qualify their ascetic or even painful implications. An article promoting Bilz's sanatorium, therefore, reassured potential clients that Bilz's sanatorium was not really a 'cold-water institution' (*Kaltwasseranstalt*), because the temperature of the water would be adjusted according to individual needs. The treatment, the author and schoolteacher Helene Winkler claimed, would not only enliven spirit and mind. It was also considerate and 'if necessary, very mild'.[38]

While *Abhärtung* was supposed to fortify the clients of Wilhelmine sanatoria against illness, it had its limits where it compromised individual comfort. This becomes even more evident if one looks at how Bilz's sanatorium administered the Schroth cure which had the reputation of being one of the most strenuous regimens offered by Wilhelmine health establishments. The Schroth cure, also known as regeneration or thirst cure, was based on the notion that in the case of chronic illnesses drastic measures were needed to raise the 'natural healing power' (*Naturheilkraft*) of the organism. The measures included, at least in theory, a strict diet, involving the withdrawal of water and other fluids. By simplifying the diet and withdrawing fluids, the digestive system would get a rest. The body could then be cleansed of its remaining phlegm and waste matter through sweating, defecation and urination. Like other forms of natural therapy, such as Louis Kuhne's water cure, the Schroth cure restored health by cleansing the body of pathogenic waste matter, thus eliminating the predisposition to a whole range of different diseases. Many people could not withstand the Schroth cure, which could last several months, and which, as Bilz's health guide warned, should only be undertaken in a sanatorium under the supervision of qualified naturopathic physicians. The regimen aimed at a rejuvenation of the juices through the creation of healthy blood. Wet packs at night tried to induce sweat and people had to adhere to a strict diet including dry bread rolls, rice, noodles, vegetables and milk products. Since the cure aimed at the cleansing of the body through the withdrawal of fluids, patients had to to drink very little.[39] The prescriptions for the cure were quite detailed and there is no need to explore them at length. What is interesting here, however, is that in Bilz's sanatorium the prescriptions for the Schroth cure were not treated as hard-and-fast rules. This was justified by the natural-therapy principle of individualised treatment: one of the dogmas of natural therapy was to tailor treatment to the individual constitutions of patients because every patient was different. This principle was one of the most important arguments used by natural therapists against orthodox medicine. Natural therapists claimed that natural therapy individualised treatments, while orthodox medicine treated patients schematically and ignored their individuality.[40] In the case of the Schroth cure, the principle of individualised treatment was used to take the sting out of some of its more torturous or ascetic aspects. The strict diet and living regime, Bilz claimed, should be modified according to the needs and nature of patients. If patients had the 'burning desire' to eat some meat, chicken or fish, they should not be denied. Alcohol was also not always frowned upon, despite the frequent condemnation of alcohol consumption in natural-therapy circles. Bilz considered one to two glasses of wine per day as acceptable, except during the so-called drinking days of the cure when patients were allowed to drink a bottle per day. While cold beer and water should be avoided, wine by contrast was justified because of its therapeutic effects. It was claimed to stimulate the nerves and blood flow.[41]

Other natural-therapy sanatoria also promised to modify their therapeutic prescriptions in accordance with the wishes of patients. Ferdinand Liskow, the owner of the Bad Sommerstein sanatorium in Thuringia, for example, pro-

moted the Schroth cure by emphasising that it was applied in a 'strictly individualised' manner that avoided the harshness of the cure.[42] However, those
patients who liked it the hard way could opt for a harsher and more ascetic
therapy (*energischste Kur*) and enjoy the full pain of the 'strict Schroth cure'.
The promotion emphasised, however, that a fasting cure was not a hunger
cure and that the patient alone decided how far they wanted to push it.[43]

Ascetic Health Reform and the Pleasures of Consumerism

The ways in which health reformers adjusted their cures for their patients
shows that natural therapists and physicians working in sanatoria had to
negotiate carefully the contradictory wishes of their wealthy bourgeois clients.
These patients had to be persuaded to participate in their cures, and could
not be forced to do anything against their wishes. Patients had to be convinced that their stay at a sanatorium would be pleasurable, and that even the
asceticism of a strict health regimen would add to their pleasure or at least not
interfere too much with their accustomed comfort level.

Instead of dwelling on the ascetic aspects of their cures, the promoters of
sanatoria emphasised the pleasant aspects of an extended stay.[44] Photographs
of furnishings and interior designs showed the comforts of individual rooms
as well as public halls for recreation.[45]

People with nervous disorders, Dr von Ehrenwall's brochure maintained,
needed entertainment as a diversion from their sanatorium routine. It recommended visits to the theatre, concerts and popular science lectures in nearby
Ahrweiler, as well as short hikes and excursions into the Ahr and Rhine valley.[46] For people who considered such excursions too strenuous, the sanatorium had purchased a small forest area with wonderful views over the Rhine
valley, which patients could reach after a short walk. Excursions and short
hikes were important aspects of a hygienic reform programme that emphasised moderate exercise. Other aspects such as dieting, while very important in
theory, seem to have received less attention in practice. The meals in Dr von
Ehrenwall's sanatorium, for example, were anything but modest: there were
two breakfasts, the first one including coffee, tea, chocolate or milk with butter and bread, the second one consisting of meat bouillon with bread. Lunch,
the main meal, consisted of soup, two courses of meat or meat and fish with
vegetables and condiments, and a sweet dessert. Dinner included warm meat
or egg dishes, or a cold plate with butter and bread, with alcoholic beverages
at the discretion of the attending physician.[47] Coffee, tea, bouillon, meat
and – under the supervision of the physician – alcohol: all these were usually
denounced in life-reform circles as dangerous irritants that weakened people's
constitutions and predisposed them to disease. Such a diet seems to be an odd

choice for a sanatorium that promoted ascetic life-reform therapies such as water cures, wet packs, air and sun bathing, massages and exercise.

This combination of luxury and asceticism makes sense if one understands the ascetic regimen in these sanatoria as part of early twentieth-century consumer culture. The sanatoria promoted their therapies as part of a socially exclusive consumer package for the wealthy. One can safely assume that patients in these sanatoria did not seek the pleasures of the living conditions of the working poor, which according to Bilz were so conducive to good health. Wilhelmine health entrepreneurs might have lauded the simplicity of rural life, but their wealthy clientele would have hardly put up with unheated rooms, bland meals and other deprivations associated with rural poverty. By contrast, the ascetic and simple life in Wilhelmine health sanatoria was based on the comfort of a carefully controlled environment. Central heating and electric light were standard in such places.[48] One sanatorium described its rooms as 'comfortable and while avoiding unnecessary luxuries adapted to the tastes of wealthy circles'.[49] Some sanatorium clients were happy to diet and exercise in moderation, and they were sometimes even happy to engage in hard physical labour; but they did so in an environment of comfort and luxury, and in the company of their social peers. The beautiful landscapes in which these sanatoria were situated and the luxurious accommodation for their clients contrasted with and emphasised the austerity of the cures and health regimens, which many people in these institutions followed.[50] In this environment patients experienced their ascetic life as something that was set apart from their everyday lives: as leisure and pleasure. For those who could afford it, the ascetic and simple life was wrapped in luxury with all the trappings of an elevated social status.

Sanatoria even presented their therapeutic applications in terms of luxurious extravagance. Catalogues gave long lists of their state-of-the-art diagnostic and therapeutic devices, ranging from simple bathing tubs in baths with central heating, complex equipment for various electrical and light therapies, to X-rays and 'radium emanators' for the inhalation of radium which supposedly helped against rheumatism, gout and other forms of chronic pain and inflammation.[51]

In Dr von Ehrenwall's sanatorium, showers and baths were an integral part of the therapeutic arsenal. However, bathing was not just something therapeutic. Bathing was something patients could indulge in for their own pleasure as long as it did not have any adverse effects on their health. The promotional material emphasised that the bathing equipment was ready at any time. All fifty hot-water bath tubs at the institution could be used simultaneously day and night.[52] There is a big irony here. In natural-therapy sanatoria, therapies became part of what puristic advocates of life-reform asceticism rejected: they were an integral aspect of the pleasures of luxury consumption.

The sanatorium was also a place where patients could socialise with their social peers, relax and meet members of the opposite sex. Despite Bilz's eulogies on the benefits of asceticism, which I have cited above, his sanatorium was such a frivolous place that the authorities tried to close it down. The ultimate reasons that led to the temporary closure of the sanatorium in early 1914 were to do with accusations about the incorrect diagnosis and maltreatment of a female patient with syphilis who lost her eyesight as a result. But the authorities in Saxony were also very worried about threats to the moral order resulting from the mingling of the sexes. In addition to his sanatorium, Bilz ran a large 'air-light bath' (*Licht-Luft-Bad*), with swimming facilities for the general public. At the request of the local police, the bath was segregated into three sections – for families, men and women – in order to avoid the mixing of single men and women.[53] While the local police could exercise some control over what was going on in the public bath, its power to enforce moral propriety in the enclosed bathing facilities of the private sanatorium was rather limited. A 1911 inspection of the sanatorium grounds confirmed official suspicions of moral and sexual impropriety. In the light-and-air bathing section of the sanatorium, young men in bathing trunks and young women in thin 'air-bathing shirts' (*Luftbadehemden*) 'consorted without shame' (*ungenierter Verkehr*). The apparently single women were photographed by men, and the changing facilities for men and women were so close that they could observe each other while undressing.[54] While such behaviour would hardly have roused an eyebrow in the 1920s – when such heterosocial intercourse between young, urban middle-class men and women was common[55] – in the more restrictive prewar period such frivolities were still worthy of an official inspection report. At the same time, meeting other young men and women in relatively informal ways was probably one of the main attractions of a longer sanatorium stay. As semi-public institutions, sanatoria provided an arena of luxury consumption which both sexes could enjoy together. As such they made a small contribution to the erosion of separate spheres for the sexes among the middle classes – a development which caused much anxiety during the late Wilhelmine period, because it smacked of women's social independence and sexual immorality.[56]

Conclusion

The wellness industry in early twentieth-century Germany demonstrated more than a bourgeois preoccupation with physical health. In expensive sanatoria, ascetic principles and practices merged with modern consumerism and hedonism. As with life-reform practices in general, natural therapy sanatoria promised their patients a transformation of their selves. An ascetic health regimen offered them a restoration of their health and vitality. They could overcome nervousness, emotional problems, or serious physical problems, and experience their transformation as a result of their discipline and hard work. Submitting to such a health regimen validated the bourgeois work ethic and gave patients the feeling that the positive outcomes of their cures were the result of their moral discipline and self-restraint. Sanatorium patients could, therefore, look with some satisfaction at their achievements. In this respect, life-reform asceticism could be a source of pleasure, as in the case of patients who had either lost or gained weight in the pursuit of a more beautiful body.[57] But patients were not only able to find personal satisfaction in the overtly ascetic aspects of a sanatorium stay. The moral implications of life reform asceticism – indicating self-discipline and strength of will – ironically served to legitimise the very opposite. They validated the pleasures of consumerism as well as the hedonistic transgression of social boundaries between the sexes. Located in rural settings, the sanatoria invoked the notion of a simple rural and ascetic life which was reinforced by the various manual occupational therapies offered to their clients. At the same time, the sanatoria always stressed their closeness to nearby cities where people could enjoy urban entertainment and shopping (see Figure 2.4). Elegant shops in Dresden, for example, offered deliveries of luxury goods to their clients in nearby sanatoria.[58]

Figure 2.4 Natural simplicity near the metropolis: Dr. Ziegelroth's sanatorium in Zehlendorf close to Berlin, 1906. © Staatsbibliothek zu Berlin, Berlin, Germany / Bildarchiv Preussischer Kulturbesitz, Berlin, Germany.

Most sanatoria saw their best times prior to the First World War. While there were still some expensive sanatoria prospering in the 1920s, many had to cope with declining visitor numbers. The reasons for this are manifold. With the loss of many of their prosperous foreign clientele after the war, many places not only lost considerable income but also much of their international glamour.[60] Equally important – and more pertinent to our question regarding the relationship between asceticism and pleasure – were fundamental changes in German society and in European societies in general. Several historians have written about the pervasive hunger for experience and pleasure that gripped European societies after the war. This postwar hedonism found its expression not only in the new postwar consumer culture, but also in changed relationships between the sexes.[61] As a result of these profound social and cultural changes, sanatoria lost their function as places where desires and pleasures were legitimated by submitting to the asceticism of a natural health regimen. To give just one obvious example, in a postwar society where urban young men and women enjoyed each other's company with little interference from their elders and social conventions, and where premarital sex was more common, young men and women of the better-off classes did not have to spend their time in Bilz's sanatorium in order to catch a glimpse of the opposite sex in an open dressing-room. The sanatoria, therefore, lost some of their uniqueness as legitimate semi-public places of leisure, consumption and pleasure.

Notes

1. F. Fritzen, *Gesünder Leben: Die Lebensreformbewegung im 20. Jahrhundert* (Stuttgart, 2006); C. Ross, *Naked Germany: Health, Race and the Nation* (Oxford, 2005); M. Möhring, *Marmorleiber: Körperbildung in der deutschen Nacktkultur, 1890–1930* (Cologne, 2004); B. Wedemeyer-Kolwe, *'Der neue Mensch': Körperkultur im Kaiserreich und in der Weimarer Republik* (Würzburg, 2004); M. Hau, *The Cult of Health and Beauty in Germany: A Social History, 1890–1930* (Chicago, 2003); K. Buchholz et al., *Die Lebensreform: Entwürfe zur Neugestaltung von Leben und Kunst um 1900* (Darmstadt, 2001); T. Rohkrämer, *Eine andere Moderne? Zivilisationskritik, Natur, und Technik in Deutschland* (Paderborn, 1999); D. Kerbs and J. Reulecke, *Handbuch der deutschen Reformbewegungen, 1880-1933* (Wuppertal, 1998); C. Regin, *Selbsthilfe und Gesundheitspolitik: Die Naturheilbewegung im Kaiserreich (1889–1914)* (Stuttgart, 1995); W.R. Krabbe, *Gesellschaftsveränderung durch Lebensreform: Strukturmerkmale einer sozialreformerischen Bewegung im Deutschland der Industrialisierungsperiode* (Göttingen, 1974).
2. Hau, *The Cult of Health and Beauty*, 44–54.
3. B. Fuhs, *Mondäne Orte einer vornehmen Gesellschaft: Kultur und Geschichte der Kurstädte* (Hildesheim, 1992); R.P. Kuhnert, *Urbanität auf dem Lande: Badereisen nach Pyrmont im 18. Jahrhundert* (Göttingen, 1984).

4. M. Frey, *Der reinliche Bürger: Entstehung und Verbreitung bürgerlicher Tugenden in Deutschland, 1760–1860* (Göttingen, 1997); U. Frevert, *Krankheit als politisches Problem: Soziale Unterschichten in Preussen zwischen medizinischer Polizei und staatlicher Sozialversicherung* (Göttingen, 1984).

5. Hau, *The Cult of Health and Beauty*, 121–23.

6. M. Lienert, *Naturheilkundiges Dresden* (Dresden, 2002), 105.

7. Ibid., 94–114; E. Freitag, *Naturheilkunde-Sanatorien in Dresden und Umgebung vom letzten Drittel des 19. Jahrhunderts bis 1945* (Dresden, 1999), 133–60.

8. Lienert, *Naturheilkundiges Dresden*, 110.

9. F.E. Bilz, *Das Neue Naturheilverfahren: Lehr- und Nachschlagebuch der naturgemäßen Heilweise und Gesundheitspflege*, 31st edn (Leipzig, 1895), 12.

10. Ibid., 9–12.

11. See, e.g., ibid., 653–65.

12. Hau, *The Cult of Health and Beauty*, 18–23.

13. Lienert, *Naturheilkundiges Dresden*, 114.

14. Freitag, *Naturheilkunde-Sanatorien*, 134

15. Lienert, *Naturheilkundiges Dresden*, 39–41, 56–59.

16. Hau, *The Cult of Health and Beauty*, 13–31, 121; N. Rose, *Inventing Our Selves: Psychology, Power and Personhood* (Cambridge, 1996).

17. Dr von Ehrenwall, *Sanatorium für Nerven und Gemütskranke* (Ahrweiler, 1907), 95.

18. Ibid., 94–5, 104–13.

19. C. Dittrich and B. von Barth Wehrenalp, *Sanatorium Frankenstein bei Rumburg. Physikalisch-diätetische Kuranstalt ersten Ranges* (Rumburg, 1912), 40, 46.

20. Ibid., 47.

21. von Ehrenwall, *Sanatorium für Nerven und Gemütskranke*, 59.

22. Ibid., 114.

23. A. Scholz, 'Ärzte und Patienten in Dresdner Naturheilsanatorien', *Medizin-Bibliothek-Information* 4,1 (2004), 16–18.

24. A. Killen, *Berlin Electropolis: Schock, Nerves, and German Modernity* (Berkeley, 2006); J. Radkau, *Das Zeitalter der Nervosität: Deutschland zwischen Bismarck und Hitler* (Munich, 1998).

25. Killen, *Berlin Electropolis*, 114–20.

26. M. Regis, 'Eine Reise durch Deutschlands Naturheilanstalten', *Reformblätter* 5 (1902), 130.

27. H. Winkler, 'Die Bilzsche Naturheilanstalt in Dresden Radebeul', in Bilz, *Das Neue Naturheilverfahren*, 1520.

28. Freitag, *Naturheilkunde-Sanatorien*, 144.

29. P.S. Ziegelroth, *Dr. Ziegelroth's Sanatorium Zehlendorf bei Berlin* (Zehlendorf, 1906), 8.

30. Ibid., 7.

31. von Ehrenwall, *Sanatorium für Nerven und Gemütskranke*, 122.

32. G. Hohorst, J. Kocka and G.A. Ritter (eds), *Sozialgeschichtliches Arbeitsbuch: Materialien zur Statistik des Kaiserreichs, 1870–1914* (Munich, 1975), 109.

33. Scholz, 'Ärzte und Patienten', 13.

34. A. Schwab, *Monte Verità: Sanatorium der Sehnsucht* (Zurich, 2003), 53–55.

35. Scholz, 'Ärzte und Patienten', 15.

36. T. Mann, *Der Zauberberg*, 16th edn (Frankfurt, 2004).

37. Bilz, *Das Neue Naturheilverfahren*, 570–72, 1405–07.

38. Winkler, 'Die Bilzsche Naturheilanstalt', 1520.

39. Bilz, *Das Neue Naturheilverfahren*, 1342–49.

40. Hau, *The Cult of Health and Beauty*, 102; Regin, *Selbsthilfe und Gesundheitspolitik*, 103.

41. Bilz, *Das Neue Naturheilverfahren*, 1343–48.

42. Regis, 'Eine Reise', 133; K. Möller and F. Liskow, *Kurbad und Waldsanatorium Bad Sommerstein: Ein Jungbrunnen in Thüringen*, 14th edn (Bad Sommerstein, 1915), 16–18.

43. Möller and Liskow, *Kurbad und Waldsanatorium*, 16.

44. Schwab, *Monte Verità*, 151–56.

45. Dittrich and von Barth Wehrenalp, *Sanatorium Frankenstein*, 31–42.

46. von Ehrenwall, *Sanatorium für Nerven und Gemütskranke*, 114–21.

47. Ibid., 123.

48. Regis, 'Eine Reise'.

49. von Ehrenwall, *Sanatorium für Nerven und Gemütskranke*, 10, 19.

50. Möller and Liskow, *Kurbad und Waldsanatorium*, 32–34; Dittrich and von Barth Wehrenalp, *Sanatorium Frankenstein*, 22–26; von Ehrenwall, *Sanatorium für Nerven und Gemütskranke*, 114–21; Ziegelroth, *Dr. Ziegelroth's Sanatorium*, 11.

51. Dittrich and von Barth Wehrenalp, *Sanatorium Frankenstein*, 26–48; Ziegelroth, *Dr. Ziegelroth's Sanatorium*, 5–7.

52. von Ehrenwall, *Sanatorium für Nerven und Gemütskranke*, 66, 79.

53. Freitag, *Naturheilkunde-Sanatorien*, 146–48, 221–24.

54. Bundesarchiv, Berlin-Lichterfelde (B/BL), R 1501 Nr. 9135, Bl. 142.

55. C. Usborne, 'The New Woman and Generation Conflict: Perceptions of Young Women's Sexual Mores in the Weimar Republic', in M. Roseman (ed.), *Generations in Conflict: Youth Revolt and Generation Formation in Germany, 1770–1968* (Cambridge, 1995), 137–63.

56. Hau, *The Cult of Health and Beauty*, 80–82.

57. Ziegelroth, *Dr. Ziegelroth's Sanatorium*, 12.

58. Freitag, *Naturheilkunde-Sanatorien*, 41.

59. Ziegelroth, *Dr. Ziegelroth's Sanatorium*, 8, cover.

60. Lienert, *Naturheilkundiges Dresden*, 58–60, 122–36.

61. H. Stoff, *Ewige Jugend: Konzepte der Verjüngung vom späten 19. Jahrhundert bis ins Dritte Reich* (Cologne, 2004); M. Eksteins, *Rites of Spring: The Great War and the Birth of the Modern Age* (Boston, 1989), 256–58.

References

Published Sources

Bilz, F.E. 1895. *Das Neue Naturheilverfahren: Lehr- und Nachschlagebuch der naturgemäßen Heilweise und Gesundheitspflege*, 31st edn, Leipzig.

Buchholz, K., et al. 2001. *Die Lebensreform: Entwürfe zur Neugestaltung von Leben und Kunst um 1900*, 2 vols, Darmstadt.

Dittrich, C., and B. von Barth Wehrenalp. 1912. *Sanatorium Frankenstein bei Rumburg: Physikalisch-diätetische Kuranstalt ersten Ranges*, Rumburg.

Eksteins, M. 1989. *Rites of Spring: The Great War and the Birth of the Modern Age*, Boston.

Freitag, E. 1999. *Naturheilkunde-Sanatorien in Dresden und Umgebung vom letzten Drittel des 19. Jahrhunderts bis 1945*, Dresden.

Frevert, U. 1984. *Krankheit als politisches Problem: Soziale Unterschichten in Preussen zwischen medizinischer Polizei und staatlicher Sozialversicherung*, Göttingen.

Frey, M. 1997. *Der reinliche Bürger: Entstehung und Verbreitung bürgerlicher Tugenden in Deutschland, 1760–1860*, Göttingen.

Fritzen, F. 2006. *Gesünder Leben: Die Lebensreformbewegung im 20. Jahrhundert*, Stuttgart.

Fuhs, B. 1992. *Mondäne Orte einer vornehmen Gesellschaft: Kultur und Geschichte der Kurstädte*, Hildesheim.

Hau, M. 2003. *The Cult of Health and Beauty in Germany: A Social History, 1890–1930*, Chicago.

Hohorst, G., J. Kocka and G.A. Ritter (eds). 1975. *Sozialgeschichtliches Arbeitsbuch: Materialien zur Statistik des Kaiserreichs, 1870–1914*, Munich.

Kerbs, D., and J. Reulecke. 1998. *Handbuch der deutschen Reformbewegungen, 1880–1933*, Wuppertal.

Killen, A. 2006. *Berlin Electropolis: Schock, Nerves, and German Modernity*, Berkeley.

Krabbe, W.R. 1974. *Gesellschaftsveränderung durch Lebensreform: Strukturmerkmale einer sozialreformerischen Bewegung im Deutschland der Industrialisierungsperiode*, Göttingen.

Kuhnert, R.P. 1984. *Urbanität auf dem Lande: Badereisen nach Pyrmont im 18. Jahrhundert*, Göttingen.

Lienert, M. 2002. *Naturheilkundiges Dresden*, Dresden.

Mann, T. 2004. *Der Zauberberg*, 16th edn, Frankfurt.

Möhring, M. 2004. *Marmorleiber: Körperbildung in der deutschen Nacktkultur, 1890–1930*, Cologne.

Möller, K., and F. Liskow. 1915. *Kurbad und Waldsanatorium Bad Sommerstein: Ein Jungbrunnen in Thüringen*, 14th edn, Bad Sommerstein.Radkau, J. 1998. *Das Zeitalter der Nervosität: Deutschland zwischen Bismarck und Hitler*, Munich.

Regin, C. 1995. *Selbsthilfe und Gesundheitspolitik: Die Naturheilbewegung im Kaiserreich (1889–1914)*, Stuttgart.

Regis, M. 1902. 'Eine Reise durch Deutschlands Naturheilanstalten', *Reformblätter* 5: 127–35.

Rohkrämer, T. 1999. *Eine andere Moderne? Zivilisationskritik, Natur, und Technik in Deutschland*, Paderborn.

Rose, N. 1996. *Inventing Our Selves: Psychology, Power and Personhood*, Cambridge.

Ross, C. 2005. *Naked Germany: Health, Race and the Nation*, Oxford.

Scholz, A. 2004. 'Ärzte und Patienten in Dresdner Naturheilsanatorien', *Medizin-Bibliothek-Information* 4(1): 13–19.

Schwab, A. 2003. *Monte Verità: Sanatorium der Sehnsucht*, Zürich.

Stoff, H. 2004. *Ewige Jugend: Konzepte der Verjüngung vom späten 19. Jahrhundert bis ins Dritte Reich*, Cologne.

Usborne, C. 1995. 'The New Woman and Generation Conflict: Perceptions of Young Women's Sexual Mores in the Weimar Republic', in M. Roseman (ed.), *Generations in Conflict: Youth Revolt and Generation Formation in Germany, 1770–1968*, Cambridge, pp.137–63.

von Ehrenwall, Dr. 1907. *Sanatorium für Nerven und Gemütskranke*, Ahrweiler.

Wedemeyer-Kolwe, B. 2004. *'Der neue Mensch': Körperkultur im Kaiserreich und in der Weimarer Republik*, Würzburg.

Winkler, H. 1895. 'Die Bilzsche Naturheilanstalt in Dresden Radebeul', in F.E. Bilz, *Das Neue Naturheilverfahren: Lehr- und Nachschlagebuch der naturgemäßen Heilweise und Gesundheitspflege*, 31st edn, Leipzig, pp.1517–20.

Ziegelroth, P.S. 1906. *Dr. Ziegelroth's Sanatorium Zehlendorf bei Berlin*, Zehlendorf.

Archives

B/BL – Bundesarchiv, Berlin-Lichterfelde, R 1501, Nr. 9135.

Part II
Social Regulation of Pleasure

Wilhelm Prager (director) and Nicholas Kaufmann (scriptwriter) 'Wege zu Kraft und Schönheit' (1924). © Friedrich-Wilhelm-Murnau-Stiftung, Wiesbaden, Germany.

3

Moving Images and the Popular Imagination: Visual Pleasure and Film Censorship in Comparative Perspective

Thomas J. Saunders

If films were an esoteric commodity for a limited audience, they would cause no more controversy than manuscripts did in the fourteenth century, before the invention of printing made possible cheap books. But films – like books – are a mass medium, so fear of their effects goes side by side with the spread of the technology that makes them possible. Out of fear grows desire for control.

—I. Bertrand, *Film Censorship in Australia*, ix.

Dreams are powerful ... and so are visions ... Censorship ensured that dreams were not turned into nightmares of doubt and distrust and that there were no alluring visions of alternative new orders.

—N. Pronay, 'The first reality: Film censorship in liberal England', 125.

In the first decades of the twentieth century, the motion picture stood at the forefront of a burgeoning entertainment industry embracing the phonograph, illustrated magazines, radio and spectator sports such as boxing, auto racing and soccer.[3] Already before the First World War movies had become the primary supplier of pleasure for the masses. In the war's aftermath they played a central role in shaping the 'jazz age', an era marked by shifting gender roles, fashions and sexual mores.[4] Offering a wide variety of vicarious experience – tragic, heroic, horrific, sentimental, comic and erotic – they attracted millions of viewers daily across Europe and America. Their enormous popular appeal, however, provoked widespread debate about the nature and impact of film entertainment. That debate found immediate focus in attempts to draw boundaries for the new medium through censorship.

The making of twentieth-century film censorship demonstrated the pervasiveness of social regulation in modern consumption culture. The social regulation of pleasure manifest in the ascetic spirit of capitalism, and in contradictory ways in the enduring complexities of sexual intimacy, was particularly conspicuous in the (capitalist) world of consumerist pleasure. As it pertained to the motion picture, it was inextricably linked to class structures and identities. Cultural and social elites were especially concerned with the moral character of a new kind of 'low culture'. For this reason censorship has often been studied as institutionalised, high-brow intervention aiming to uphold morality, social welfare and political stability.[5]

Although such concerns are familiar from a long history of official attention to print material, theatre and art, motion pictures posed novel challenges to high-brow censors. The chief of these, apart from the speed with which the new medium became pervasive a century ago, was the broad appeal and assumed impact – visual, emotional and behavioural – of moving images. The attraction and power of images themselves were hardly new – as witnessed, for instance, by the intense war of images in the Reformation. But the moving photographic image brought visual pleasure and influence together in an unprecedented way. The projection of moving photographs on screens captured the eye, drawing viewers inexorably into the world they witnessed. Early observers generally assumed that world to be so realistic that viewers identified closely with it. The viewing experience was believed to enhance this illusion: communal viewing in darkened rooms intensified the reality effect and conditioned filmgoers to absorb the images without critical reflection. Since moving images were generally credited as a potent stimulus to the imagination, their impact on behaviour, particularly the behaviour of those considered most impressionable – children and youth – appeared unparalleled. The U.S. National Catholic Welfare Conference Bulletin formulated somewhat dramatically a widely shared conviction when, in 1919, it wrote that 'the influence of motion pictures upon the lives of our people is greater than the combined influence of all our churches, schools, and ethical organisations'.[6] In other words, the new medium risked undermining bourgeois cultural norms.

The encounter of high-brow culture and a new form of visual pleasure did not, however, signify merely prohibition, repression and coercion. Censorship evolved in a social context involving the interests of film-makers and cinema audiences, with the latter partially represented by associations committed to enhancement of artistic quality and moral acceptability. Official censorship bodies therefore operated in conjunction with other interests as much as they acted as coercive authorities, even where they required cuts to a film or prohibited an entire motion picture. In this respect censorship operated as a creative social agency rather than a purely restrictive one. As praxis, censorship spoke about what was inappropriate, about the risks and dangers associated with the new medium. Nonetheless, it acknowledged, indeed presumed, that going to the cinema was a pleasurable pastime. Even early opponents of the motion picture recognised that the movies provided the masses with diversion from, and compensation for, the physically demanding and mentally deadening routine of everyday life. In this regard, by acknowledging cinema's role in the life of the masses, they were also expressing concern about the workings of the pleasure principle in the modern world. Censorship stimulated as well as contained the educative powers associated with visual pleasure. Indeed, it could be argued that the lure of the new medium derived centrally from the creative tension between the promise and perils of cinema as negotiated between censorship authorities and viewers.

Seen from this perspective, censorship not only participated in regulating the content of cinema but also helped to shape the early twentieth-century imagination as a whole. It did so while constantly balancing the pleasures of viewing – the sensual eye – with moral and social responsibility – the ascetic mind. Although the formal task of early film censorship was not to deny visual pleasure, censorship mediated the relationship between visual pleasure and contemporary anxieties about its nature and social impact. Without theorising how cinema 'structures ways of seeing and pleasure in looking',[7] censors tried to regulate the relationship between 'pleasure in looking' and the images which created that pleasure. Their intervention in this relationship admitted that pleasurable viewing included images which could prove dangerous or harmful, particularly those of crime, sexual indulgence and political revolt. Their efforts therefore addressed, in the first instance, the power of moving images to stimulate and influence the imagination. Their aim was to refine visual pleasure by erecting safeguards against specific kinds of images, those seen as having power to stimulate or arouse the imagination in inappropriate ways or to dangerous ends. This involved them in adjudicating the relationship between moving images, on the one hand, and viewers' imaginations on the other.

The Machinery of Censorship

The mechanisms by which motion pictures were regulated suggest both the possibilities and limitations of shaping visual pleasure. One response to the attraction and perceived influence of the cinema could have been to regulate it directly through public ownership. This, after all, was the preferred mode for radio as it developed in the 1920s. The primary impetus here paralleled that behind censorship of motion pictures: to secure public welfare (and the health of the nation) by overseeing the provision of appropriate information and entertainment. The airwaves were to be used to educate and ennoble as well as entertain, but not jeopardise national morality and social harmony.[8] On this model, regulation of film could have been fundamentally prescriptive rather than proscriptive, a monopolisation of the images to be projected on movie screens. Official or semi-official agencies could have governed the film industry to ensure that film's power to entrance and influence served public interests.[9]

Although the idea of the nationalisation of cinema drew some attention after the First World War, direct public ownership or oversight of motion-picture production was attempted only in authoritarian states such as Nazi Germany and Soviet Russia, though even there it operated under market constraints. These derived partly from the formative and extended period in which the movies were in private hands. Whereas radio was largely born under public authority, from the start film had been the plaything of private, and increasingly capitalised, interests. The interwar authoritarian states which challenged this mode of operation faced interlocking creative and financial challenges.[10] The other major constraint followed from the fact that the motion picture was an international commodity, eagerly traded across state boundaries. The language barrier associated with print and radio, and the limitations of radio's effective broadcasting range in the early years, were not encountered by the movies. By the 1920s, Hollywood had become the principal global supplier of movie entertainment. Thus the rationale for public ownership in one country could only be sustained if at the same time the import of motion pictures from other countries, especially the United States, was strictly regulated or banned. Not surprisingly, the pervasiveness and influence of American movie entertainment figured prominently in interwar debates about cinema – not least in Russia, Germany and Italy – where Hollywood pictures, though popular, were eventually banned or sharply restricted.[11]

The prevalence of private ownership in the means of production, distribution and exhibition of motion pictures meant that control assumed other forms. In some cases the regulative bodies were constituted by the industry, initially voluntary and often acquiring the aura of public authority. In others they were directly constituted by the state and answered to government ministries.[12] Despite this difference, they shared responsibilities and approaches, proceeding with a mixture of rating, cutting and banning. One should not, of course, understand these proscriptive tools as unrelated to prescriptive impulses. How regulative bodies rated films and what they objected to pointed clearly to preferred treatments. Over time the judgments of these bodies also acquired normative status by which film-makers could anticipate ratings and gauge the line between acceptable and unacceptable treatments, just as lawyers gauge the possibilities of certain lines of argument from legal precedents. From this perspective, the difference between intervention at the pre-production stage, typical of authoritarian states and some systems of self-regulation, and censorship of completed films does not alter the principles by which censors operated.

The impetus behind the regulatory apparatus, whether industry-sponsored or state-mandated, had a similar provenance across Europe and North America. Where the motion picture was not directly subordinated to an official ideology, as in Stalinist Russia or Hitler's Germany, pressure to oversee and reform it came principally from a wide circle of educational, cultural and religious associations, with women often playing active roles. From the early years of cinema these groups became attentive to the appeal of the movies and anxious about their influence. The first decades of film history saw a drawn-out and often acrimonious confrontation between branches of the industry and the social and moral reformers committed to preserving public morality and national welfare. Social workers, pedagogues, pastors and priests were organised and enjoyed public influence in drawing attention to the dangers of the new medium and pressing for state controls. In addition to the overriding aim of restricting what was considered deleterious, especially for young people, these associations showed intermittent interest in harnessing the power of cinema to constructive ends. Attracted by the educational potential of the motion picture, some of them sought to exploit visual pleasure to bring a range of scientific, technological and geographic knowledge to both children and general audiences.[13]

Among the multitude of reform associations, the best known and most influential with a focus on cinema was the Legion of Decency, an organisation of American Catholics established in 1934.[14] The Legion built on efforts in the United States and Europe to co-ordinate Roman Catholic interests to place boundaries on visual pleasure. One precursor was a committee organised by the French Catholic Church in 1927 to monitor and classify motion pictures for Catholic viewers and thereby apply pressure on the industry. The classification system used a six-point scale ranging from films suitable for general viewing ('1') to those appropriate for adults only ('3b'), to those described as 'fundamentally pernicious' ('6'). Apart from concern about depiction of the Church, the leading source of offense was sexuality. This included everything from scanty dress to scenes of seduction and indications of sexual relations outside marriage. The work of the French committee included dissemination of these ratings to parishes, but it also branched out to enlist exhibitors prepared to accept its film choices. Participation varied widely, but in some regions up to 25 per cent of the cinemas worked within the guidelines offered by the committee. Its efforts, however, never approached the effectiveness of its subsequent American counterpart, perhaps in part because the French state focused on the political influence of cinema and resisted an age-appropriate classification system.[15]

The Legion of Decency also developed a rating scheme to provide its supporters with guidance on what films to frequent and what ones to avoid. Although neither its objectives nor methods were new, it acquired unprecedented clout. In the heyday of the Hollywood studio system it organised between seven and nine million American Catholics to condemn 'vile and unwholesome moving pictures' and to pledge avoidance of all movies offensive to 'decency and Christian morality'. It enjoyed a public profile and support in persuading producers to work with its rating scheme. Guidelines of which the industry had previously approved became much harder to ignore when they were backed by such a show of unity. In 1936 the Legion received emphatic public endorsement from Pope Pius XI in an encyclical addressing motion pictures ('With Vigilant Care'). Pius XI held it up as a model for co-ordinating the concerns of the Church hierarchy and the people on an issue of crucial moral and social importance.[16]

Just as the impetus behind censorship of the cinema had common impulses, the organisation of censorship and categories by which objectionable material was enumerated show considerable overlap across national borders. Although there were distinctive emphases, a comparative survey indicates that in Europe and America censors targeted very similar material.[17] In postwar Vienna, (police) censors rejected motion pictures which jeopardised public order and safety, offended religious sensibilities, distorted reality, had immoral or coarse influences, or damaged Austria's reputation or its diplomatic ties.[18] Weimar Germany first abolished all forms of censorship and then quickly excepted cinema in response to a flood of 'enlightenment films' – the counterpart of British 'health propaganda' – offering sensational treatments of prostitution and venereal disease. The new national censorship law of 1920 refused permits to films which could 'endanger public order and security, offend religious sensibilities, foster brutality or immorality or compromise Germany's reputation or its relations with foreign states'. The law provided even more comprehensive terms for restricted films: persons up to the age of eighteen were not to be admitted to screenings from which there was cause to fear a 'harmful effect on the moral, spiritual or physical development or overstimulation of the imagination of young people'.[19]

French censorship was likewise formalised on a national basis after the First World War, though it still permitted local authorities to ban films considered a threat to public order within their jurisdictions. It took 'decency' as its primary standard, prohibiting undue eroticism and brutality. In addition to guarding morality, the national board sought to protect the prestige of the armed forces, religious feelings and political stability. In the course of the 1930s increasing emphasis fell upon preventing the exhibition of films damaging national prestige and those representing criminal, especially armed, violence.[20] Under fascism, the Italian law of 1923 instituted, as later in Nazi Germany, a form of pre-censorship. Scripts were not to contain indecent or morally offensive scenes, incitements to social conflict, cruelty to animals, suicide or crime, or anything detrimental to national institutions or international relations.[21] In the early Soviet Union the state balanced concern for anti-Bolshevik tendencies and 'pornography'. From 1923 onwards film scripts required state clearance. The entertainment offered by domestic feature-film production therefore generally met state requirements; bans fell mostly on foreign films, whose popularity, however, overshadowed that of domestic features. From the late 1920s the imposition of Stalinist controls made it not only increasingly difficult to gain pre-approval, contributing to a catastrophic decline in film production, but also prevented the commercial release of perhaps a third of the feature films produced over the next decade.[22]

Co-ordinated regulation of film content in Britain was initiated by the film industry before the First World War to forestall state censorship and, as elsewhere, to override the multiple interventions of municipal authorities. In the early 1920s the British Board of Film Censors (BBFC) acquired broad sanction so that its rulings became generally binding. Its second chair described its task as preventing the release of anything 'calculated to demoralise an audience'. In 1917 its working rules were detailed in forty-three points, three-quarters of which broadly addressed moral questions. Among other things these prohibited portrayal of prostitution, premarital and extramarital sex, sexual perversion, incest, seduction, nudity, venereal disease, orgies, swearing, abortion, brothels and white slavery.[23] Its mandate was sufficiently comprehensive to address the challenging moral, social and political issues which were to concern it in the interwar period.[24] That comprehensiveness was duplicated in four simple principles adopted by the Commonwealth Censorship Board in Australia, refusing licenses to films which were: blasphemous, indecent or obscene; likely to be injurious to morality, or encourage or incite crime; likely to be offensive to any ally of Great Britain; or depicted any matter the exhibition of which, in the opinion of the Board, was not in the public interest.[25] The likelihood of a deleterious influence therefore sufficed to impose a ban.

In the United States, as in many other countries, censorship was initially exercised by local authorities. Against these, and to prevent state regulation, the industry took repeated steps at self-regulation. The National Board of Review, founded in New York in 1909, was an early coalition of film distributors/exhibitors and the city's People's Institute (reformers from educational, clerical and women's groups), which screened and classified motion pictures. Although the Board of Review took pains to distinguish its work from that of censors, it did recommend bans and cuts or modifications to films before approving them. Its working rules prohibited obscenity, indecency, blasphemy, libel, detailed depiction of crime and scenes which would have a 'deteriorating tendency on the basic moralities or necessary social standards'.[26]

The subsequent development of state censorship boards, and the threat of their proliferation, brought renewed efforts at self-regulation from the industry. In the early 1920s negative publicity for Hollywood and growing pressure for official censorship spurred establishment of the Motion Picture Producers and Distributors Association (MPPDA) under the presidency of Will Hays. The MPPDA adopted a detailed code of 'don'ts and be carefuls' in 1927 which itemised eleven topics which were out of bounds – including profanity, 'licentious or suggestive nudity', sex hygiene, ridicule of the clergy, and wilful offense to any nation, race or creed – and twenty-five subjects requiring circumspect treatment – among them arson, theft, brutality, cruelty to children or animals, and rape.[27] Three years later these were formalised in the famous Motion Picture Production Code (Hays Code). Although long on detail, the Hays Code did not provide a magic solution to the challenge of reconciling the interests of the industry and social and moral reformers: the discrepancy between its promises and the objectives of the latter was an important impetus behind the formation of the Legion of Decency.[28]

Negotiating Pleasure

This overview of the forms and aims of film regulation suggests a number of conclusions about how visual pleasure was to be constructed. First, although the aim was ostensibly to ennoble the medium, and its audience, the operating mode remained largely reactive and prohibitive in nature. Apart from the German system for rewarding artistically and pedagogically valuable pictures with tax relief (administered by a separate body), the approach negated more than it affirmed. Review boards and censors operated in this regard like a court of law, focusing on the illicit and on ways to control or banish it. Second, although in some cases the offensive material was itemised in great detail, the guidelines were so broad and comprehensive that they offered interest groups and censors enormous discretionary powers to object, cut or ban films, and considerable latitude to producers to protest their good intentions. Operative concepts as loose as 'demoralisation', 'indecency' and 'immorality' inevitably generated argument between interested parties about what did or did not present such a risk. Third, cutting across the categories was a general concern for children and youth, a concern which largely transcended political or associational differences. Consequently, most jurisdictions employed a rating system which prohibited those under certain ages from viewing a significant portion of the films otherwise approved for exhibition (or required adult supervision). Fourth, censors paid close attention to political and diplomatic sensibilities as well as social, moral and religious values.[29] The exercise of political censorship, which occasionally generated enormous public conflict, discouraged the production of controversial material (film producers also had a monetary incentive to prefer themes attractive to the widest possible audience). In practice, treatment of social morality – sexuality and crime – which was both permissible and hedged with numerous restrictions, commanded much of the censors' attention, particularly as film-makers challenged the limits of what was considered acceptable.

Insofar as they were mediating the relationship between filmic images and public imaginations, censors were not conducting a monologue, nor even just a dialogue between themselves and the industry. They were engaged in multilateral negotiations involving the state, the film industry, educational, cultural and religious groups and, indirectly, the silent mass of cinema goers. Whether review boards operated directly under state auspices or at arm's length, and whether or not they allocated representation to spokespersons for these various groups, they provided a crucial site for the contestation of social, cultural and religious values. They participated directly – and often frankly, despite their bureaucratic practices, behind-the-scenes bargaining and laconic formulations – in the crucial debates of their time: on sexuality (prostitution, venereal disease, birth control, abortion and eugenics), women's roles and the family, youth culture and criminality, the authority of the state, and the role of technology in shaping social development. Paradoxically, they also operated, at least with respect to their broad objectives, on a remarkably consensual basis. Continual wrangling over the interpretation of regulations should not obscure the fact that virtually all parties in the debate paid lip service to the principles of social welfare and healthy entertainment. On pragmatic grounds, producers and exhibitors preferred the regularised oversight and rating of motion pictures to the interventions of multiple local authorities or pressure groups. Consequently, as much as they frequently challenged censors' decisions, they benefited from the predictability censorship provided to conduct business effectively.

One party enjoyed only a shadow existence at the negotiating table: the audience. But although absent, it loomed large in the discussion. Since it could speak only indirectly, by frequenting or avoiding movie theatres, its inclinations and interests were appropriated by the other partners to the discussion. These partners additionally assumed responsibility for imagining the impact of motion pictures on viewers. While the moving images presented the raw data for scrutiny, the imagined effect of these images on the audience mattered most and provided the ultimate rationalisation for censorship. A certain doubling of roles therefore surfaced in censors' deliberations. While determining what images provided appropriate pleasure, however trivial and formulaic, they also imagined the impact of the images and the viewing experience on behaviour.

The concern over the effect of films on their audience was more clearly enunciated in some regulations than in others, but the principle itself was essentially universal. It had several implications. Evaluation of impact meant attention to the context, sequence and balance of shots within a film. For instance, the depiction of social rebellion or criminal activity could be dangerous or harmless depending on how it was framed. At the simplest level, crime or immoral behaviour was not to be sanctioned or glorified: treatments, and especially endings, needed to lead viewers to draw appropriate moral conclusions.[30] Framing of the narrative also included geographic, temporal and cultural distance. A motion picture set in a remote time or culture with exotic customs was generally perceived as having less potential to impact on viewers' behaviour than one set in proximate and familiar settings. This presumed distancing effect meant that censors showed greater tolerance of nudity, violence or political unrest insofar as these were perceived as appropriate to the setting.[31]

Context could include the narrative impulse or source for a film. In some jurisdictions the treatment of respectable literature or religious themes, so long as 'in good faith and with artistic merit', would predispose censors to sympathy; in others it was understood as a transgression against good taste.[32] But neither counted in isolation. Producers had no difficulty finding eminent sources that challenged the bounds of propriety. Many of the great works of Western literature, not least the Bible and Shakespeare, included material that no film censor would pass uncut. Cecil B. de Mille, for instance, adept at modern tales of extra-marital dalliance and adultery, walked a fine line in combining biblical vice, titillation, and virtue, while exploiting the temporal and cultural distancing these provided, in films such as *The Ten Commandments* (1923), *The King of Kings* (1927) and *The Sign of the Cross* (1932).[33] The estimation of literary and artistic merit also played a role. Since effect was cumulative rather than limited to specific scenes, objectionable elements in a film could be countered by treatments judged artistic or educational; negative elements could be outweighed or redeemed by positive ones.

Concern for the effect of movies on viewers involved regulators in imagining the emotional and behavioural responses of cinema goers: in this regard they gave attention to the link between the screen and the audience which has become an important thread of film scholarship. Although the review boards did not generally indulge in discussions of the relationship between what was pleasurable and what was prohibited, in mediating between film and audience they did more than worry that inappropriate images could create pleasurable experiences. An examination of their judgments indicates that they imagined multiple audiences and multiple kinds of visual pleasure. Indeed, what otherwise appears as inconsistency, even contradiction, in their decisions can be explained in part by reference to the different audiences they imagined being exposed to the varieties of visual pleasure provided by cinema.

It has already been emphasised that motion pictures attracted regulatory attention out of high regard for their ability to captivate and influence, for good and ill. Cinema's reputation also rested on its ability to attract a mass audience, overriding distinctions of national origin, social rank, gender, age, education or culture. Yet in speaking on behalf of cinema goers, censors reaffirmed these distinctions. The Hays Code offers a useful point of departure for framing this issue since it provided, in addition to detailed guidelines, systematic moral underpinnings for its prohibitions. This statement of principles, initially unpublished, related the unique characteristics of the medium to its audience. It worked from the premise that cinema was an art, but one distinguished from all others by the breadth of its audience. As an art which was universally appreciated and understood it raised special concerns of content, treatment and impact. 'Most arts appeal to the mature. This art appeals at once to every class, mature, immature, developed, undeveloped, law abiding, criminal … The exhibitors' theatres are built for the masses, for the cultivated and the rude, the mature and the immature, the self-respecting and the criminal'.[34] Additionally, the fact that movies played to large audiences was understood to heighten the inherent powers of suggestion enjoyed by the medium.

According to the statement explaining the principles, the Hays Code's primary interest was to address the social and moral implications of a medium whose 'vividness of presentation' entertained such a mass audience. Recognizing that film was simultaneously an art of mass pleasure and a source of moral development, the Hays Code attempted to distinguish between depictions in which evil or sin was suitably repellent and those in which evil was attractive. Initially it tried to do this on the grounds of subject matter. In the former category it placed 'murder, most theft, many legal crimes, lying, hypocrisy, cruelty et cetera'; in the latter, 'sex sins' and 'sins and crimes of apparent heroism' (banditry, organised crime, revenge). But it subsequently had to admit that repulsion and attraction were not neatly separable on the basis of subject matter. Some of the ambiguity was attributable to the specific filmic treatment offered, though the fundamental question of how the medium could both offer visual pleasure and provoke selective repulsion was elided.

In attempting to explain this disturbing ambiguity, the statement of principles shifted emphasis to the composition of movie audiences. In respect to sexual themes and treatments it argued that 'many scenes cannot be presented without arousing dangerous emotions on the part of the immature, the young, or the criminal classes'.[35] Among the three audience groups identified here, the second appears the most straightforward. The first suggests a group of people older in years but deficient in moral development. The term 'criminal classes' conflates illicit behaviour and a social category. It presumably encompasses not just those with criminal pasts but those seen as otherwise predisposed to criminality. In current parlance the first two groups would be 'at risk'; the third would be a threat to society. These three groups should not, however, be understood as the only ones vulnerable to 'dangerous emotions' (overstimulation or arousal) from certain depictions on the screen. In its rationale for proscribing nudity or semi-nudity, the Code imagined yet another audience, one that was 'normal', even mature. For the 'normal man or woman' or the 'average audience', nudity still had a suggestive and immoral effect.

The average or normal audience identified in the Hays Code was imagined and invoked not only in America. It served as the nominal benchmark for censors adjudicating the impact of films in many jurisdictions. But if on the one hand it typecast viewers, suggesting considerable homogeneity, on the other hand it implied the existence of sub-groups and the possibility of pleasure from scenes that should have provoked other responses. Take, for instance, the response of the British Board of Film Censors to the 'health film' or 'social hygiene film' during and after the First World War. These films – which were notably produced in the United States and Germany as well, where they were also a source of much controversy – warned against the dangers of prostitution and unprotected sex. In wartime their primary aim was to protect servicemen from venereal disease, but by treating with unprecedented frankness a topic otherwise out of bounds in the cinema they confronted censors with a sharp dilemma. The British response was to categorise them as propaganda or educational material and prohibit their exhibition in movie theatres. They were approved instead for special-purpose screenings addressing the relevant target audience. Since movie theatres served a mixed audience, much less sophisticated than that of the regular theatre and consisting of many children and youths, they were seen as a venue for entertainment, but not controversial or sensitive subject matter.[36]

The British solution did not, of course, resolve the question of whether an audience viewed films about sexual themes as education or eroticism, and thus how to regulate the relationship between film image and public imagination. This in turn was a special case of the problem apparent in the rationalisation of the Hays Code discussed above: On what terms and for what audiences did any depiction of 'sin' create moral repulsion? How could censors fix how a film would be read by its audience(s) when these could not be conveniently segregated by class, education or moral inclinations?[37] In American practice, reinforced by the Hays Code and the Legion of Decency, filmic texts employed conventions permitting variable readings according to the maturity and sophistication of the audience. The point was not to fix how a film would be read but to open a filmic text, within the terms of the Code, to divergent readings.[38] Visual and verbal double-entendres, one part of this strategy, can be seen as manipulations or circumventions of the Code. But they also represent a negotiation of the multiple audiences which, all parties to the efforts at regulation understood, sought distraction and amusement in the motion picture.

Three Cases: *Maisie's Marriage*, *Captain Kidd* and *The Count of Monte Christo*

The relationship between filmic text, social context and the censors' imaginings of audiences' readings of a film represented the essential nexus in evaluating the line between appropriate and inappropriate visual pleasure. A specific British case illustrates the challenges censors negotiated. In 1923 the BBFC reviewed a domestic feature loosely based on a very popular book by Marie Stopes, *Maisie's Marriage* (1918). The book offered frank and for the era remarkably explicit advice on sexual fulfillment and birth control. The movie was constructed as a romantic drama, thus formally satisfying the criterion that it should be entertainment rather than propaganda or education. However, it was submitted to the BBFC under the same title as the book, thereby directly associating it with the controversial best-seller and suggesting that an otherwise innocuous film story masked discussion of issues considered inappropriate for general movie audiences. The Board passed the film with minor cuts but insisted that its title be changed and that it not reference Marie Stopes. As Annette Kuhn argues in her discussion of the case, the attempt to dissociate the film from Stopes ultimately backfired, as so often with censors' interventions, and provided publicity for the film.[39] Indirectly, however, Kuhn confirms that the fluidity of meanings – between entertainment and propaganda – in this British film paralleled the indeterminacy by which Hollywood served a diverse audience. Whether or not a conscious strategy, *Maisie's Marriage* offered different meanings to different audiences. In balancing entertainment and propaganda it exploited a familiar narrative formula and various levels of awareness of the issues addressed by Stopes's book. The conclusion Kuhn draws – 'the conflict was never really about the film's content; it was about the conditions under which it was constructed as a film with a particular message'[40] – confirms that the censors' anticipation of why a film would exert appeal and how it would be read were inseparable from considerations of audience composition.

The language with which German censors approached audiences differed somewhat from that of the Hays Code and the BBFC, but here too the imagined viewer provided the essential point of reference. The formal basis for considering the audience was the principle that a motion picture be evaluated on both its objective and its subjective appropriateness – what could be described as subject matter and treatment, on the one hand, and the (presumed) influence on the audience, on the other.[41] The first represented censors' opinions of the film; the second censors' imagination of audience reception and what impact a film would have upon behaviour. The latter was ultimately decisive, though clearly it could not be divorced from the former. Tying the film to its impact on the audience, the censors used the following formulation with respect to depictions of violence: a film is brutalising 'when its exhibition poses the direct danger of deadening the emotional life of a normal, average human being or of awakening latent brutal instincts to the point that internal resistance to evil collapses and the desire to emulate what's shown is stimulated'.[42] In matters of (sexual) morality, a film was objectionable if there was 'sufficient probability of a direct risk that it would adversely affect the moral feeling and thinking of an average movie-goer'.[43]

Viennese censors, although generally very taciturn in their judgments, likewise imagined and spoke for a number of audiences. They too gave no overt suggestion of intent to deprive viewers of visual pleasure: their explicit rationalisation for cutting or banning films was irritation, disgust or repulsion provoked by sensuality, brutality or the depiction of criminal activities. After the First World War their focus fell largely on violence and crime. Depictions which could be construed as providing lessons in criminality as well as brutality, torture, murder or graphic fights and bloodletting occupied them more than sensuality. Sometimes offensiveness was tied explicitly to viewers' sensibilities, or at least the sensibilities of one segment of viewers. In certain cases, above all in the banning of scenes of bullfights – a subject widely rejected elsewhere – judgments referred to that part of the audience with humane instincts, implying a part whose inclinations were otherwise. In other cases negative decisions were clearly grounded in the sensitivities of social groups committed to the ethical and cultural ennoblement of the nation.[44] Occasionally the judgments admitted, as did the American Hays Code, the coexistence of conflicting impulses. In July 1923 a German film was rejected because its 'numerous scenes of coarse and brutal violence appear[ed] such as to offend moral feelings, arouse the instincts of the viewers and give offence'.[45] A similar rationale applied in a judgment which simultaneously described a film as repulsive and as calculated to create nervous excitement and an appetite for sensationalism.[46] Recognition of the divergent impulses generated by motion pictures, depending in part upon the composition of their audiences, therefore implicated censors in balancing the tension between legitimate pleasure and dangerous desires.

How censors imagined audiences related also, not surprisingly, to the wider set of circumstances within which they made their decisions. This is vividly illustrated by German censors' response to the return of American film entertainment to domestic cinemas in the early 1920s. Banned during the First World War, Hollywood movies began to appear in Germany in considerable numbers in 1921. Prominent among them were slapstick comedies, and fast-paced sensationalist and western films featuring wild brawls and gunfights. Reports from critics on audience reactions and the commentaries offered by censors indicate that viewers were stunned by the speed, intensity and violence of these films. Both critics and censors alternated between dismissing them as harmless because they were farcical, remote from reality and without dramatic coherence, and cutting or banning them because of their physical brutality. Initially censors tended towards the former, considering the events portrayed to be so unrealistic from a German perspective that viewers could not be negatively influenced by them. They did, however, see the coarseness and brutality of the films as a potentially 'serious social danger for the lower part of the population'.[47]

As Germany experienced rising levels of political and criminal violence in the context of diplomatic crises and spiraling inflation, censors became increasingly cautious in assessing the impact of such entertainment. In early 1923 the board banned a Charlie Chaplin short, a mix of the usual barrage of kicks, flying bricks and punches, for its coarseness and lack of compensating values, despite the fact that the entire affair was clearly not meant to be taken seriously. Although this decision was overturned on appeal, it offers a measure of the growing sensitivity to violence in public life.[48] The contemporaneous assessment of an American action film took this sensitivity a step further. In this case the censorship board rejected a film as brutalising and immoral on the grounds that 'such an excess of bestial brutality and nerve-wracking frightfulness' could harm the health of viewers by plaguing their imaginations with horrible images.[49]

So far the case for rejecting these American imports rested on an assessment paralleling that of Viennese censors or the framers of the Hays Code: the motion pictures in question were repellent or disgusting. But what proved disturbing, and the occasion for a rare admission on the part of the German board, was that American sensationalism and brutality evidently exerted a popular attraction comparable to that of eroticism. In 1923, the year of deep socio-economic crisis, the appeal board banned four feature-length installments of a serial film, *Captain Kidd*, because these offered nothing other than violence and sensationalism. It recommended drastic cuts, suggesting that the equivalent of two feature films be reconstructed from the original four. The distributor met the censors half-way, condensing the four films into three. However, the censors rejected these again. In justifying the ban they described the overall impression of the string of fights, hold-ups and beatings as cheap or trashy. That assessment did not meet the technical requirements for imposing a ban. The following rationale provided a substitute:

> The Board is aware that American films which deal with such inferior subject matter are particularly enjoyed by German audiences. This enjoyment indicates that healthy instincts have been dulled and thus demonstrates demoralisation as described by the Motion Picture Law. The expectation that these films would be especially successful in Germany is also apparent from the appellant's statement that he faced strong competition and paid an unusually high fee to acquire distribution rights for these films.[50]

Here the anticipation of visual pleasure, deduced from unnamed sources and from the testimony of a distributor, figured directly in the decision to ban the film. As with a comparable American feature, characterised as a combination of sensationalism, falsehood and sentimentality, the appeal board clearly expressed distaste: 'experience shows the population enjoys such trashy material'.[51]

Such a forthright confession of a fundamental divide between censors' and audiences' understandings of visual pleasure was relatively unusual. Similarly infrequent, given that censors had little cause to comment on pictures that were approved, were explicit commendations of appropriate entertainment, particularly as it engaged viewers' imaginations. However, in the German case the appeal board had occasion to exercise a broader perspective in responding to decisions by the initial review panel. In 1922 the latter imposed a rating on an American adaptation of the classic Alexandre Dumas novel, *The Count of Monte Cristo*, which restricted it to adult viewers. It argued that strong suspense and the dramatic intensity of a number of scenes would overstimulate youthful imaginations.[52] On appeal the decision was overturned on two fundamental grounds: The quality of the film, and the importance of cultivating the imagination of the youth. On the first count: 'The film has wonderful shots, whose composition leaves a strong artistic impression. It captivates, demands imaginative engagement from its viewers and is resolved in a morally satisfying fashion'. In commenting on its suitability for young people the board offered a pithy assessment of the role of the imagination in personal development and creativity:

> Imagination, that is, the ability to work with new ideas, to elaborate on a visual image, to develop one's own inventiveness or heighten a feeling, is valuable for youths and for adults. A person who misuses this capacity we call a dreamer; a person who develops this capacity into a talent we call an artist. It's in the national interest to give youth ample room to develop their imaginations.

According to the board, this included exposing them to filmic images of fright and horror from familiar legends and fairy tales. Sexual or erotic themes presented the chief danger to the youthful imagination, but were not of concern in this film.[53]

The case of *The Count of Monte Cristo* raises intriguing questions about the relationship between visual pleasure in cinema and inherited thematic and narrative conventions familiar to the early twentieth century. Early film censors were raised in a pre-cinematic world. In this case Dumas's work, a very popular nineteenth-century novel, was clearly familiar to them. Insofar as its motion-picture adaptation respected the original tale, and recreated it effectively, their designation of it as having a positive influence on youths indicates that the compass within which visual pleasure could be considered beneficial was largely set by precedents familiar to them from the age before cinema and by assumptions outside the filmic text. Not the least of these were conventions of narrative pleasure familiar from novels and plays, and now also provided by cinema.

The importance of this wider context for the assessment of what constituted appropriate visual pleasure can be illustrated by an Italian feature film loosely based on another familiar source, the biblical Song of Solomon. The liberties taken by the plot – the development of the love affair of Solomon and the Shulamite woman, and the murder of the latter by one of Solomon's jealous wives – did not themselves motivate negative decisions by either of the German censorship panels. Their judgments condoned filmic adaptation of the biblical love story. However, the lower board objected to the thorough eroticisation of the tale, seeing in it a misrepresentation of the original. On these grounds it judged the film immoral and offensive to 'the religious sensibilities of the majority of both the rural and urban population'.[54] The appeal board agreed in this case but offered a subtle refinement of this judgment. The essential problem lay not in the film's preoccupation with sexual passion, a theme within the bounds of filmic representation. Rather, it lay in the coarse and inadequate nature of that representation, particularly in the acting, when based on such a treasured work of religious literature. 'The biblical tales belong to a culture which is millennia old and based on a strong moral foundation. An inadequate depiction of these tales, lacking moral earnestness and failing to comprehend their cultural value, offends the moral feelings of the people'.[55] In short, the film ran foul of both censorship boards because, unlike *The Count of Monte Cristo*, it was seen as a travesty of its religious and literary source.

Conclusion

Censors' regulation of visual pleasure in motion pictures was deeply embedded in contextual and intertextual considerations which resist the apparently neat categorisations of the various codes by which they operated. The codes provide important guides to the kinds of borders censors patrolled, but they are less revealing than censorship practice for identifying the boundaries of visual pleasure. Even a document like the Hays Code, which attempted detailed delimitation of forbidden territory, can mislead as much as inform. The contortions through which censors sometimes went to justify their decisions, not unlike those of producers protesting their observance of the regulations, therefore invite deconstruction, but those decisions cannot be viewed in isolation, either from each other or from the wider context.

Censors participated with state authorities, film reformers, film-makers, critics and indirectly with audiences in adjudicating the varieties, values and intensity of motion-picture entertainment. They were one party negotiating over the nature of the shots, scenes and the narratives provided by motion pictures. All parties agreed that the movies were to engage mass audiences, and thus stimulate or excite the popular imagination. There was also broad consensus that there were limits to the kind and intensity of the stimulation they should provide. Moving images had the capacity to exceed those limits and thus required restraints. To protect the viewer from 'overstimulation', whether associated with sensuality, political ideology, violence or crime, censors helped define the nature and proportions of pleasurable viewing. Evaluating movies as entertainment for the masses, they authorised images consistent with their perception of the imaginative horizons and behavioural responses of 'average' or 'normal' cinema goers.

Notes

1. R. Maltby (ed.), *Passing Parade: A History of Popular Culture in the Twentieth Century* (New York, 1989), 32–52; L. Abrams, 'From Control to Commercialisation: The Triumph of Mass Entertainment in Germany 1900–1925', in T. Ginsberg and K. Thompson (eds), *Perspectives on German Cinema* (New York, 1996), 643–59.
2. T. Saunders, 'The Jazz Age', in G. Martel (ed.), *A Companion to Europe 1900–1945* (Oxford, 2006), 343–58.
3. For useful reflections on this approach, see: A. Kuhn, *Cinema, Censorship and Sexuality, 1909–1925* (London, 1988), 2–6; P. Corrigan, 'Film Entertainment as Ideology and Pleasure: Towards a History of Audiences', in J. Curran and V. Porter (eds), *British Cinema History* (London, 1983), 29.
4. F. Walsh, *Sin and Censorship: The Catholic Church and the Motion Picture Industry* (New Haven, 1996), 19.
5. L. Mulvey, 'Visual Pleasure and Narrative Cinema', *Screen* 16,3 (1975), 7.
6. R. Fortner, *Radio, Morality, and Culture: Britain, Canada and the United States, 1919–1945* (Carbondale, 2005); K. Führer, 'A Medium of Modernity? Broadcasting in Weimar Germany', *Journal of Modern History* 69,4 (1997), 722–53; D. Scannell and D. Cardiff, *A Social History of British Broadcasting*, vol. 1 (Oxford, 1991).

7. P. Mosley, *Split Screen: Belgian Cinema and Cultural Identity* (Albany, 2001), 52–54.

8. P. Kenez, *Cinema and Soviet Society from the Revolution to the Death of Stalin* (London, 2001), 26–46, 114–19; M. Phillips, 'The Nazi Control of the German Film Industry', *Journal of European Studies* 1 (1971), 37–68.

9. V. de Grazia, 'Mass Culture and Sovereignty: The American Challenge to European Cinemas, 1920–1960', *Journal of Modern History* 61,1 (1989), 53–87; T. Saunders, *Hollywood in Berlin: American Cinema and Weimar Germany* (Berkeley, 1994); D. Youngblood, *Movies for the Masses: Popular Cinema and Soviet Society in the 1920s*, (Cambridge, 1992), 50–64, 73.

10. R. Maltby, 'Censorship and Self-regulation', in G. Nowell-Smith (ed.), *The Oxford History of World Cinema* (Oxford, 1997), 235.

11. L. Grieveson, *Policing Cinema: Movies and Censorship in Early-Twentieth-Century America* (Berkeley, 2004), 18–21; G. Stark, 'Cinema, Society, and the State: Policing the Film Industry in Imperial Germany', in G. Stark and B. Lackner (eds), *Essays on Culture and Society in Modern Germany* (College Station, 1982), 122–64.

12. Walsh, *Sin and Censorship*; J. Skinner, *The Cross and the Cinema* (Westport, 1993); G. Black, *Hollywood Censored: Morality Codes, Catholics, and the Movies* (Cambridge, 1994).

13. C. Crisp, *The Classic French Cinema 1930–1960* (Bloomington, 1993), 255–59.

14. C. Carlen (ed.), *Papal Encyclicals*, 5 vols (Ann Arbor, 1990), 3: 517–23.

15. See the comparative survey of legal foundations in N. Hunnings, *Film Censors and the Law* (London, 1967).

16. *Entscheidungen der Wiener Filmzensur* 9 (2002), vii.

17. P. Jelavich, *Berlin Alexanderplatz: Radio, Film, and the Death of Weimar Culture* (Berkeley, 2006), 128–30; J.P. Barbian, 'Filme mit Lücken: Die Lichtspielzensur in der Weimarer Republik', in U. Jung (ed.), *Der deutsche Film: Aspekte seiner Geschichte von Anfängen bis zur Gegenwart* (Trier, 1993), 52–58; Saunders, *Hollywood in Berlin*, 26–30.

18. P. Monaco, *Cinema and Society: France and Germany during the Twenties* (New York, 1976), 48–52; Crisp, *The Classic French Cinema*, 250–51.

19. E. Mancini, *Struggles of the Italian Film Industry during Fascism, 1930–1935* (Ann Arbor, 1985), 26–27.

20. Kenez, *Cinema and Soviet Society*, 30, 127–40.

21. R. Low, *The History of the British Film 1918–1929* (London, 1971), 55–57; J. Richards, *The Age of the Dream Palace: Cinema and Society in Britain, 1930–1939* (London and Boston, 1984), 92–93; J. Robertson, *The British Board of Film Censors* (London, 1985), 7.

22. N. Pronay, 'The First Reality: Film Censorship in Liberal England', in K. Short (ed.), *Feature Films as History* (Knoxville, 1981), 113–37; J. Richards, 'The British Board of Film Censors and Content Control in the 1930s', *Historical Journal of Film, Radio and Television* 1,2 (1981), 95–116; 2,1 (1981), 39–48.

23. Bertrand, *Film Censorship in Australia*, 48.

24. E. Bowser, *The Transformation of Cinema, 1907–1915* (Berkeley, 1990), 48–52; E. de Grazia and R. Newman, *Banned Films* (New York, 1982), 10–15.

25. M. Vieira, *Sin in Soft Focus: Pre-code Hollywood* (New York, 1999), 215.

26. R. Maltby, 'More Sinned Against than Sinning: The Fabrications of "Pre-code Cinema"', *Senses of Cinema* 29 (2003); de Grazia and Newman, *Banned Films*, 20–35.

27. Pronay, 'The First Reality', 119–20.

28. Cynics observed that film-makers could satisfy this principle by serving a menu of 95 per cent vice and 5 per cent redeeming virtue. See the discussion in Black, *Hollywood Censored*, 57–58.

29. D. Andrew, *Mists of Regret: Culture and Sensibility in Classic French Film* (Princeton, 1995), 166–68.

30. I. Bertrand, *Film Censorship in Australia*, 63–64.

31. S. Higashi, *Cecil B. DeMille and American Culture* (Berkeley, 1994).

32. Vieira, *Sin in Soft Focus*, 216. Cf. British censors: 'The audience at a cinema is very differently constituted from that of a theatre, being composed largely of young people and family parties … This consideration obviously imposes on the Board other canons of criticism' (Robertson, *The British Board of Film Censors*, 20); and German censors: 'A theatrical production is open only to relatively few people, most of whom, moreover, are mature; by contrast, a film attracts the great mass of the population belonging to all educational levels' (Jelavich, *Berlin Alexanderplatz*, 135).

33. Vieira, *Sin in Soft Focus*, 217.

34. Kuhn, *Cinema, Censorship and Sexuality*, 49–74.

35. Ibid., 42.

36. Maltby, 'Censorship and Self-regulation', 242.

37. Kuhn, *Cinema, Censorship and Sexuality*, 75–83.

38. Ibid., 89–90.

39. Cf. Bertrand, *Film Censorship in Australia*, 97.

40. Film-Oberprüfstelle, *Pietro, der Korsar*, 6.

41. Film-Oberprüfstelle, *Paragraph 1717*, 3.

42. *Entscheidungen der Wiener Filmzensur* 8: 66, 8: 62, 8: 70.

43. *Entscheidungen der Wiener Filmzensur* 8: 84.

44. *Entscheidungen der Wiener Filmzensur* 8: 170, 8: 267.

45. Film-Oberprüfstelle, *Der Zirkuskönig I*, 2–3; *Der Zirkuskönig IV*. For this and the following discussion, see Saunders, *Hollywood in Berlin*, 98–101.

46. Film-Oberprüfstelle, *Chaplin sitzt im Hühnerstall*.

47. Film-Oberprüfstelle, *Das Rätsel von San Francisco*.

48. Film-Oberprüfstelle, *Kapitän Kidd, Urkunde ohne Schrift*, 2.

49. Film-Oberprüfstelle, *Rose der Nacht*, 2.

50. Filmprüfstelle, *Der Graf von Monte Christo*, 3.

51. Film-Oberprüfstelle, *Der Graf von Monte Christo*, 1–3.

52. Filmprüfstelle, *Aus König Salomos Liebesleben*, 2.

53. Film-Oberprüfstelle, *Aus König Salomos Liebesleben*, 2–3.

54. Film-Oberprüfstelle, *Aus König Salomos Liebesleben*, 2.

55. Film-Oberprüfstelle, *Aus König Salomos Liebesleben*, 2–3.

References

Published Sources

Abrams, L. 1996. 'From Control to Commercialisation: The Triumph of Mass Entertainment in Germany 1900–1925', in T. Ginsberg and K. Thompson (eds), *Perspectives on German Cinema*, New York, pp.643–59.

Andrew, D. 1995. *Mists of Regret: Culture and Sensibility in Classic French Film*, Princeton.

Barbian, J.P. 1993. 'Filme mit Lücken: Die Lichtspielzensur in der Weimarer Republik', in U. Jung (ed.), *Der deutsche Film: Aspekte seiner Geschichte von Anfängen bis zur Gegenwart*, Trier, pp.51–78.

Bertrand, I. 1978. *Film Censorship in Australia*, St Lucia.

Black, G. 1994. *Hollywood Censored: Morality Codes, Catholics, and the Movies*, Cambridge.

Bowser, E. 1990. *The Transformation of Cinema, 1907–1915*, Berkeley.

Carlen, C. (ed.) 1990. *Papal Encyclicals*, 5 vols, Ann Arbor.

Corrigan, P. 1983. 'Film Entertainment as Ideology and Pleasure: Towards a History of Audiences', in J. Curran and V. Porter (eds), *British Cinema History*, London, pp.24–35.

Crisp, C. 1993. *The Classic French Cinema 1930–1960*, Bloomington.

De Grazia, V. 1989. 'Mass Culture and Sovereignty: The American Challenge to European Cinemas, 1920–1960', *Journal of Modern History* 61(1): 53–87.

De Grazia, E., and R. Newman. 1982. *Banned Films*, New York.

Fortner, R. 2005. *Radio, Morality, and Culture: Britain, Canada and the United States, 1919–1945*, Carbondale.

Führer, K. 1997. 'A Medium of Modernity? Broadcasting in Weimar Germany', *Journal of Modern History* 69(4): 722–53.

Grieveson, L. 2004. *Policing Cinema: Movies and Censorship in Early-Twentieth-Century America*, Berkeley.

Higashi, S. 1994. *Cecil B. DeMille and American Culture*, Berkeley.

Hunnings, N. 1967. *Film Censors and the Law*, London.

Jelavich, P. 2006. *Berlin Alexanderplatz: Radio, Film, and the Death of Weimar Culture*, Berkeley.

Kenez, P. 2001. *Cinema and Soviet Society from the Revolution to the Death of Stalin*, London.

Kuhn, A. 1988. *Cinema, Censorship and Sexuality, 1909–1925*, London.

Low, R. 1971. *The History of the British Film 1918–1929*, London.

Maltby, R. 1997. 'Censorship and Self-regulation', in G. Nowell-Smith (ed.), *The Oxford History of World Cinema*, Oxford, pp.235–48.

——— 2003. 'More Sinned Against than Sinning: The Fabrications of "Pre-code Cinema"', *Senses of Cinema*, nr. 29 November/December. http://www.sensesofcinema.com.

——— (ed.) 1989. *Passing Parade: A History of Popular Culture in the Twentieth Century*, New York.

Mancini, E. 1985. *Struggles of the Italian Film Industry during Fascism, 1930–1935*, Ann Arbor.

Monaco, P. 1976. *Cinema and Society: France and Germany during the Twenties*, New York.

Mosley, P. 2001. *Split Screen: Belgian Cinema and Cultural Identity*, Albany.

Mulvey, L. 1975. 'Visual Pleasure and Narrative Cinema', *Screen* 16(3): 6–18.

Phillips, M. 1971. 'The Nazi Control of the German Film Industry', *Journal of European Studies* 1: 37–68.

Pronay, N. 1981. 'The First Reality: Film Censorship in Liberal England', in K. Short (ed.), *Feature Films as History*, Knoxville, pp.113–37.

Richards, J. 1981. 'The British Board of Film Censors and Content Control in the 1930s', *Historical Journal of Film, Radio and Television* 1(2): 95–116; 2(1): 39–48.

——— 1984. *The Age of the Dream Palace: Cinema and Society in Britain, 1930–1939*, London and Boston.

Robertson, J. 1985. *The British Board of Film Censors*, London.

Saunders, T. 1994. *Hollywood in Berlin: American Cinema and Weimar Germany*, Berkeley.

——— 2006. 'The Jazz Age', in G. Martel (ed.), *A Companion to Europe 1900–1945*, Oxford, pp.343–58.

Scannell, D., and D. Cardiff 1991. *A Social History of British Broadcasting*, vol. 1, Oxford.

Skinner, J. 1993. *The Cross and the Cinema*, Westport.

Stark, G. 1982. 'Cinema, Society, and the State: Policing the Film Industry in Imperial Germany', in G. Stark and B. Lackner (eds), *Essays on Culture and Society in Modern Germany*, College Station, pp.122–64.

Vieira, M. 1999. *Sin in Soft Focus: Pre-code Hollywood*, New York.

Walsh, F. 1996. *Sin and Censorship: The Catholic Church and the Motion Picture Industry*, New Haven.

Youngblood, D. 1992. *Movies for the Masses: Popular Cinema and Soviet Society in the 1920s*, Cambridge.

Other Sources

Entscheidungen der Wiener Filmzensur, 1922–1925; republished Vienna, 2002.

Filmprüfstelle, Berlin, Zensurentscheidungen. 1920-1938: http://www.deutsches-filminstitut.de.

Film-Oberprüfstelle, Berlin, Zensurentscheidungen. 1920-1938: http://www.deutsches-filminstitut.de

4

'The Wo that Is in Marriage': Abstinence in Practice and Principle in British Marriages, 1890s–1940s

Lesley A. Hall

Among his many apothegems on relations between the sexes, the Anglo-Irish dramatist, social commentator and wit George Bernard Shaw (1856–1940) remarked: 'Marriage is popular because it combines the maximum of temptation with the maximum of opportunity'.[1] It is a paradox entirely in keeping with Shaw's reputation as the master of the paradoxical that his marriage to Charlotte Payne Townsend, a union of companionship and friendship between two individuals who shared numerous interests in political and social reform, is generally considered by his biographers to have been lacking in sexual ardour, and was probably never consummated. This might be considered a manifestation of particular personal idiosyncrasies, since Shaw is noted for his ascetic habits: strict vegetarianism, the reform dress of Dr Jaeger, teetotalism and non-smoking.

However, it is more productive to locate this relationship within a wider context of contemporary attitudes towards sexuality within marriage and practices of sexual restraint within it than to attribute it to personal peculiarities or neuroses. Shaw and his wife were far from a unique case among intellectuals and artists of their period, as biographies demonstrate. Carmel Quinlan has suggested that there were a number of instances of similarly sexless marriages among reforming circles in Ireland (which would have been known to Shaw and Payne Townsend) during the late nineteenth century.[2] While in some cases a partially or completely sexually inactive marriage was due to the fact that one partner was primarily interested in the same sex, as in the case of C.R. and Janet Ashbee, this was far from universally true.[3]

Ascetic practices within and around marriage at this time were based on the making of conscious choices in the realm of the sexual. These choices were determined by a variety of factors: pragmatism, politics, and, paradoxically, the pursuit of pleasure. Rather than taking sexual desire and behaviour as a given, practices of self-restraint meant that sexuality became an area to be given thought, where calculations of risk had to be made and new sensibilities in the matter developed. While initially it might seem that this attitude of prudence was singularly negative, a plausible case can be argued for its value in making sex a matter for deliberate consideration. Far from repressing sexuality entirely, practices of restraint made sexual practice a much more conscious matter, even if this was at first in the direction of avoidance not merely of indulgence but of any phenomena that might prove dangerously arousing. This may be seen as one facet of Norbert Elias's concept of the "civilising process": the internalisation of standards of behaviour imposing self-restraint over the natural instincts of the individual through the action of social and cultural pressures (Elias 1978).

Prudential Restraint and its Costs

Recent scholarship by historians of demography and sexuality has persuasively suggested that a culture of sexual restraint was prevalent in later nineteenth-century Britain, and endured throughout a 'long Victorian era', which did not finally terminate until circa 1960. While there were numerous groups within society with different attitudes and practices, the overall tendency was towards careful management of the dangerous sexual urge rather than its reckless indulgence. The relatively late age of marriage prior to the 1950s meant that young people had to control their sexual urges throughout adolescence and young adulthood, so that by the time they married they were in the habit of self-restraint.[4]

Men had some leeway under this system. Undoubtedly some kept mistresses, but since the late age of marriage was due to the need to be in a secure financial situation before setting up a conjugal household, it is doubtful whether many were in a position to set up a discreet non-marital establishment either. Who resorted to prostitutes, when and how often, is a question that the historian is unable to answer: evidence from early twentieth-century surveys tends to suggest that a significant, perhaps the greater, proportion of their clientele consisted of married men, although in general the composition of prostitutes' clientele is something of a mystery.[5] Moral scruples or fear of disease or blackmail might have held back some men from bought sex. Masturbation was regarded as a pernicious habit leading to all sorts of deleterious consequences to health and sanity, and it seems very probable that the negative associations of self-abuse had a more general effect on male attitudes to sexuality.[6] Medical authorities warned against the dangers of excessive carnal indulgence even within marriage.[7]

There were solidly pragmatic reasons underlying this fear of over-indulgence. Beyond what might be considered low levels of sexual frequency in a largely anti-sensual culture, there were also compelling reasons for deliberate abstinence within marriage, such as rational calculation of economic factors for limiting the size and consequent expense of the family, or, indeed, the preservation of the wife's health from the debilitation of over-frequent pregnancy. Recent work on the discernable demographic decline in Britain from 1870 onwards has increasingly demonstrated that this was brought about less by the use of contraceptive devices or even clandestine abortion than by the practice of complete or partial abstention from sexual relations within marriage. Contraceptives were not easy to obtain, the expense placed them beyond the reach of many, they were clumsy and unaesthetic, and this all added to the moral revulsion against deliberate limitation of births by artificial means, exemplified by several scandals.[8]

Married couples wishing to limit their families were thus thrown back upon what were seen as 'natural' expedients. While these might have included coitus interruptus (withdrawal), medical opinion considered this deleterious. It is also a practice that to be effective requires a considerable degree of restraint and self-control on the part of the man, and is not likely to be effectively practised by the sexually ignorant or inhibited, which many British men during this period were. Many couples therefore practised abstention for longer or shorter periods. The most-cited Victorian medical expert on the matter, William Acton, advocated once a fortnight as being consistent with good health, but other authorities were yet more stringent, advising that intercourse should only take place specifically for the purpose of procreation at very wide intervals.[9]

Couples might have been influenced in the timing and frequency of intercourse by notions of the 'safe period'. Unfortunately the relationship between menstruation and ovulation was misunderstood until this was clarified in 1929, through the work of the Japanese and German scientists Ogino and Knaus. Prior to this date, any alleged safe period was likely to have been calculated using a system which actually identified as 'infertile' what were potentially the least safe days of a woman's cycle. Janet Farrell Brodie, however, undertook a very interesting analysis of the application of the usual nineteenth-century calculation of what was believed to constitute the safe period to differing cycle lengths, and argues that for certain women it might have been effecacious, or at least tended to delay further pregnancy, in spite of its fallacious underpinnings.[10] Anything that lowered coital frequency would probably have reduced the likelihood of conception.

Well into the twentieth century there is evidence that a significant number of couples were practising abstention for contraceptive purposes for substantial periods during their married life. The thousands of letters from both men and women received by the highly influential writer of marriage advice and birth-control advocate Marie Stopes, following the publication of her book *Married Love* in 1918 and throughout the interwar years, quite often mentioned the practice:

> I have by the greatest exercise of self-denial kept our family down to three, without any artificial checks but it has been a very great trial.[11]

> We have had no union ever since the child was conceived over 5 years ago.[12]

> [A]fter my third … I vowed never to have any more connection, and he was so good.[13]

Many correspondents complained about the lack of helpful information from medical practitioners (this was usually sought by the male partner, at least prior to the establishment, from the 1920s onwards, of dedicated birth control clinics which focused on women as the object of their attentions):

> I have asked two family doctors for information in respect to an auxiliary preventative but have had no satisfactory answer.[14]

> I have spoken to three different doctors, and they appear to have little knowledge of this subject, or are prejudiced, or in too great hurry to be bothered.[15]

But even many doctors knew of no more reliable method than abstention to manage the size of their own families, as the surviving responses to Stopes's 1922 questionnaire on contraceptive practices among the medical profession revealed. Several reported abstaining for long periods (up to fifteen years) as the only method of deliberate limitation they practised.[16]

The extent to which prolonged avoidance of conjugal intimacy disrupted relationships can be discerned from such comments as:

> We are unable to live together in case I should fall pregnant … my husband has now got an appointment abroad and we would like to spend a few days together before he goes but as we have not lived together for 7 months, I am afraid, it would be disastrous.[17]

Only once since then have I allowed my husband sexual relations and then I was so afraid that I got up early the next morning and walked 14 miles, in a snow storm absolutely distracted.[18]

I would like my Husband to satisfy his Desires yet I am terrified at the thought anytime he comes near me and it causes unpleasant scenes in the Home.[19]

[A]lthough I have been married 15 years, 14 years out of that my husband has had no married pleasure at all and I am afraid it is making me sour and irritable.[20]

[M]y husband tells me to control and hold myself in check. Well I can, but we do without kisses, and oh, lots of other little things that help to make life pleasant, then I get depressed, my husband gets ill-tempered, we quarrel, make it up and afterwards I am in torment.[21]

In one letter to Stopes, the husband explained that he had taken a job in northern Nigeria for fear of the dangers of further pregnancies from the intercourse both partners desired: 'I came out here in the hope that both of us might get over our desires and be able to live together again without being worried that way'. This had not happened.[22] Work using oral history testimony also indicates that abstinence played a significant role in the limitation of families throughout the interwar period: '[S]ome had only one or two children. They used self-restraint and so avoided conception by going without sex. Many men used the garden for odd jobs or kept an allotment to keep their minds occupied and off sex'.[23] Kate Fisher has suggested that men's role as good responsible husbands included taking care of their wives by ensuring that they did not fall pregnant too often, either through refraining from intercourse altogether or by controlling themselves and withdrawing before ejaculation (which would have had a significant impact on their own enjoyment of the act).[24]

'I Dread to See Night Time Coming'

While the fear of untimely pregnancy was one that affected both husbands and wives, it is clear that the fear was far greater among wives. It is sometimes assumed that the fear of pregnancy completely obviated any sexual desire or possibility of sexual pleasure in women but the letters received by Stopes testify to a more nuanced picture of differences in individual response. Some women found refraining from intercourse a personal strain:

I am very passionate as well as he, and we have been so wonderfully happy and I do so want to make this happiness last.[25]

> Living as we have to do … is wearing my nerves to pieces.[26]

> With the love we bear each other its [*sic*] impossible to put passion entirely out of our lives.[27]

Nonetheless, the borderline between fear of pregnancy and more general sexual repugnance was a fuzzy one, and the first might cause the second. It is clear that for many women in Britain, lack of sexual interest if not complete revulsion was more or less standard, particularly when husbands did not feel it necessary to restrain themselves or consider that their wives might experience pleasure in the act and therefore take measures to induce it. The views of the matter that Leonora Eyles, a socialist and women's magazine 'agony aunt', gleaned from working-class women make this vividly clear: '"I shouldn't mind married life so much if it wasn't for bedtime". This remark has been made to me on five separate occasions, all of which are very vividly impressed upon my memory, because, before I was married, it puzzled me intensely … afterwards it seemed astonishing to me'.[28] As one of the women put it: 'It does seem rotten, somehow, never able to call your body and soul your own! I don't mind being a man's beast of burden all day, but I do think a woman might get her nights to herself'.[29] Another woman welcomed the outbreak of the First World War and the departure of husbands to the front: 'You do get your nights to yourself, and no fear of another blooming kid … [W]ait till you've been to bed over three thousand nights with the same man … and had to put up with everything. Then you'd be blooming glad the old Kayser went potty'.[30]

Women were brought up in ignorance of their own bodily functions, and it was the rule rather than the exception for them to be unaware of what would take place on the wedding night, with sometimes traumatic results influencing the rest of married life. A Lincoln woman reported her mother telling her in the 1930s: 'When you get married, there are certain things your husband will require from you. It's not nice and you'll just have to put up with it'.[31] Another one remembered: 'Our mother didn't say anything about what to expect to my sister when she got wed, and on her wedding night she came home in an awful state, running across the field in her nightie … [S]he told me dad that he [her husband] had tried to do something terrible to her'.[32] Fisher points out in her analysis of responses to her own oral history research that it was considered highly inappropriate for a woman with any claim to respectability to reveal either any sexual knowledge she might have or evidence of sexual desire, should she experience it, something likely to militate against any satisfactory sexual adjustment.[33]

This all indicates a culture in which passive endurance of, and compliance with, the husband's demands was simply seen as part of marriage for women. Mary Stocks alluded to the statements often heard in early birth-control clinics that 'a good husband was often summed up as one "who seldom troubles me" or "only troubles me once a week"'.[34] Acquiescing to this 'troubling' might even be considered a form of ascetic practice and self-sacrifice undertaken by wives in the interests of conjugal harmony: in her 1928 volume *Enduring Passion,* Stopes described wives who, faced with over-frequent demands for sex by their husbands, 'gallantly try to meet it and *act* the daily part'.[35] One of Eyles's informants, put up with the demands of a husband who was a 'dreadful little man': '[A] vague sense of fulfilling her duty … made her do it; she thought a woman who drove her husband to other women was immoral; her reasoning went no further than that'.[36] Veteran birth-controller and pioneer in marriage guidance Helena Wright summed up this mindset when describing the women who, when asked whether they enjoyed sex with their husbands, replied: 'Why, doctor? *What is there to enjoy?*' These women 'endure intercourse quite patiently, for the sake of the husband's pleasure, but … would be relieved if it never happened again'.[37]

An ethos of self-sacrifice and uncomplaining endurance is certainly suggested by comments in letters to Stopes, and recorded in the comments of Sutton's informants. For many women, it is clear that sex was something they underwent for their husbands' sake rather than for any enjoyment they might experience themselves:

> I have never at any time had a desire to be with a man and even with my husband I never get any sensation or feeling.[38]

> I cannot expect my husband to cease cohabiting with me, for my part I would not mind at all.[39]

> I simply dread to see night time coming however tired I am because I am always dreading my husband wanting is [*sic*] wishes fulfilled.[40]

> My old man got it every night for years. That's why I'm so exhausted. The only pleasure I got out of it was the children. How could you tell him he wasn't doing it right? You know what men are: right about everything. I never got any pleasure from it.[41]

As late as the 1940s, Moya Woodside and Eliot Slater found in their survey of working-class marriage that the women they interviewed frequently had a 'negative attitude [which] quite often reaches a low point in one of boredom, even dislike, and a desire to get it over: "I'm not keen", "I don't think there's anything in it" … "my heart's not in it", "it's the one part of marriage I could do without"'. Husbands were praised in terms that recall those familiar to Stocks, such as 'he's very good, he doesn't bother me much', 'he's not lustful', 'he wouldn't trouble you at all', 'he's pretty good that way; if I say no, he doesn't go on'. Slater and Woodside made explicit the concept of wifely compliance with their husband's sexual desires as being undertaken in the interests of conjugal harmony rather than in the expectation of personal gratification in their analysis of the responses they received: 'Several times the phrase recurred, "I've never refused him", often said with pride. Compliance is seen as an anchor for the husband, keeping his affection at home. Passive endurance is shown in such phrases as "he's happy", "I try to be accommodating", "it's a satisfaction for him"'.[42]

'A Marked Distaste to Marriage … as Something Low and Sensual'

This state of affairs was seen by many women as simply the way things were, something that they had, as individuals, to come to terms with. Some silently endured, others devised strategies to avoid their husbands' demands for sex, such as staying up at night 'just finishing' domestic tasks until their husband had fallen asleep. However, late nineteenth and early twentieth-century feminist campaigners openly articulated as a political and social question the problems arising out of the mismatch between the desires of the husband and the feelings of the wife towards these desires.

A social purity movement evolved during the final decades of the nineteenth century aiming to improve the morality of society by imposing a single, high moral standard for respectable men and women, to replace the existing double standard that considered male immorality a mere peccadillo. While this attacked the sexual exploitation of women in prostitution, there was also a critical analysis of marriage and the power differential between husband and wife. 'Conjugal rights', late nineteenth-century reformers argued, were a brutally intimate exercise of the domination enjoyed by men within society at large.[43] This presented an ideology of restraint as a political and ethical matter.

The religious thinker and leading social purity reformer Ellice Hopkins asked the following question:

> Whilst the sight is so familiar of wives with health broken down and life made a burden, possibly even premature death incurred, by their being given no rest from the sacred duties of motherhood, to say nothing of the health of the hapless child born under such circumstances, can we wonder that the modern woman often shows a marked distaste to marriage and looks upon it as something low and sensual?[45]

Similar views were advanced by Annie Besant, who came from a very different background to Hopkins. A secularist, socialist and Malthusian campaigner, who had left her husband (and subsequently lost custody of her children following the publication of her manual on birth control, which was prosecuted for, though not convicted of, obscenity), Besant was widely regarded as a loose and fallen woman.[46] She wrote in her polemical work *Marriage*: 'A married woman loses control over her own body; it belongs to her owner, not to herself; no force, no violence, on the husband's part in conjugal relations is regarded as possible by the law … The English marriage law sweeps away all the tenderness, all the grace, all the generosity of love, and transforms conjugal affection into a hard and brutal legal right'.[47]

Several of these reformers argued that intercourse in marriage should therefore take place solely for the purposes of procreation. The extreme Edwardian social-purity feminist Frances Swiney took the position that 'no woman can with safety to her own health and that of her child, incur the pains of childbirth year after year. The interval for complete recuperation between the birth of each child should be at least three years'. Was it, she asked, 'too much to expect the same amount of reasonable consideration from the Anglo-Saxon husband towards his wife, as is shown by many races of so-called savages in their marital relations; where, after the birth of a child, the husband voluntarily separates from the wife for a prescribed period?'[48] Lucy Re-Bartlett advocated that the act of union should 'be limited to the interests of creation as being the only use for it into which altruism enters in', and in these circumstances wives would not 'feel indignity or humiliation … in the act of union' since they would not be giving themselves 'to their husbands only, but always to God and to the race'.[49]

Other writers during the Edwardian period saw spinsterhood not as a despised condition of failure to marry, but as a proud political gesture of independence and resistance. Cicely Hamilton stated the position thus: 'Under present conditions, it is not easy for a self-respecting woman to find a mate with whom she can live on the terms demanded by her self-respect. Hence a distinct tendency on her part to avoid marriage'.[50] She suggested: 'In many runs of life the lack of a husband is no longer a reproach; and some of us are even proud of the fact that we have fought our way in the world without aid from any man's arm … when we are assured that we have lost the best that life has to offer us, we are not unduly cast down'.[51]

The charismatic leader of the Women's Social and Political Union, Christabel Pankhurst, similarly claimed that:

> nowadays … unmarried women have a life full of joy and interest. They are not mothers of children of their flesh, but they serve humanity, they can do work that is useful or beautiful. Therefore their life is complete. If they find a man worthy of them, a man fit physically and morally to be their husband, then they are ready to marry, but they will not let desire, apart from love and reason, dominate their life or dictate their action.[52]

Feminists of this era did not necessarily deny that women were capable of experiencing sexual desire and pleasure, just that they were better at controlling it in the interests of the social good. Pankhurst even claimed that: 'women have the satisfaction of knowing that their subjection has brought them at least one great gain – a gain they will not surrender when the days of their subjection are over. The mastery of self and sex, which either by nature or by training women have, they will not yield up'.[53] The pioneer woman doctor Elizabeth Blackwell argued: 'physical passion is not in itself evil, on the contrary it is an essential part of our nature. It is an endowment which like every other *human* faculty, has the power of high growth'.[54]

Nonetheless, 'under the effect of training to a moral life and the action of public opinion, a great body of women in our own country constantly lead a virtuous life, frequently in spite of physical instincts as strong as those of men'.[55] Therefore, the argument went, with appropriate training and a change in public opinion, men too ought to be able to control themselves and lead lives of restraint and virtue. As Cicely Hamilton put it: 'we are more or less politely incredulous when we are informed that we are leading an unnatural existence ... not because we have no passions, but because life to us means a great deal more than one of its possible episodes'.[56] The novelist Olive Schreiner similarly commented: 'consciousness of great impersonal ends, to be brought, even if slowly and imperceptibly, a little nearer by her action ... gives to many a woman strength for renunciation, when she puts from her the lower type of sexual relationship, even if bound up with all the external honour a legal bond can confer'.[57] The agenda here was to change the perception of spinsterhood from something shameful to a status behind which lay a deliberate political and moral choice. This, of course, bore the implication that if a woman did eventually decide to marry it was a positive choice for a particular male comrade and partner, rather than one made out of desperation and fear of being 'left on the shelf'.

Discipline for Pleasure

The instances cited above all tend to position abstinence within a discourse of negativity about the erotic: even when pleasure and desire were associated with the sexual act, fear and anxiety over a range of potential undesired consequences were pervasively expressed. There are recorded instances where the abandonment of sexual interaction within marriage seems to have been something of a relief to the couple. Inhibition, lack of knowledge and consequent ineptitude in the act, fears and anxieties – all meant that sex was for many neither a simple gratification nor an uncomplicated pleasure.

Men confessed to Marie Stopes that their wives' distaste or passivity had a negative effect on their own enjoyment. There is evidence that many sensitive men of the later nineteenth and early twentieth century had internalised views of marriage as being about the victimisation of women by brutish male lusts, or at least that male sexual demands were an imposition on the decent woman. They wished to dissociate themselves from this model of selfish masculinity, sometimes even to the extent of forswearing carnal interactions in wedlock altogether.[58] The correspondence received by Marie Stopes expresses the enormous revelation it was to men that their wives might enjoy and actively participate in sexual intercourse, and the joy with which they greeted this enlightenment.[59]

Nonetheless, there are hints in some of the writings of sexual reformers of the late nineteenth and early twentieth century of the idea that self-restraint as an erotic discipline could lead to an improved and meaningful sexual life. Havelock Ellis, the leading English sexologist, argued strongly against the negativity of debates about sexual abstinence in a chapter on the topic in *Sex in Relation to Society*, volume six of his *Studies in the Psychology of Sex*. In his view, 'asceticism is the virtue of control that leads up to erotic gratification, and chastity is the virtue which exerts its harmonising influence in the erotic life itself'. Thus, 'properly understood, asceticism is a discipline, a training, which has reference to an end not itself'. It should 'subserve the ends of vital activity, which cannot be subserved by a person who is engaged in a perpetual struggle with his own natural instincts'.[60] In Ellis's view, chastity was 'the natural instinct of dignity and temperance; in part it is the art of touching the things of sex with hands that remember their aptness for all the fine ends of life'.[61] He concluded that: '[the] artificially magnified conception of the sexual impulse is fortified by the artificial emphasis placed upon asceticism. We may learn the real place of the sexual impulse in learning how we may reasonably and naturally view the restraints on that impulse'.[62]

However he also argued that 'reckless and promiscuous indulgence' was also antithetical to the true art of love. He suggested that 'absence is needed to maintain the keen freshness and fine idealism of love', and that married lovers who were obliged to meet for brief periods between long absences enjoyed 'a lifelong succession of honeymoons'.[63] This does suggest a possible alternative reading of the practice of sexual restraint within marriage: if abstinence was experienced not as a constant nagging burden of temptation to which the couple might occasionally give in, but as something embodied in a series of special if infrequent encounters between a loving couple, this would change the meaning of the practice considerably. Evidence for this, however, would be hard to come by.

Ellis also emphasised the importance of restraint and consideration on the part of the male: 'the need for delay and considerate skill', 'he must hold himself in complete restraint lest he should fall into the fatal error of yielding to his own impulse of domination'.[65] He also reiterated the need for courting the woman prior to intercourse, and quoted an unnamed woman as stating that: 'the man who thinks this prolonged courtship previous to the act of sex union wearisome, has never given it a trial. It is the approach to the marital embrace, as well as the embrace itself, which constitutes the charm of the relation between the sexes'.[66]

A concept of moderation, rather than total rigid abstinence, with quality rather than quantity as the desideratum, was adumbrated by women writing marriage advice in the era just after the First World War. They were strongly influenced both by preceding feminist debates and by the kind of views expressed by Ellis (which were themselves influenced by contemporaneous feminist writings).[67] Marie Stopes's epoch-making *Married Love* was published during the final months of the war. Like Ellis, she gave central importance to the need for men to woo their wives prior to union, rather than rushing ahead intent on their own gratification: 'when the man tries to enter a woman whom he has *not* wooed to the point of stimulating her natural physical reactions of preparation, he is endeavouring to force his entry through a dry-wall opening too small for it. He may thus cause the woman actual pain, apart from the mental revolt and loathing she is likely to feel for a man who so regardlessly uses her'.[68]

In *Enduring Passion* (1928), her sequel to *Married Love*, Stopes argued: 'A woman's potential happiness in sex life is deadened or killed outright by demands, which are so frequent and so regardless of her own needs and requirements that they crush spontaneity and happiness'.[69] Stopes argued that women experienced periodic recurrences of natural desire. However, 'woman … has had to mould herself to the shape desired by man wherever possible, and she has stifled her natural feelings and her own deep thoughts as they welled up'. That is, she has had to make herself sexually available on male terms. While men were aware of the rhythms of menstruation and pregnancy, 'the subtler ebb and flow of woman's sex has escaped man's observations or his care', and thus a man found 'only caprice in his bride's coldness when she yields her sacrificial body while her sex-tide is at the ebb'.[70] Husbands tended to have 'regular habits of intercourse … claiming [their wives] both when [they] would naturally enjoy union and when it is to some degree repugnant', and this 'tended to flatten out the billowing curves of the lines of … natural desire'.[71] On the basis of this theory, she suggested that husbands should endeavour to engage in intercourse at approximately fortnightly intervals to take advantage of the 'high tide' of female desire, carefully observing their wives for the signs.[72]

Without going so far as to claim this kind of biological basis for her prescriptions, the doctor Isabel Hutton suggested in *The Hygiene of Marriage* (1923) that husbands should not insist on intercourse when their wives did not want it, and that 'frequent intercourse is debilitating, and, by rendering the act somewhat commonplace, takes away, to some extent, its beauty'. But by over-frequent intercourse, Hutton meant more than once or twice a week, though she cautioned that individuals and couples differed greatly.[73]

This was very different from the line promoted by Mary Scharlieb, a pillar of the Edwardian social-purity movement and one of the first women to qualify in medicine. In *Straight Talks to Women* (1923) she advocated a rule of 'nine months pregnancy, nine months lactation, six months sexual holiday' during which intercourse would not take place.[74] There was a new valuation of the possibility of female sexual pleasure in the works of the younger generation of writers such as Stopes and Hutton. Restraint was to be based on mutual consideration and respect, and was primarily about the male educating and disciplining himself to be a good lover, rather than Scharlieb's perception of 'true unselfish love and of self-control' in men consisting of 'subdu[ing] their bodies ... to keep them under' in order that they could 'deny themselves so as to permit their beloved a time for recuperation'.[75]

Eyles summed up this new ideal of asceticism as the path to a higher degree of enjoyment: 'continual pandering to an impulse robs it of thrill or pleasure. The only people who find pleasure in the indulgence of any desire are those who have practised asceticism ... the slow storing up of energy during a time of quiet to be spent in a happy outburst'.[76]

The greater weight of erotic discipline was laid on the man in this new vision of conjugal pleasure, since he was the one who was 'making what should be a feast into a dreary penance' and 'spoiling his own pleasure' through over-insistence on his conjugal 'rights'.[77] He was not only to restrain himself from routine gratification of 'a surface need, quickly satisfied, colourless, and lacking beauty', instead trading these 'few moments of physical pleasure' for 'realms of ever-expanding joy and tenderness',[78] in a new regimen of more occasional and considered intercourse. He had also to restrain the impetuosity of his response during the act itself. Firstly, the husband had to 'woo her before every separate act of union' to 'rouse, charm, and stimulate her to ... local readiness', with the beneficent result from his point of view being 'an immense increase of sensation from the mutuality thus attained'.[79] Then,

> even after a woman's dormant sex feeling is aroused and all the complex reactions of her being have been set in motion, it may even take as much as from ten to twenty minutes of actual physical union to consummate her feeling, while two or three minutes often completes the union for a man who is ignorant of the need to control his reactions, so that both may experience the added benefit of a mutual crisis to love.[80]

Women, however, also had to discipline themselves to this new regime of conjugal pleasure. They had 'to learn to regard sex life in marriage, not only as a duty to the man they love, but as something to be joyfully shared between them'.[81] Women had to make up their minds to put themselves into a frame of mind to find sexual intercourse pleasurable: 'She must decide with all her strength that she *wants* her body to feel all the sensations of sex with the greatest possible vividness'.[82]

Although this new genre of marriage manual held out the promise of sensually enjoyable conjugality, the evidence from letters received by Stopes, from the Slater and Woodside survey, and other contemporary sources,[83] indicates that for many couples well into the middle years of the twentieth century, the truth of their marital experience was closer to Freud's gloomy observation that 'it is scarcely credible … what a degree of renunciation, often on both sides, is entailed by marriage, and to what narrow limits married life – the happiness that is so ardently desired – is narrowed down'.[84]

Notes

1. Shaw's remark is taken from *Man and Superman* (1903), and quoted in E. Knowles (ed.), *The Oxford Dictionary of Quotations*, 6th edn (Oxford, 2004).
2. C. Quinlan, *Genteel Revolutionaries: Anna and Thomas Haslam and the Irish Women's Movement* (Cork, 2002).
3. F. Ashbee, *Janet Ashbee: Love, Marriage and the Arts and Crafts Movement* (Syracuse, 2002).
4. S. Szreter, *Fertility, Class and Gender in Britain, 1860–1940* (Cambridge, 1996); H. Cook, *The Long Sexual Revolution: English Women* (Oxford, 2004); K. Fisher, *Birth Control, Sex, and Marriage in Britain 1918–1960* (Oxford, 2006).
5. Anon., *Downward Paths: An Inquiry into the Causes which Contribute to the Making of the prostitute / with a foreword by A. Maude Royden* (s.l., 1916); G. Hall, *Prostitution: A Survey and a Challenge* (London, 1933).
6. L. Hall, *Hidden Anxieties: Male Sexuality 1900–1950* (Oxford, 1991); L. Hall, 'Forbidden by God, Despised by Men: Masturbation, Medical Warnings, Moral Panic and Manhood in Britain, 1850–1950', *Journal of the History of Sexuality* 2,3 (1992), 365–87.
7. R. Porter and L. Hall, *The Facts of Life: the Creation of Sexual Knowledge in Britain, 1650–1950* (New Haven, 1995).
8. P. Fryer, *The Birth Controllers* (London, 1965), 123–31, 169–72; S. Chandrasekhar, *'A Dirty Filthy Book': The Writings of Charles Knowlton and Annie Besant on Reproductive Physiology and Birth Control and an Account of the Bradlaugh–Besant Trial* (Berkeley, 1981); R. Ledbetter, *History of the Malthusian League, 1877–1927* (Columbus, 1986).
9. Porter and Hall, *The Facts of Life*, 79–86.

10. J. Brodie, *Contraception and Abortion in Nineteenth-century America* (Ithaca, 1994), 79–86.

11. Marie Stopes Papers, Wellcome Library for the History and Understanding of Medicine, London (MS/WL/L): PP/MCS/A.147 CEGJ 1923.

12. MS/WL/L – PP/MCS/A.148 RHK 1924.

13. MS/WL/L – PP/MCS/A.110 Mrs HG n.d.

14. MS/WL/L – PP/MCS/A.197 LBP 1918.

15. MS/WL/L – PP/MCS/A.90 JAF 1927.

16. Marie Stopes Papers, Department of Manuscripts, British Library, London (MS/BL/L) – Additional Manuscript 58562: BL Add Mss.

17. MS/WL/L – PP/MCS/A.180 Mrs AFM 1920.

18. M. Stopes (ed.), *Mother England: A Contemporary History Self-written by Those Who Have Had No Historian* (London, 1929), 9.

19. Ibid., 11.

20. Ibid., 37.

21. Ibid., 156.

22. MS/WL/L – PP/MCS/A.249, DFSW 1919.

23. M. Sutton, *'We Didn't Know Aught': A Study of Sexuality, Superstition and Death in Women's Lives in Lincolnshire during the 1930s, 40s and 50s* (Stanford, 1992), 53.

24. K. Fisher, '"She Was Quite Satisfied with the Arrangements I Made": Gender and Birth Control in Britain 1910–1950', *Past and Present* 169 (2000), 161–93; K. Fisher and S. Szreter, '"They Prefer Withdrawal": The Choice of Birth Control in Britain, 1918–1950', *Journal of Interdisciplinary History* 34 (2003), 263–91; Fisher, *Birth Control*.

25. Stopes, *Mother England*, 53.

26. Ibid., 115.

27. Ibid., 136.

28. L. Eyles, *The Woman in the Little House* (London, 1922), 129.

29. Ibid., 130–31.

30. Ibid., 132.

31. Sutton, *'We Didn't Know Aught'*, 48.

32. Ibid., 43.

33. Fisher, *Birth Control*.

34. M. Stocks, *My Commonplace Book* (London, 1970), 162.

35. Stopes, *Enduring Passion*, 31.

36. Eyles, *The Woman in the Little House*, 131.

37. H. Wright, *More About the Sex Factor in Marriage* (London, 1947), 14–15, original emphasis.

38. Stopes, *Mother England*, 11.

39. Ibid., 85.

40. Ibid., 145.

41. Sutton, *'We Didn't Know Aught'*, 50.

42. E. Slater and M. Woodside, *Patterns of Marriage: A Study of Marriage Relationships in the Urban Working Classes* (London, 1951), 165–76.

43. L. Bland, *Banishing the Beast: English Feminism and Sexual Morality, 1885–1914* (London, 1995); E. Bristow, *Vice and Vigilance: Purity Movements in Britain Since*

1700 (Dublin, 1977); L. Hall, 'Hauling Down the Double Standard: Feminism, Social Purity, and Sexual Science in Late Nineteenth-Century Britain', *Gender and History* 16,1 (2004), 36–56; A. Hunt, *Governing Morals: A Social History of Moral Regulation* (Cambridge, 1999); J. Walkowitz, *Prostitution and Victorian Society: Women, Class and the State* (Cambridge and New York, 1980).

45. J. Hopkins, *The Power of Womanhood or Mothers and Sons: A Book for Parents, and those in Loco Parentis* (London, 1899), 143. On Hopkins, see: S. Morgan, *A Passion for Purity: Ellice Hopkins and the Politics of Gender in the Late-Victorian Church* (Bristol, 1999).

46. A. Nethercot, *The First Five Lives of Annie Besant* (London, 1961); A. Nethercot, *The Last Four Lives of Annie Besant* (London, 1963).

47. A. Besant, *Marriage, As it Was, As it Is, and As it Should Be: A Plea for Reform* (London, 1882), 13–14.

48. F. Swiney, *The Awakening of Women or Woman's Part in Evolution* (London, 1908), 118–19.

49. L. Re-Bartlett, *The Coming Order* (London, 1911), 57.

50. C. Hamilton, *Marriage as a Trade* (London, 1909), 240–41.

51. Ibid., 226.

52. C. Pankhurst, *The Great Scourge and How To End It* (London, 1913), 131–32.

53. Ibid., 132.

54. E. Blackwell, *Counsel to Parents on the Moral Education of their Children* (London, 1882), 52, original emphasis.

55. Ibid., 75.

56. Hamilton, *Marriage as a Trade*, 241.

57. O. Schreiner, *Woman and Labour* (London, 1911), 127.

58. Quinlan, *Genteel Revolutionaries*.

59. Hall, *Hidden Anxieties*, 62–113; Porter and Hall, *The Facts of Life*, 202–23; L. Hall, 'Impotent Ghosts from No-man's Land, Flappers' Boyfriends, or Crypto-patriarchs? Man, Sex and Social Change in 1920s Britain', *Social History* 21,1 (1996), 54–70.

60. H. Ellis, *Studies in the Psychology of Sex, Volume VI: Sex in Relation to Society* (Philadelphia, 1910), 175.

61. Ibid., 176.

62. Ibid., 177.

63. Ibid., 562.

65. Ibid., 547, 549.

66. Ibid., 546.

67. Hall, 'Hauling Down the Double Standard'.

68. M. Stopes, *Married Love: A New Contribution to the Solution of Sex Difficulties* (London, 1918), 47, original emphasis.

69. M. Stopes, *Enduring Passion: Further New Contributions to the Solution of Sex Difficulties, Being the Continuation of Married Love* (London, 1928), 30.

70. Stopes, *Married Love*, 19–20.

71. Ibid., 27–28.

72. Ibid., 42–43.

73. I. Hutton, *The Hygiene of Marriage* (London, 1923), 69–70.

74. M. Scharlieb, *Straight Talks to Women* (London, 1923), 130.

75. Ibid.

76. Eyles, *The Woman in the Little House*, 140.

77. Ibid.

78. Stopes, *Married Love*, 20, emphasis removed.

79. Ibid., 48.

80. Ibid., 50.

81. Hutton, *The Hygiene of Marriage*, 33.

82. H. Wright, *The Sex Factor in Marriage: A Book for Those Who Are, or Who Are About to Be, Married* (London, 1930), 31, original emphasis.

83. L. Hall, 'Eyes Tightly Shut, Lying Rigidly Still and Thinking of England? British Women and Sex from Marie Stopes to Hite', in M. Martin and C. Nelson (eds), *Sexual Pedagogies: Teaching Sex in America, Britain, and Australia, 1879–2000* (Basingstoke, 2003), 53–71.

84. S. Freud, '"Civilised" Sexual Morality and Modern Nervous Illness', in *Civilisation, Society and Religion* (Harmondsworth, 1985), 53.

References

Published Sources

Anon. 1916. *Downward Paths: An Inquiry into the Causes which Contribute to the Making of the prostitute / with a foreword by A. Maude Royden* , s.l.

Ashbee, F. 2002. *Janet Ashbee: Love, Marriage and the Arts and Crafts Movement*, Syracuse.

Besant, A. 1882. *Marriage, As it Was, As it Is, and As it Should Be: A Plea for Reform*, London.

Blackwell, E. 1882. *Counsel to Parents on the Moral Education of their Children*, London.

Bland, L. 1995. *Banishing the Beast: English Feminism and Sexual Morality, 1885–1914*, London.

Bristow, E. 1977. *Vice and Vigilance: Purity Movements in Britain Since 1700*, Dublin.

Brodie, J. 1994. *Contraception and Abortion in Nineteenth-century America*, Ithaca.

Chandrasekhar, S. 1981. *'A Dirty Filthy Book': The Writings of Charles Knowlton and Annie Besant on Reproductive Physiology and Birth Control and an Account of the Bradlaugh–Besant Trial*, Berkeley.

Cook, H. 2004. *The Long Sexual Revolution: English Women*, Oxford.

Elias, N. 1978, *The Civilizing Process, Vol. I: The Development of Manners*, New York.

Ellis, H. 1910. *Studies in the Psychology of Sex, Vol. VI: Sex in Relation to Society*, Philadelphia.

Eyles, L. 1922. *The Woman in the Little House*, London.

Fisher, K. 2000. '"She Was Quite Satisfied with the Arrangements I Made": Gender and Birth Control in Britain 1910–1950', *Past and Present* 169: 161–93.

———— 2006. *Birth Control, Sex, and Marriage in Britain 1918–1960*, Oxford.

Fisher, K., and S. Szreter. 2003. '"They Prefer Withdrawal": The Choice of Birth Control in Britain, 1918–1950', *Journal of Interdisciplinary History* 34: 263–91.

Freud, S. 1985[1908]. '"Civilised" Sexual Morality and Modern Nervous Illness', in *Civilisation, Society and Religion*, Pelican Freud Library Vol. 12, Harmondsworth, 33–55.

Fryer, P. 1965. *The Birth Controllers*, London.

Hall, G. 1933. *Prostitution: A Survey and a Challenge*, London.

Hall, L. 1991. *Hidden Anxieties: Male Sexuality 1900–1950*, Oxford.

———— 1992. 'Forbidden by God, Despised by Men: Masturbation, Medical Warnings, Moral Panic and Manhood in Britain, 1850–1950', *Journal of the History of Sexuality* 2(3): 365–87.

———— 1996. 'Impotent Ghosts from No-man's Land, Flappers' Boyfriends, or Crypto-patriarchs? Man, Sex and Social Change in 1920s Britain', *Social History* 21(1): 54–70.

———— 2003. 'Eyes Tightly Shut, Lying Rigidly Still and Thinking of England? British Women and Sex from Marie Stopes to Hite', in M. Martin and C. Nelson (eds), *Sexual Pedagogies: Teaching Sex in America, Britain, and Australia, 1879–2000*, Basingstoke, pp.53–71.

———— 2004. 'Hauling Down the Double Standard: Feminism, Social Purity, and Sexual Science in Late Nineteenth-century Britain', *Gender and History* 16(1): 36–56.

Hamilton, C. 1909. *Marriage as a Trade*, London.

Hopkins, J. 1899. *The Power of Womanhood or Mothers and Sons: A Book for Parents, and those in Loco Parentis*, London.

Hunt, A. 1999. *Governing Morals: A Social History of Moral Regulation*, Cambridge.

Hutton, I. 1923. *The Hygiene of Marriage*, London.

Knowles, E. (ed.) 2004. *The Oxford Dictionary of Quotations*, 6th edn, Oxford.

Ledbetter, R. 1986. *History of the Malthusian League, 1877–1927*, Columbus.

Morgan, S. 1999. *A Passion for Purity: Ellice Hopkins and the Politics of Gender in the Late-Victorian Church*, Bristol.

Nethercot, A. 1961. *The First Five Lives of Annie Besant*, London.

———— 1963. *The Last Four Lives of Annie Besant*, London.

Pankhurst, C. 1913. *The Great Scourge and How To End It*, London.

Porter, R., and L. Hall. 1995. *The Facts of Life: The Creation of Sexual Knowledge in Britain, 1650–1950*, New Haven.

Quinlan, C. 2002. *Genteel Revolutionaries: Anna and Thomas Haslam and the Irish Women's Movement*, Cork.

Re-Bartlett, L. 1911. *The Coming Order*, London.

Scharlieb, M. 1923. *Straight Talks to Women*, London.

Schreiner, O. 1911. *Woman and Labour*, London.

Slater, E., and M. Woodside. 1951. *Patterns of Marriage: A Study of Marriage Relationships in the Urban Working Classes*, London.

Stocks, M. 1970. *My Commonplace Book*, London.

Stopes, M. 1918. *Married Love: A New Contribution to the Solution of Sex Difficulties*, London.

———— 1928. *Enduring Passion: Further New Contributions to the Solution of Sex Difficulties, Being the Continuation of Married Love*, London.

———— (ed.) 1929. *Mother England: A Contemporary History Self-written by Those Who Have Had No Historian*, London.

Sutton, M. 1992. '*We Didn't Know Aught': A Study of Sexuality, Superstition and Death in Women's Lives in Lincolnshire during the 1930s, 40s and 50s*, Stanford.

Swiney, F. 1908[1905]. *The Awakening of Women or Woman's Part in Evolution*, London.

Szreter, S. 1996. *Fertility, Class and Gender in Britain, 1860–1940*, Cambridge.

Walkowitz, J. 1980. *Prostitution and Victorian Society: Women, Class and the State*, Cambridge and New York.

Wright, H. 1930. *The Sex Factor in Marriage: A Book for Those Who Are, or Who Are About to Be, Married*, London.

———— 1947. *More About the Sex Factor in Marriage*, London.

Archives

MS/BL/L – Marie Stopes Papers, Department of Manuscripts, British Library, London.

MS/WL/L – Marie Stopes Papers, Wellcome Library for the History and Understanding of Medicine, London

5

Asceticism in Modern Social Thought

Henk de Smaele

'A civilization that succumbs to the fascination of asceticism and embraces religious or philosophical gospels of self-denial is not likely to increase its wealth very much'.[1] This remark, made in 1951 by the Canadian-Austrian economic historian Karl Ferdinand Helleiner, clearly suggested that asceticism can be very attractive to societies, and that they can easily 'succumb' to its appeal.[2] Helleiner believed that 'a society that is dominated by ascetic ideals' – note the use of the word 'dominated' here – 'will, generally, be less interested in accumulation and innovation than one whose members give free rein to their appetites'.[3] In this common-sense belief, however, 'a curious sociological paradox' was hidden.[4] Helleiner admitted that the social cultivation of ascetic ideals not only fetters consumption and restrains economic growth, but also encourages important 'capitalist' attitudes, such as thrift and deferring satisfaction, both important prerequisites for the modern economic idea of accumulation. 'Accustomed to balance future benefits against present sacrifices', Helleiner argues, 'the Christian ascetic developed the very mental traits which, if transferred to the economic field, enabled him to save and accumulate'. He concludes that 'Christianity – and not only its later Puritan variety – must be classified among the positive factors of economic growth'.

Throughout history, the Christian stress on the moral value of labour has caused an 'asceticism of work' that reinforces the 'asceticism of underconsumption'.[5] It was a 'paradox that man, through the practice of self-denial, should have increased his capacity to produce the very satisfactions which he was so eager to renounce'.[6] As history shows, asceticism was not necessarily an obstacle to social modernisation and economic development. On the contrary, it appears to have been an essential step in the emergence of modern capitalism. Rather than contradicting it, asceticism fuelled modernisation.

Since the late eighteenth century, many social theorists have defined asceticism as a crucial means of social regulation. Helleiner cites the work of famous theorists – such as Adam Smith, Edward Gibbon, Thornstein Veblen and Max Weber – to underline his point, demonstrating that asceticism is an important concept in intellectual reflection on the nature and development of modern society. These social theorists have explicitly and frequently referred to either the restraining or the beneficial effects of promoting ascetic ideals to advance society. In social theory, asceticism was often defined as a crucial trait of modern society. Since asceticism explained capitalism's birth and triumph, it almost became synonymous with progress. In Weber's lessons about the social regulatory powers of asceticism, the concept even came close to 'society'. In the societal imagination, so it seemed, the social future and the social whole were easily anchored in asceticism. Contrary to the life reformers whose heritage has been studied in the previous section of this volume, these social theorists amalgamated asceticism with social regulation. In their eyes, asceticism was to be found at society's very core.

In this chapter I will focus on the different and contradictory meanings that have been attributed to 'asceticism' in modern social thought, and I will demonstrate that authors have defined asceticism as an 'anti-social', 'primitive', or 'retrograde' ideal, as well as a 'social', 'civilising', and 'progressive' principle. It can be argued that Friedrich Nietzsche, for one, saw asceticism as an individual way out of the homogenising tendencies of modern life, as a way of masculine self-mastery, a strategy of resistance against the standardisation of capitalist and industrial societies, and as a means to restore personal autonomy.[7] Far more conspicuous and influential, however, is Nietzsche's critique of the fundamental, omnipresent and destructive role that the 'ascetic priest' has played in human history, making ascetic ideals the leading social principles, turning the Earth into the *asketische Stern* ('the ascetic star').[8] Arguably, Nietzsche did not condemn 'asceticism' as such, and he even considered it as a strategy of resistance, but he nonetheless criticised current ascetic ideals and held the preachers of asceticism responsible for the creation of the 'sick herd'.

Paradoxically, to distance oneself from this 'sick herd', one has to fly into the desert, to become a solitary ascetic. In this chapter I am not so much concerned about asceticism as a flight into the desert more about the way it can be used as an individual strategy to save the modern self. This chapter will focus on the assumed relationship between 'modern (industrial, capitalist) society' and 'asceticism'.

As far as possible, I will stick to those authors and texts that explicitly refer to 'asceticism' or 'ascetic ideals'. This does not mean, however, that I will attempt a real *Begriffsgeschichte* ('history of concepts'). Rather than trying to determine how different authors defined the concept itself, or to map the shifts in how it has been defined over the years, I will explore the intellectual debates and contexts in which the concept of asceticism was introduced.

Many canonised – as well as other more forgettable – social theorists seemed to need the concept of asceticism in their work and apparently found it an adequate, clarifying notion. No doubt I could have included other – equally interesting – examples, but these escaped my attention. In analysing the significance of asceticism in the history of social thought, I will also refer to texts in which the word itself does not appear.

The theories on the value of asceticism in contemporary societies were closely linked to other important debates, such as the significance of religion, the desirability of capitalism, and the nature of humanity. Often – and as the examples of Helleiner and Nietzsche have shown – the notion of asceticism introduces strong assumptions about gender. Just as the individual ascetic can be cast in the role of the sturdy desert saint or the religious fanatic, the 'ascetic nation' could either be compared to the 'manly' Spartan republic or depicted as a 'feminised' and 'hypnotised' herd of weaklings.

From Religious Cult to Social Life

The religious origins of asceticism seem obvious. Emile Durkheim included the ascetic rites in *The Elementary Forms of Religious Life* (1912). In his search for the basic features of religious phenomena, Durkheim distinguished between negative and positive forms of religious cults. Negative rites can act as a taboo; they have a crucial role in separating the sacred from the profane and in protecting the sacred from being profaned. Restrictions and abstentions are inherent in all religious systems. But negative rites can also have positive effects. By forcing the individual to withdraw from the profane and to sacrifice their profane interests, they are to some extent 'sanctified' and can achieve closer contact with the sacred. This explains the importance of asceticism and suffering in religious life: 'suffering is the sign that ... certain of the bonds attaching [the individual] to his profane environment are broken; so it testifies that he is partially freed from his environment'.[9]

So far, Durkheim's Christian contemporaries could more or less agree. Devout authors insisted on the importance of asceticism and self-sacrifice as paths to sanctification and salvation. However, they would have been less pleased by Durkheim's comments on the secular functions and meanings of religious asceticism, for as he observed: 'Asceticism not only serves religious ends. Here, as elsewhere, religious interests are but the symbolical form of social and moral interests'.[10]

In every ordered society, individual desires and appetites had to be disciplined, restrained and sacrificed, and natural instincts repressed. 'So there is an element of asceticism inherent in social life that will survive all mythologies and dogmas; it is an integral part of every human culture. And it is this asceticism that is, fundamentally, the *raison d'être* and the justification of the asceticism that religions have preached at all times'.[11] Therefore, asceticism is not only a basic characteristic of religious life; it is also a defining element of social life.

Countless other nineteenth and twentieth-century Western authors pointed out this extra-religious, societal significance of asceticism. In *The Golden Bough* (1922), James George Frazer commented on 'primitive' religious rules of restraint:

> Perhaps the self-restraint which these and the like beliefs, vain and false as they are, have imposed on mankind, has not been without its use in bracing and strengthening the breed. For strength of character in the race and the individual consists mainly in the power of sacrificing the present to the future, of disregarding the immediate temptations of ephemeral pleasure for more distant and lasting sources of satisfaction.[12]

The view was widely shared in anthropology that 'culture implies the repression of instincts'.[13] It was only possible for individuals to live together in more or less organised societies if restrictions were imposed on their sexual (and other) passions, energetic impulses and desires. In 'primitive' societies, religious awe was needed to ensure that people observed these restrictions, which were formulated as sacred laws, taboos and ascetic rules.

Capitalism and Asceticism

So it seems that asceticism was a primal social principle that helped create 'primitive' culture. But some theories outlined the importance of religious, Christian asceticism in the development of modern capitalism as well. The most famous of these is Weber's thesis that the asceticism of Calvinism, Pietism, Methodism and Puritanism contributed to the emergence of the modern capitalist spirit. According to Weber, 'asceticism was carried out of monastic cells into everyday life, and began to dominate worldly morality', and by doing so 'did its part in building the tremendous cosmos of the modern economic order'.[14] Paradoxically, 'since asceticism undertook to remodel the world and to work out its ideals in the world, material goods have gained an increasing and finally an inexorable power over the lives of men as at no previous period in history'.[15] Thus, according to Weber, religious asceticism has played an essential role in constructing the 'iron cage' of capitalism.[16]

For Weber, the spirit of capitalism is the 'idea of a duty of the individual towards the increase of his capital, which is assumed as an end in itself'.[17] In the 1844 manuscripts, the young Karl Marx was already exploring the logic of capitalism along similar lines, and he too needed the concept of asceticism. In a sharp and biting passage on 'Human requirements and division of labour under the rule of private property', he described the 'scientific creed' of the capitalist political economist who 'reduced the worker's need to the barest and most miserable level of physical substance' and 'counted the most meagre form of life as the standard':

> To him [the political economist], therefore, every *luxury* of the worker seems to be reprehensible, and everything that goes beyond the most abstract need – be it in the realm of passive enjoyment, or a manifestation of activity – seems to him a luxury. Political economy, this science of *wealth*, is therefore simultaneously the science of renunciation, of want, of *saving*, and it actually reaches the point where it *spares* man the *need* of either fresh air or physical *exercise*. This science of marvellous industry is simultaneously the science of *asceticism*, and its true ideal is the *ascetic* but *extortionate* miser and the *ascetic* but *productive* slave. … Thus political economy – despite its worldly and voluptuous appearance – is a true moral science, the most moral of all the sciences. Self-renunciation, the renunciation of life and of all human needs, is its principal thesis. The less you eat, drink and buy books; the less you go to the theatre, the dance hall, the public house; the less you think, love, theorise, sing, paint, fence etc, the more you *save* – the greater becomes your treasure which neither moths nor rust will devour – your capital.[18]

In this particular passage, Marx did not refer to the possible religious origins of the capitalist theory of asceticism, nor did he speak of any Christian complicity in preaching or enforcing proletarian self-sacrifice. In other texts, however, Marx did make these anti-religious claims. For him, it was perfectly obvious that the moral messages of Christianity contributed to the general acceptance of an impoverished proletariat. Marx's statements on the 'narcotic' functions of religion in his *Contribution to the Critique of Hegel's Philosophy of Right* (1844) are so famous that they do not need to be repeated here.

Nietzsche was another philosopher who repeatedly and explicitly referred to the narcotic effects of the religious ascetic sermon. He believed that one of religion's general traits was to stun the sufferer (and to exercise power over them by doing so), and Christianity in particular provoked his wrath. Nietzsche's diatribes against Christian morals and asceticism were closely linked with his denunciation of capitalism and modern mass society in which everyone was turned into 'industrious ants'.[19] In the third treatise of the

Genealogy of Morals (1877), Nietzsche included 'mechanical labour' as one of the typical features of the ascetic society:

> Mechanical activity and what's associated with it – like absolute regularity, meticulous and mindless obedience, a style of life set once and for all, filling in time, a certain allowance for, indeed, training in, "impersonality", in forgetting oneself, in *"incuria sui"* – how fundamentally, how delicately the ascetic priest knew how to use them in the struggle with suffering! Especially when it involved the suffering people of the lower classes, working slaves, or prisoners (or women, most of whom are simultaneously both – working slaves and prisoners) what was needed was a little more than the minor art of changing names, of re-christening, so as to make those people in future see a favour, some relative good fortune, in things they hated.[20]

During the interwar period, the leading British philosopher Bertrand Russell denounced the 'foolish asceticism' of capitalism (and, for that matter, Soviet communism) and its work ethic in much the same way.[21]

However, such ideas about the function of religious and capitalist asceticism were by no means the exclusive preserve of exceptional social thinkers such as Durkheim, Weber, Marx and Nietzsche. A host of other – less memorable – authors developed and circulated similar theories on the disciplining effect of ascetic ideals in modern industrial societies. For instance, in an essay on social control, first published in 1898, Stanford professor Edward Alsworth Ross remarked that 'the secret of asceticism is this: *it is the regime that tames men for social life*. Society through the ascetic priest attacks the egoistic instincts seeking to hamstring the primitive impulses of lust, greed, and pride, the chief mischief-makers among associated men'.[22] However, taming natural instincts for the sake of society is not without danger. 'Narcotics are dangerous, and it is impossible to drug an entire people without an occasional overdose ... But once its terrible toxic power is realized, asceticism administered in more cautious doses is capable of beneficent effects'.[23] Commenting more specifically on Western society, Ross remarked that 'the doctrines of Jesus, since the excesses of monasticism passed away, have fostered a readiness to self-sacrifice which has been of vast ethical benefit to European civilization', but then he immediately added that no further proof was needed that 'the ascetic view of the "world" is an illusion'.[24] Asceticism is based on a positive appreciation of pain and suffering, and, according to Ross, 'the worship of pain has never contributed an element of solid worth to human life which might not have been added through the gradual enlightenment of the judgment and the elevation of taste'.[25]

Most authors optimistically noted that growing social welfare and the progress of science and culture would signal the end of the need for restraint and asceticism. The 'pain economy' would give way to a 'pleasure economy' – to use the popular vocabulary of the American economist and philosopher Simon Nelson Patten – in which, according to Ross and the American sociologist Lester Frank Ward, the need for negative ethical rules would decline.[26]

There was widespread debate on the 'narcotic' function of religion and asceticism. 'It is no figure of speech to call certain mental states "narcotic" in character', the American scholar Ernest Groves remarked.[27] 'Religion has for the defeated and distracted individual the function that we know in these modern days belongs especially to the neurosis. It affords a refuge, at what cost matters not, from the bitter facts of life'.[28] In particular, religion was a perfect tranquilliser for women, who had less access to other drugs like alcohol. Groves also distinguished between the different forms of religious sedation, stating that, 'the socially dangerous character of the narcotic element in religion can hardly escape one. It appears, for example, in asceticism'.[29] However, with its low esteem of worldly pleasures and its promise of future happiness to soften the blow and prevent social unrest, and with too strong an emphasis on resignation, religion could easily turn into a cult of asceticism and weakness, sucking all virile energy out of the nation. Instead of strengthening people's character and will-power, asceticism might have a weakening, 'feminising' effect.

On this point, authors could find ammunition in the cultural criticism of Nietzsche and Schopenhauer, and in Darwinist writings. Most social theorists, however, rejected such radical anti-Christian and 'naturalistic' arguments, acknowledging that human beings' bestial inclinations needed to be disciplined. According to Mabel Atkinson, 'the problem of the future … is to unite the pagan with Christian character, and it turns out that, after all, the true superman must have in him more than a dash of the Christian saint'.[30]

In his 1901 essay on 'The truth in ascetic theories of morality', the philosopher Henry Wilkes Wright declared that 'it was a correct understanding of the facts of human experience which led so many of our great moral teachers to emphasise the existence of the "natural man", the suppression of whose desires and inclinations is necessary to moral development'.[31] Wright added that 'asceticism intelligently directed is the *sine qua non* of moral progress'.[32]

Luxury and Civilisation

Asceticism was an important concept in nineteenth and early twentieth-century social thought. Although the cited writings are very different, they all consider ascetic values as central elements needed to form disciplined citizens and dedicated workers and deemed it irrelevant whether or not the individual motives for resignation and restraint were genuinely religious. The fundamental meaning of asceticism was based on society's need for control and organisation, and this stress on the social function of ascetic ideals challenged certain eighteenth-century, Enlightenment, visions of ethics and political economy.

Although this book focuses on the late nineteenth and the early twentieth century, it is useful to discuss some earlier and contrasting ideas on the relationship between luxury and civilisation, in order to get a better understanding of the later writings. Bernard Mandeville's influential *Fable of the Bees* (1714) had developed the famous paradox that 'private vices' yielded 'publick benefits'. Egoism was no obstacle to social coherence, a 'truth' equally propounded by Adam Smith and many other exponents of the Scottish Enlightenment,[33] who spoke positively about luxury and consumption, challenging moralistic discourses on the importance of sobriety.

In an essay on luxury, originally published in 1742, David Hume upheld that 'the increase and consumption of all the commodities, which serve to be the ornament and pleasure of life, are advantages to society'. He admitted that 'innocent luxury' could easily turn into 'vicious luxury', but maintained that 'in a nation where there is no demand for such superfluities, men sink into indolence, lose all enjoyment of life, and are useless to the public'. Hume consciously contradicted the jeremiads of 'severe moralists' who warned against the 'feminising' effects of modern opulence and comfort. While 'the refinement of the arts' betrayed a softening of the morals and manners, this did not imply that the civilised, commercial societies needed to 'fear, that men, by losing their ferocity, will lose their martial spirit, or become less undaunted and vigorous in defence of their country or their liberty. The arts have no such effect in enervating either the mind or body'.

Hume explicitly referred to the 'effeminacy of the Italians', since the adoption of exquisite, Italian male fashions by the English aristocracy had become a symbol of extravagant consumption. The so-called 'macaronis' were satirised as effeminate fops, who exemplified the weakening of virtuous citizenship caused by the modern craving for luxury and consumption.[34] Hume acknowledged that the Italians were effeminate and lacking in 'courage and martial spirit', but refused to accept that this 'degeneracy' was caused by 'their luxury, politeness, or application to the arts'. Hume also had to admit that 'libertine love, or even infidelity to the marriage-bed' are 'more frequent in polite ages, when it is often regarded only as a piece of gallantry', while 'drunkenness, on the other hand, is much less common' in civilised, commercial societies, and alcohol abuse is 'a vice more odious, and more pernicious, both to mind and body'.[35]

The eighteenth-century philosophical tendency to downplay the importance of individual morality for general well-being went together with a harsh criticism of the traditional Christian stress on restraint, self-sacrifice, and indeed asceticism. An author of the Enlightenment like Hume ridiculed the 'monkish virtues' of celibacy, mortification, humility and self-denial.[36]

The historian Edward Gibbon, who wrote critically and mockingly about early Christian ascetic principles in *The Decline and Fall of the Roman Empire* (1776–1788), was partly influenced by his dislike of contemporary forms of religious zeal and puritan lifestyles.[37] This is particularly noticeable where Gibbon attacks the Christian 'fathers' for their radical rejection of every kind of earthly pleasure and for their 'abhorrence of every enjoyment which might gratify the sensual, and degrade the spiritual, nature of man'.[38] He added bitingly: 'The loss of sensual pleasure was supplied and compensated by spiritual pride'.[39]

According to many eighteenth-century writings on political economy, progress and welfare stemmed from the individual's desire for pleasure and consumption. The authors of these texts were deliberately seeking a 'scientific' and secular explanation of public morals, toning down moralist discourses of 'good' and 'evil', blurring the boundaries between 'vice' and 'virtue', and weakening the antagonism between 'selfishness' and 'public good'.[40] In Hume's aforementioned essay, he states that 'the bounds between the virtue and the vice cannot here be exactly fixed'.[41]

Mandeville made a similar point earlier, but he did not completely deny the possibility and heroism of 'true' virtuousness, arguing that the publicly acclaimed 'virtuous citizen' was quite often driven by a selfish desire for praise and honour, rather than by genuine virtuousness and self-denial. He added that public welfare and order were shaped by man's vicious nature. In an essay added to the 1723 edition of the *Fable of the Bees*, he concluded:

> I flatter myself to have demonstrated that, neither the Friendly Qualities and kind Affections that are natural to Man, nor the real Virtues he is capable of acquiring by Reason and Self-Denial, are the Foundation of Society; but that what we call Evil in this World, Moral as well as Natural, is the grand Principle that makes us sociable Creatures, the solid Basis, the Life and Support of all Trades and Employments without Exception: That there we must look for the true Origin of all Arts and Sciences, and that the Moment Evil ceases, the Society must be spoiled, if not totally dissolved.[42]

Victorian Saints and Gender Trouble

In short, according to some Enlightenment thinkers, asceticism was an anti-social principle that hampered the development of culture and society, and the contrast with the views of the nineteenth and early twentieth-century social theorists mentioned above can hardly be greater. With Stefan Collini, one can argue that nineteenth-century social and political thought was typified by a new stress on morality, self-control and restraint, exemplified by the cult of 'altruism'.[43]

The term 'altruism' was coined in the 1850s by Auguste Comte and quickly became current in nineteenth-century philosophical vocabulary throughout Europe and the United States. Ironically, in British and American intellectual circles, the concept of altruism was very suitable for theorists who tried to reconcile religious ideas with modern social science.[44]

Generally speaking, Victorian thought was 're-moralised' and had more religious overtones than the philosophy of the Enlightenment. The belief that private vice could create public benefit was seriously flawed, and the Victorian authors stressed the importance of commonly-shared ideals of restraint, morality and austerity. Moral philosopher Wright summarised widespread ideas, when he wrote in 1901 that 'the ascetic aspect of morality is no passing phenomenon, but an essential element necessarily involved in a process which consists in the adjustment of the individual into a larger whole'.[45]

Even authors with clearly anti-religious or anti-clerical sympathies acknowledged that asceticism was inextricably linked with the modern reality of capitalism and social organisation. It appeared that rather than being opposed to the modern world of mass consumption and unlimited spending, asceticism was one of its defining elements.[46] Most authors therefore felt deeply ambiguous about its social value: it was somehow necessary, and yet dangerous. It was part of the social problem, and at the same time a key element in its solution.

It became increasingly difficult to believe – as some Enlightenment authors had thought – that the sinister aspects of asceticism could be 'overcome' by destroying its religious, superstitious foundations. For authors like Nietzsche, it was obvious that ascetic ideals had permeated all aspects of modern life, not least the spheres of learning and science. As mentioned above, a flight into the desert was all that was left.

As James Eli Adams has maintained, the 'desert saint' was one of the ideal types of Victorian manhood.[47] Indeed, the debate on masculinity has very similar ambiguities as those connected with asceticism,[48] and 'manliness' and 'austerity' have been closely related concepts since the late eighteenth century. The middle classes cultivated the image of 'manly simplicity' in opposition to earlier, aristocratic representations of the gallant and polite gentleman.[49]

The ideal Victorian man was sober, independent, self-controlled, hard-working, straightforward, responsible and virtuous. It is generally assumed that the nineteenth-century religious revival contributed to the construction of the austere patriarch, but the image of manly simplicity could as well fit older republican notions of masculine virtue and citizenship.[50] Austere, ascetic manliness was contrasted with so-called feminine weakness and dependence – exemplified by women's consumerism, their craving for luxury and fashion, and their capriciousness – and, much worse, with the effeminate behaviour of the male dandy.

But the image of austere and simple masculinity could just as easily be reversed. The industrious and disciplined bourgeois man was as much an object of satire and mockery as he was a praiseworthy role model. The responsible housefather was 'domesticated' and 'tamed'. Had he not lost his virile will-power and surrendered to the alliance of feminists, preachers, and intellectuals, that despicable bunch of male traitors and eunuchs?

As Lucy Bland has demonstrated, the 'banishing of the beast' was an important goal of nineteenth-century feminism.[51] As feminists strove to abolish the moral double standard and to generalise the 'feminine' standard, resisting this attempt to 'feminise' men was an easy and obvious way to reaffirm one's own masculine identity. Instead of banishing the beast within, men started to discover, cultivate and unleash their animal masculinity. Tarzan was no less an icon of early twentieth-century masculinity than the desert saint.[52]

To remodel oneself and to adapt to the Tarzan-like image, however, involved a renewed ascetic disciplining of the body. Breaking out of the restraints imposed by modern capitalist society (as Tarzan fans desired),[53] implied accepting further restraints. Perceptive observers during the interwar period remarked that athletic, soldierly images of manhood were on the rise and were attractive to numerous people. Entire nations became obsessed with this 'Spartan form of austerity' (to quote Russell in a 1935 essay on *The Ancestry of Fascism*), 'dazzled by the vision of glory, heroism, and self-sacrifice' and 'blind to their serious interests, and in a blaze of emotion [allowed] themselves to be used for purposes not their own'. Russell, the social democrat, called this 'the psychopathology of Nazidom',[54] and criticised liberal bourgeois capitalism for its 'foolish asceticism', which was challenged by a National Socialist form of asceticism (as well as by a no less ascetic communist alternative). According to Russell, fascist leaders generated 'mass hysteria'. The sufferers were seduced, lost every form of 'intellectual sobriety in favour of some delusive will o' the wisp'.[55] In Russell's analysis, the followers of the fascist, austere, masculine ideal were turned into emotional, anti-rational, hysterical and thus feminised men. He preached the return to 'a universal and impersonal standard of truth', to 'intellectual sobriety'.[56] Another ascetic (and manly) ideal, indeed.

Concluding Remarks

While some eighteenth-century authors of the Enlightenment thought that asceticism was part of the old, dark, Christian world that had to be overcome by a new, rational and brilliant age, nineteenth-century intellectuals were less sure that such a break with the past was possible or even desirable. They laid bare the deeply ingrained continuities and historical inextricabilities between religious ascetic ideals on the one hand, and the rise of consumerism, capitalism and modern social organisation on the other. This insight led to ambiguous feelings and perplexities.

For some – probably most – social theorists, it was reassuring to think that capitalism was not all about greed and egoism, but as much about self-restraint and self-denial. Western capitalist society was the outcome of the Christian age of civilising morals, not a brute and barbarous system of pure exploitation and lack of ethics.

For critical thinkers, however, the Christian, ascetic element in capitalism was far from reassuring. It contributed to the idea that radical social reform was somehow impossible, that the face of the 'enemy' was ever changing. So-called 'historical ruptures' turned out to be a delusion, and slave morality indestructible. Only the very strong, really austere individual could transcend the weakening force of capitalist society. Human society was only made possible by imposing restraint and asceticism; it needed more asceticism and restraint to resist the herd and to live apart.

Notes

1. K.F. Helleiner, 'Moral Conditions of Economic Growth', *Journal of Economic History* 11,2 (1951), 100.
2. Karl Ferdinand Maria Helleiner was born in Vienna in 1902. He worked as an archivist in Sankt-Pölten from 1928 till 1938, and then emigrated to Canada, where he taught at the University of Toronto from 1942 onwards. He died in Toronto in 1984.
3. Helleiner, 'Moral Conditions', 100.
4. Ibid., 103.
5. Ibid., 105.
6. Ibid., 104.
7. T.T. Roberts, '"This Art of Transfiguration is Philosophy": Nietzsche's Asceticism', *Journal of Religion* 76,3 (1996), 402–27.
8. F. Nietzsche, *The Genealogy of Morals*, [1887], III §11.
9. E. Durkheim, *Les formes élémentaires de la vie religieuse* (Paris, 1991), 535.
10. Ibid., 537.
11. Ibid.
12. J.G. Frazer, *The Golden Bough: A Study in Magic and Religion* (London, 1993), 139.
13. B. Malinowski, *Sex and Repression in Savage Society* (London, 2001), 145.
14. M. Weber, *The Protestant Ethic and the Spirit of Capitalism* (New York, 1958), 181.
15. Ibid., 181–82.
16. Ibid., 181.
17. Ibid., 47.

18. K. Marx, 'Human Requirements and Division of Labour Under the Rule of Private Property', in K. Marx and F. Engels, *Collected Works*, 50 vols (London, 1975–2005), 3:309, original emphasis.

19. R.J. Antonio, 'Nietzsche's Antisociology: Subjectified Culture and the End of History', *American Journal of Sociology* 101 (1995), 10.

20. Nietzsche, *The Genealogy of Morals*, III §18.

21. B. Russell, *In Praise of Idleness and Other Essays* (London, 2004), 8.

22. E.A. Ross, 'Social Control: XI', *American Journal of Sociology* 3,4 (1898), 508, original emphasis.

23. Ibid., 510.

24. Ibid.

25. Ibid., 511.

26. L.F. Ward, 'Utilitarian Economics', *American Journal of Sociology* 3,4 (1898), 520–36.

27. E.R. Groves, 'An Unsocial Element in Religion', *American Journal of Sociology* 22,5 (1917), 657.

28. Ibid., 658.

29. Ibid., 660.

30. M. Atkinson, 'The Struggle for Existence in Relation to Morals and Religion', *International Journal of Ethics* 18,3 (1908), 310.

31. H.W. Wright, 'The Truth in Ascetic Theories of Morality', *Philosophical Review* 10,6 (1901), 610.

32. Ibid., 613.

33. Of course, I am not arguing that, according to Smith, humans are only capable of selfishness, nor that Smith is in complete agreement with Mandeville (which he is clearly not). It is correct, however, that Smith's moral philosophy supposes that 'natural selfishness contributes to the well-being of all' and that 'Smith, like Mandeville, argues that consumption helps distribute the necessities of life' (J.R. Weinstein, *On Adam Smith*, Belmont, 2001, 54).

34. D. Wahrman, 'Gender in Translation: How the English Wrote their Juvenal, 1644–1815', *Representations* 65 (1999), 19–21.

35. D. Hume, *The Philosophical Works*, 4 vols (Edinburgh, 1826) 3: 302–16.

36. P. Gay, *The Enlightenment: An Interpretation. The Science of Freedom* (New York and London, 1977), 193–94. Stephen Holmes, the historian of political thought, remarks in this context: 'For both Hume and Voltaire, the "rehabilitation" of self-love was inseparable from an attack on Christian severity and asceticism' (S. Holmes, *Passions and Constraint: On the Theory of Liberal Democracy*, Chicago, 1995, 60–61).

37 B.W. Young, '"Scepticism in Excess": Gibbon and Eighteenth-century Christianity', *Historical Journal* 41,1 (1998), 189–90.

38 E. Gibbon, *The Decline and Fall of the Roman Empire*, 12 vols (New York, 1906), 2: 305.

39 Ibid., 2: 307.

40 Holmes, *Passions and Constraint*, 47–48.

41 Hume, *The Philosophical Works*, 3: 315.

42. B. Mandeville, *The Fable of the Bees: Or Private Vices, Publick Benefits*, ed. F.B. Kaye, 2 vols (Oxford, 1924), 1: 369.
43. S. Collini, *Public Moralists: Political Thought and Intellectual Life in Britain* (Oxford, 1991).
44. L.J. Budd, 'Altruism Arrives in America', *American Quarterly* 8,1 (1956), 41–43.
45. Wright, 'The Truth in Ascetic Theories', 613.
46. Today's critics of modern capitalism also note this paradox. To quote from Belgian philosopher Johan Moyaert: 'We realise insufficiently how our so-called "consumer society" rests on an ascetic mentality' (J. Moyaert, *Kritiek van de ascetische rede*, Brussels, 2004, 85).
47. J.E. Adams, *Dandies and Desert Saints: Styles of Victorian Masculinity* (Ithaca, 1995).
48. Nineteenth-century discourses on masculinity were much more ambiguous than is usually suggested in historical literature on 'hegemonic' masculinity (e.g., G.L. Mosse, *The Image of Man: The Creation of Modern Masculinity*, Oxford, 1996). This is a point I have made elsewhere: H. de Smaele, 'Een beeld van een man. Mosse en het moderne mannelijke stereotype', *Tijdschrift voor Genderstudies* 9,3 (2006), 5–18.
49. J. Tosh, *Manliness and Masculinities in Nineteenth-century Britain* (Harlow, 2005), 83–102.
50. Mosse, *The Image of Man*.
51. L. Bland, *Banishing the Beast: Feminism, Sex and Morality* (London, 1995).
52. J.F. Kasson, *Houdini, Tarzan and the Perfect Man: The White Male Body and the Challenge of Modernity in America* (New York, 2001).
53. Kasson quotes Edgar Rice Burroughs, the inventor of Tarzan: 'We wish to escape not alone the narrow confines of city streets for the freedom of the wilderness, but the restrictions of man made laws, and the inhibitions that society has placed upon us. We like to picture ourselves as roaming free, the lords of ourselves and of our world; in other words, we would each like to be Tarzan. At least I would; I admit it' (Kasson, *Houdini, Tarzan*, 159).
54. Russell, *In Praise of Idleness*, 59, 67.
55. Ibid., 70.
56. Ibid., 71.

References

Adams, J.E. 1995. *Dandies and Desert Saints: Styles of Victorian Masculinity*, Ithaca.
Antonio, R.J. 1995. 'Nietzsche's Antisociology: Subjectified Culture and the End of History', *American Journal of Sociology* 101(1): 1–43.
Atkinson, M. 1908, 'The Struggle for Existence in Relation to Morals and Religion', *International Journal of Ethics* 18(3): 291–311.
Bland, L. 1995. *Banishing the Beast: Feminism, Sex and Morality*, London.
Budd, L.J. 1956. 'Altruism Arrives in America', *American Quarterly* 8(1): 40–52.
Collini, S. 1991. *Public Moralists: Political Thought and Intellectual Life in Britain*, Oxford.

De Smaele, H. 2006. 'Een beeld van een man: Mosse en het moderne mannelijke stereotype', *Tijdschrift voor Genderstudies* 9(3): 5–18.

Durkheim, E. 1991[1912]. *Les formes élémentaires de la vie religieuse*, Paris.

Frazer, J.G. 1993[1922]. *The Golden Bough: A Study in Magic and Religion*, London.

Gay, P. 1977. *The Enlightenment: An Interpretation. The Science of Freedom*, New York and London.

Gibbon, E. 1906. *The Decline and Fall of the Roman Empire*, 12 vols, New York.

Groves, E.R. 1917. 'An Unsocial Element in Religion', *American Journal of Sociology* 22(5): 657–62.

Helleiner, K.F. 1951. 'Moral Conditions of Economic Growth', *Journal of Economic History* 11(2): 97–116.

Holmes, S. 1995. *Passions and Constraint: On the Theory of Liberal Democracy*, Chicago.

Hume, D. 1826. *The Philosophical Works of David Hume*, 4 vols, Edinburgh.

Kasson, J.F. 2001. *Houdini, Tarzan and the Perfect Man: The White Male Body and the Challenge of Modernity in America*, New York.

Malinowski, B. 2001[1927]. *Sex and Repression in Savage Society*, London and New York.

Mandeville, B. 1924[1723]. *The Fable of the Bees: Or Private Vices, Publick Benefits*, ed. F.B. Kaye, 2 vols, Oxford.

Marx, K. 1975[1844]. 'A Contribution to the Critique of Hegel's Philosophy of Right: Introduction', in K. Marx and F. Engels, *Collected Works*, London, 3: 175–187.

Marx, K., 1975[1844]. 'Human Requirements and Division of Labour Under the Rule of Private Property', in K. Marx and F. Engels, *Collected Works*, London, 3: 306-321.

Mosse, G.L. 1996. *The Image of Man: The Creation of Modern Masculinity*, Oxford.

Moyaert, J. 2004. *Kritiek van de ascetische rede*, Brussels.

Nietzsche, F. 2009 [1887]. *On the Genealogy of Morals: A Polemical Tract*, trans. I. Johnston, Arlington.

Roberts, T.T. 1996. '"This Art of Transfiguration is Philosophy": Nietzsche's Asceticism', *Journal of Religion* 76(3): 402–27.

Ross, E.A. 1898. 'Social Control: XI', *American Journal of Sociology* 3(4): 502–19.

Russell, B. 2004[1932, 1935]. *In Praise of Idleness and Other Essays*, London.

Tosh, J. 2005. *Manliness and Masculinities in Nineteenth-century Britain*, Harlow.

Wahrman, D. 1999. 'Gender in Translation: How the English Wrote their Juvenal, 1644–1815', *Representations* 65: 1–41.

Ward, L.F. 1898. 'Utilitarian Economics', *American Journal of Sociology* 3(4): 520–36.

Weber, M. 1958. *The Protestant Ethic and the Spirit of Capitalism*, trans. T. Parsons, New York.

Weinstein, J.R. 2001. *On Adam Smith*, Belmont.

Wright, H.W. 1901. 'The Truth in Ascetic Theories of Morality', *Philosophical Review* 10(6): 601–18.

Young, B.W. 1998 '"Scepticism in Excess": Gibbon and Eighteenth-century Christianity', *Historical Journal* 41(1): 179–99.

Part III
Aesthetics and Distinction

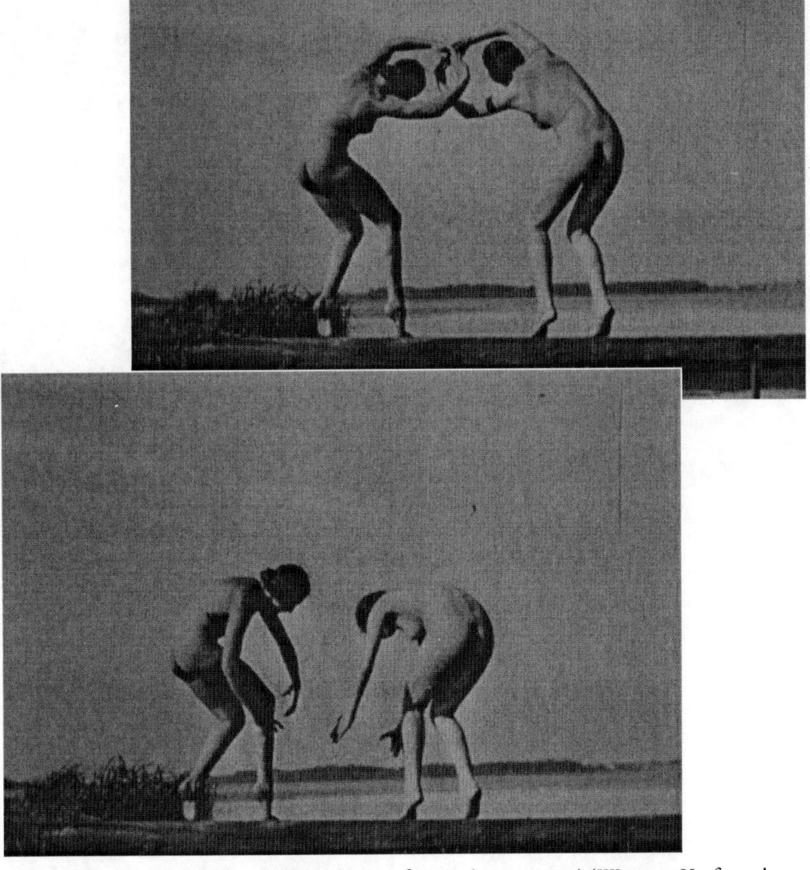

Wilhelm Prager (director) and Nicholas Kaufmann (scriptwriter) 'Wege zu Kraft und Schönheit' (1924). © Friedrich-Wilhelm-Murnau-Stiftung, Wiesbaden, Germany.

6

Adolf Loos and the Doric Order

Wessel Krul

In memory of Margrith Wilke (1958–2007)

Asceticism may be practiced for a variety of reasons, but one enduring motive is a desire to gain or restore power. In this guise it turns out to be a conspicuous ingredient in the early history of the modernist movement in architecture. While the study of late nineteenth and early twentieth-century European culture has often concentrated on its 'decadent' aspects, the *fin de siècle* was also the age of imperialism, militarism, and a growing confidence in ever-expanding new technology. Alongside the discourse of aesthetic and moral refinement and distinction runs one of aggressive dominance. Neurasthenia and hypersensitivity were fashionable symptoms of modern life, but many contemporary observers stressed that these regrettable weaknesses should be combated, not indulged in. The 1890s and early 1900s were marked as much by the 'will to power' as by psychological introspection and individual expression. Sometimes one attitude was transformed into the other almost overnight. As legend has it, after the trial of Oscar Wilde in 1895, the carnations worn by fashionable young men suddenly disappeared, replaced by Union Jacks flying in the streets of London.[1]

As a preparation for self-defence, asceticism clearly is a sign of the 'desire for power'. Practical considerations, such as sacrificing private pleasure to the common good, are, however, only part of the story. Asceticism can act as a means to power in a still more elementary sense: when it is used as a form of magic. Refraining from food or sleep or other bodily comforts, and especially from sexual or other types of contact with human beings, enables the practitioner to build up a reservoir of strength which gives him extraordinary powers. By rejecting everything that is 'luxurious', the ascetic conquers the material world. His abstinence enables him to retain all the energy that would be dissipated and lost in normal life.[2]

Ornament and Crime

The two approaches to power through asceticism – discipline and magic – cannot always be strictly separated. Demonstrations of collective strength and power, themselves often based on a willingness to sacrifice private concerns, are usually accompanied by signs and symbols, and when these are inspired by asceticism, a form of magical thinking is often present.

As a case in point, I want to focus on one of the reactions against the supposed *fin de siècle* decadence of the Habsburg Empire. In Vienna, the artists, architects and designers grouped around the Wiener Secession (Vereinigung bildender Künstler Oesterreichs), and afterwards the Wiener Werkstätte, developed a refined, elegant and highly ornate contemporary style. In their quest for an art that would be a fitting expression of their own age, they violently rejected the eclecticism and historicism of the earlier generation. But they also rejected the mechanised ornamentation of industrial mass-production. Their aim was to 'suffuse life with beauty', which meant adopting aesthetic quality as the highest standard in life, and proffering the cultivated and sensitive individual as a model for society at large. Their ideal was a civilisation in which all the visible elements of public and private life would harmonise with one another.

In the art and architecture of Josef Maria Olbrich, Josef Hoffmann, Koloman Moser, and Alfred Roller, even the smallest details became part of a grand design, enveloping and absorbing the human subject, just as the bodies of the sitters are turned into a decorated surface in the portraits by Gustav Klimt. Although the Viennese artists preferred geometric to floral or vegetative forms, the principle of a total, all-encompassing style remained the same as in other European varieties of art nouveau.[3]

The ideal of universal harmony, and the aesthetisation of life in general, implied dissolving the boundaries between public and private spheres. The cultivated person had to set an example to the world, and the uncultivated person had to be educated by coming into contact with an aesthetically balanced environment. In murals by Klimt, expressly meant as public art, references to the erotic sphere replaced the traditional, but by now highly controversial references to the greatness of the Austrian state and the various nationalities of which it was made up.[4]

After the turn of the century, a new group of artists and writers denounced this aesthetisation of life as a decadent delusion, as one more unrealistic façade, similar to the rich ornamentation decorating the earlier official buildings in the historicist style. The best-known of these attacks is an essay by the architect Adolf Loos: 'Ornament und Verbrechen' ('Ornament and Crime'), first presented as a lecture in 1910, and published (in French) in 1913 after Loos had delivered his lecture again in Munich, Berlin and Vienna. The original German version was not published until 1929, but was reprinted in

1931, at the height of the modernist movement in architecture.[5] From then on it came to be regarded as one of the founding texts, even a manifesto, of incipient modernism, even though it was not the first stage in the debate on ornament, or even the clearest statement of Loos's position.

It remains, however, a remarkable piece of polemic. Although he did not use the expression, Loos's aims can be summarised as 'less is more'. In contrast to most of his contemporaries, Loos did not give pride of place to ornament, but instead preached a 'radical abstinence', an asceticism in design which, he thought, would raise the quality and aesthetics of modern life to a higher level.

Loos was almost forty years old when he first described ornament as a 'crime'. By that time, he was a well-known personality in Viennese artistic circles. As a young man, he had cut a figure as a dandy, a connoisseur of English and American fashion, and one of the best-dressed men in town. He was feared for his sharp wit and for his relentless criticism of the dominant principles of Viennese art nouveau.

From 1898 onwards, he published polemical articles and satirical vignettes against what he saw as an ever-widening epidemic of ornamentation. In 1909, his career as an architect, which until then had been rather low-key, gained momentum.[6] Loos had just embarked on the building that would make him famous, if only because no inhabitant of Vienna could avoid it: the shop and apartment complex for the men's tailoring firm of Goldman and Salatsch, situated on a corner of the Michaelerplatz, in front of Fischer von Erlach's baroque Michaelertor wing of the imperial palace. The building horrified the public because of its flattened, almost undecorated façade, and it soon became known as 'the house without eyelids'. Perhaps as a reaction to this, Loos now stated his opinions on contemporary art and architecture even more vehemently than before.

In his essay, Loos took a strictly evolutionary line of reasoning. Traditionally, the use of ornament had been defended on the grounds that it was universally used by so-called 'primitive peoples', and therefore originated from a basic human impulse. Owen Jones opened his *Grammar of Ornament* (1856) with a chapter on 'the ornament of savage tribes', arguing that because it was based on instinct, 'primitive' ornament was 'necessarily true to its purpose'. In this sense, modern society should take it as a source of inspiration: 'If we would return to a more healthy condition, we must even be as little children or as savages'.[7] Jones's message was heard in Vienna as well, where his work (in German translation) was used as a standard text at the Kunstgewerbeschule (School of Design) until the 1890s.[8]

Loos turned this argument on its head: precisely because ornamentation originated in 'primitive' instincts, it should be banned from modern civilised society. In contemporary Europe, the 'primitive' pleasure in ornamentation still survived among the lower classes: farmers and seafaring men, gypsies, criminals, madmen and imbeciles. This decorative impulse resulted in earrings, tattoos, graffiti, in bodily deformations and obscene scribblings on walls.

The time had arrived to cut the thread that connected the arts to these lower forms of expression. Ornament had to do with fear, aggression, superstition, scatology, and above all sexuality; in short, with sentiments which, in the civilised world, belonged to the private sphere and should not be shown in public.

> The first-born ornament, the cross, was of erotic origin. The first work of art, the first artistic act, was smeared by the first artist on a wall, to be relieved of his superfluities. A horizontal line: the lying woman. A vertical line: the man penetrating her. The man who created this experienced the same urge as Beethoven, he was in the same heaven in which Beethoven created his Ninth Symphony. But when someone of our time smears the walls with erotic symbols, expressing his inner urges, he is either a criminal or a degenerate.[9]

The cultivated person – Loos usually referred to the English 'gentleman' as a model – was someone who hid himself behind a mask of imperturbable correctness, in dress, in manners and in behaviour, and who arranged his home to show the same restraint. 'Primitive' man might express his emotions in decorating his body, his tools and his house, but the modern gentleman presented a smooth and unruffled appearance in society, and reserved his emotions for private occasions. His feelings were far too complex to be reflected in ornamental patterns. 'Modern man uses his dress as a mask. His individuality is so immensely strong, that it cannot be expressed in clothing anyway'.[10]

The private houses Loos designed in the course of his career were based on the same principle: they were conceived as boxes with a plain, screen-like and undecorated exterior, containing a rich, though unornamented interior, where luxurious materials formed the background against which the private fancies of the owners could be acted out.[11] The progress of civilisation led to an ever sharper distinction between outside and inside, between the public and the private. The use of ornament in design and architecture was a regression, an unacceptable intrusion of private matters into the public sphere. 'Cultural evolution is identical with the removal of ornamentation from functional objects'.[12]

Asceticism and Aestheticism

Loos's prescriptions seemed, at least in external matters, to favour an austere, angular style, based on self-control, self-denial and restraint. In the modernist movement, Loos's essay was read as an outright condemnation of all ornamentation. Loos became known as the great ascetic of contemporary architecture.

A conference organised in Vienna in 1985, which took Loos's work as a starting point, was given the title 'Ornament und Askese' ('Ornament and Asceticism').[13] But by that time the modernist tradition had run its course. Some of the contributors confirmed the existing view of Loos as one of the severest critics of the self-indulgent aestheticism of *fin de siècle* culture. Carl Schorske, for instance, regarded Loos and the journalist Karl Kraus, with whom Loos had many ideas in common, as 'the last Puritans', defenders of what were in their opinion, 'the manly virtues of reason, ethics and honest truth'. But Schorske also stressed the turn towards the private in Loos's work, and recognised that his interiors were designed for a life of luxury, intimacy and pleasure, including erotic pleasure.[14] Loos's biographer Rukschcio even denied that there was anything ascetic about Loos at all,[15] arguing that he was in no way interested in abstinence, sacrifice or self-castigation. He supported his opinion by pointing to one of the statements in Loos's seminal essay: 'The representative of ornament believes that my urge towards simplicity is a kind of chastisement. No, venerable professor at the School of Design, I am not chastising myself! It's just more to my taste this way'.[16]

It was not Loos's intention to minimise pleasure, but to refine and intensify it. In general, more recent studies tend to interpret his work as one of the possible varieties of *fin de siècle* aestheticism, rather than a rejection of it.[17] In fact, with a subtle dialectic, Loos's pronounced preference for finely grained, polished and costly materials can be seen as the ultimate in ornamentation. This effectively turns Loos's essay into 'a eulogy on "the ornament of the absence of ornament"'.[18]

But the pendulum may have swung too far the other way. If I return to the idea of Adolf Loos as an ascetic, I am not attempting to re-establish the principles of modernism, or to deny that much progress has been made in understanding Loos in his historical context. The use of beautiful forms and surfaces to maximise visual and sensual pleasure was obviously extremely important to him. In this respect, his work was a continuation of that of both his predecessors and his contemporaries. Loos was no absolute enemy of ornament, and he certainly was not a functionalist either; he was an aesthete in his own right.

Nevertheless, his polemic against ornamentation was not just a literary device to scandalise his audience. There is a sentence in Loos's essay which betrays some of his underlying obsessions: 'The lack of ornament is a sign of intellectual power'.[19] Power and distinction mattered to Loos, not only as a means to all sorts of other pleasures, but also as something to be enjoyed in itself. To attain this power, one had to keep oneself under tight control, and not waste energy on superfluous things. It was just one step from the decadent artist, who invaded public space with his private sympathies and sentiments, to the degenerate and the madman. To mix private and public life was a fatal weakness, as the distinctive English gentleman, the builder of empires, understood all too well.

Even if Loos did not fully detach himself from the preoccupation with aesthetics which marked the Viennese fin de siècle, he was certainly a radical in relation to the values of his time. He had no patience with the ideal of 'the beautiful life', as it was practiced by the artists from the circle of the Wiener Secession. His declared enemy was the architect Josef Hoffmann, whom he pursued in his journalism as a decadent and a degenerate. For Loos, as we have seen, there was no difference between degeneration and the savagery of the so-called 'lower cultures'. Therefore Hoffmann could be dismissed as a 'state-subsidised Papuan'.[20]

In the debate on the problems of modern society, Loos consistently took the side of those who defended strength, manliness, order and discipline. His sources of inspiration were Friedrich Nietzsche, whose influence is immediately evident in the style of Loos's writing, and authorities such as Max Nordau, the great accuser of degeneration, and Otto Weininger, with his desperate struggle against effeminacy. Loos detested the *vie de bohème*, the nostalgic yearning for the glories of the past, the cultivation of neurotic sensitivities, the 'sentimentality of women'. Every time a choice had to be made between artistic and intellectual introspection on the one hand, and the disciplined life of sports, travel and machinery on the other, Loos chose the latter.

There were several options for those who, like Loos, were convinced that modern culture should seek a radical remedy for its problems. A well-known and oft-tried solution was to go 'back to basics', to return to nature or to an earlier stage of civilisation. If the complexities of modern society resulted in confusion, repression and neurosis, the solution lay in simplification and directness of expression. Many contemporary pleas for a healthier life presented their aims, in a tradition going back to Rousseau or even to classical antiquity, as a return to an existence according to natural laws.

These ideas frequently took the form of primitivism, when the way of life and the arts of non-Western societies were extolled as examples of a direct expression of natural humanity. Primitivism could be a revolutionary instrument to break through the stifling conventions of European civilisation. This was the course favoured by all expressionists, from Les Fauves in France, led by Matisse, to the Blaue Reiter group in Germany, which included Kandinsky, Arp and Klee. Picasso's *Demoiselles d'Avignon* (1907), with its abrupt changes of perspective and its apparently crude suggestion of African masks, was painted not long before Loos wrote his famous essay. Picasso's work was yet another example of how the search for renewal led to an attempt to see the world through the eyes of children or savages.

Loos was not a systematic enemy of expressionism, as is clear from his moral and financial support of an artist like Oskar Kokoschka, who painted his portrait in 1909.[21] In 1912 Loos published several short pieces in the expressionist journal *Der Sturm*. But at least in theory, he despised everything primitive. He saw his ascetic aesthetics not as a return to a natural simplicity or to an idealised earlier stage, but as an important step forward in the progressive march of civilisation.

Figure 6.1 Adolf Loos's portrait by Oskar Kokoschka, 1909 © Nationalgalerie, Berlin, Germany / SABAM, Brussels, Belgium.

In Loos's opinion, rejecting ornamentation had nothing to do with primitivism. The main characteristic of 'primitive' art was not simplicity but a proliferation of surface decoration. Loos saw his plea for an assertive and dynamic sobriety as a completely modern sign of refinement. He was an energetic sportsman himself, a swimmer, tennis player and dancer, and his essay was one of the many contemporary eulogies of a modern dynamism, a move away from the stuffiness, the fears, the inhibitions and encumbrances of the Victorian age. In many respects, 'Ornament and Crime' was closer to the exultation of the machine age in Marinetti's *Futurist Manifesto* (1909) than to the primitivism that inspired the successive avant-garde movements in France and Germany.

Ornament and Power: The Chicago Tribune Project

Loos wanted to be a radical, but a strictly modern radical, one who was not nostalgic for an organic or primitive past. The 'intellectual power' derived from the 'lack of ornament' was a purified power, energetic, agile and elegant, unburdened by historical reminiscences or sentimental considerations. It was the result of mental restraint, of self-possession, of concentrating on essentials. But is it possible to show such strength without introducing symbols of power? Even if Loos rejected the kind of primitivism he associated with 'savagery', he could not completely free himself from a tradition of representing power in elementary, primitive, phallic forms. And what exactly was the object of this power? What kind of dominance did Loos have in mind?

Loos's shop and apartment building on the Michaelerplatz in Vienna met with generalised public incomprehension, as the 'naked' upper part of the exterior was deemed an unacceptable modernist extravaganza. The city council tried to promote a plan by another architect to redecorate the façade, to bring it into line with the baroque and neo-baroque buildings elsewhere along the square.

Figure 6.2 Loos's shop and apartment building on the Michaelerplatz in Vienna, 1908. © Getty Images.

There were also critics who thought Loos was dishonest and untrue to his own principles. One of them even spoke of the Goldman and Salatsch building as 'thoroughly un-modern'.[22] Loos had flanked the entrance to the tailor's shop with four Doric columns in white and green *cipollino* marble from the Greek island of Euboia (Evvia), even though it was well-known that the complex was constructed in reinforced concrete, and the lintel over the entrance was strong enough to carry the façade without the support of columns. The white-and-green Doric columns, and the decoration of the entrance with slabs of the same marble, were therefore nothing but ornamentation. Of course, Loos hastened to declare that his columns were functional, if only as additional supports, in case of an emergency.[23] But it was clear that his campaign against ornamentation was targeted at the way in which others, Josef Hoffmann in particular, applied it, and did not preclude his own version. Around the corner of the façade, Loos added English-style bay-windows on the second floor, which again were flanked by Doric columns, this time very small and obviously non-functional. And in the interior of the shop Loos masked the construction behind rich panels of polished mahogany.

Why would coloured Doric columns be particularly expressive of the elegant self-restraint, the reserved stylishness featured by Loos's favourite tailor? And what was the 'intellectual power' symbolised by this non-ornamental ornamentation?

Proof that the Doric column occupied a special place in Loos's imagination appeared in a spectacular manner just over a decade later. In 1922, the *Chicago Tribune*, the largest newspaper in the American Midwest, announced a competition for the design of a new office building. A large number of both famous and obscure architects sent in their projects, including Loos.[24] Although his proposal never progressed beyond the design stage, his version of the Chicago Tribune Tower has become an icon of modernist architecture, even to the point where Loos as the inventor is often forgotten.

The new office building for the *Chicago Tribune* was planned as a modern high-rise structure or skyscraper. Most, though not all, of the designs submitted for the competition were in the form of square towers, including the neo-gothic design by Howells and Hood which was finally selected and built. Loos, however, presented a design for a circular building in the shape of one gigantic Doric column, rising from a square 'pedestal' or building block that was to be ten storeys high.[25] The exterior was to be executed in black granite, brick and terracotta. The entrance was flanked by two smaller Doric columns, rising two storeys high. The free-standing column as a whole supported nothing. It was crowned with a Doric, that is a flat and unadorned, capital, which was left empty and was not used as a base for any type of sculpture or other decoration.

Loos's sensational and highly memorable design is sometimes explained by a verbal pun. After all, a newspaper is printed in columns, so why not use a column as a symbol of everything the *Chicago Tribune* stood for?[26] The empty

Figure 6.3 Adolf Loos's design for the Chicago Tribune Tower, 1922.

capital crowning the column may have been aimed at creating a special visual effect. From a distance, the column would be seen as supporting the sky, which not only gave a new meaning to the concept of the 'skyscraper', but also underlined the symbolic function of the building. One thing, however, was obvious: this seemed to be a massive return to the ornament.[27] Was it a sudden manifestation of something repressed? Or was Loos repeating the statement he had made shortly before the first World War with the columns on the façade of the Goldman and Salatsch building on the Michaelerplatz, but now on an enormous scale? It is certain that he was not thinking of his project as a joke or a passing fancy. He was convinced of the importance of his design, not only for the present but also as a model for the future. 'The great Greek Doric column will be built. If not in Chicago, then in another town. If not for the *Chicago Tribune*, then for somebody else. If not by me, then by another architect'.[28]

It is easy to explain Loos's design of an enormous phallic object as the result of private obsessions. In 'Ornament and Crime', as elsewhere in his writings, there is a remarkable insistence on cleanliness and purity, a fear of contamination. This probably originates in biographical circumstances. At the age of twenty-two Loos had contracted a type of syphilis after being taken to a brothel by one of his uncles, and although he was supposed to be cured after a treatment of several months, his health always remained precarious. By the 1920s, he had become almost completely deaf.

Loos was a restless man, not only in his constant travelling, but also in his love affairs. Maybe he felt the need to make a show of strength and sexual potency in his architecture as well. But if his project for the Chicago Tribune Tower was inspired by such feelings, this would have completely ignored his own injunctions never to mix the private and the public, let alone expressing his secret urges in scribblings on the wall. He would, in his own opinion, have become a 'criminal' or a 'degenerate' himself.

As a public statement, an expression of political feelings, his project was above all a sign of respect for the United States. Loos had lived in America from 1893 to 1896. He had visited the famous Chicago World Fair of 1893, and after a period in which he earned a living by various menial jobs – such as a dishwasher, carpenter and so on – he found a job in an architect's office. Although he never revisited the country, he always held a positive image of the United States, and sometimes thought of himself as an American.[29] In 1903 he had tried, in his rather sarcastic manner, to introduce the American way of life to the Habsburg Empire with a short-lived journal, *Das Andere: Zeitschrift zur Einführung abendländischer Kultur in Österreich* ('Something different: journal for the introduction of Western civilisation into Austria'). The idea was not just political satire, but part of his attempt to quell a sense of decadence. At the time, a large segment of the Austrian intelligentsia still entertained the optimistic view that the Empire could be modernised and transformed into a new and more enlightened political system, a federation of republics perhaps, in which the multinational principle would be maintained. Loos was one of them.

Although he was in constant conflict with official Austrian cultural policy, Loos took the universal idea of the Empire for granted, and like his enemies at the Wiener Secession he thought of art, in his case modernist art, as something transcending national differences. Perhaps the Habsburg Empire might still be turned into a United States of Central Europe. At least, like so many others, Loos did not foresee the total collapse of the Empire in 1918 and its subsequent reorganisation along strictly nationalist lines.

Shortly after the First World War, Loos became involved in a project for the development of a Viennese new suburb, predominantly composed of social housing. It was a very serious attempt on his part to work on a public project, and to contribute to a spirit of republican reconstruction in Austria. Other modernist architects tried to impose their message of austere design and functionality upon a larger public as well, as Sofie De Caigny demonstrates in the next chapter. But all too soon Loos ran into difficulties with the organising committee, which preferred large housing complexes to the smaller one-family houses he proposed. In the postwar economic depression, other commissions in his own country were not readily available. In 1922, Loos decided to settle in France, where he was well-known in the modernist circle of L'esprit nouveau. His project for the Chicago Tribune Tower was submitted from his address on the Côte d'Azur, and for that reason it was classified as a 'French contribution'.

In his comments on his submission, Loos stressed that his proposal was completely in line with the architectural principles he had always maintained. As he said, he more or less expected others to reproach him 'for becoming untrue to my principles. I have, however, not abandoned them, and I am totally at one with my project'.[30] His Doric column was not an ornament, because it did not introduce private feelings into the public sphere. Its intended statement was entirely public, and therefore political in nature. Loos's villas functioned as masks or screens, behind which the owners could live their private lives without interference from, or intrusion on, the outside world. For that reason they were free of ornamentation. But his public buildings accentuated their public function with an appropriate symbolism.[31] The Goldman and Salatsch building of 1909–1911 demonstrated perfectly how Loos imagined the different architectural expression of the two spheres. The upper part, consisting of private apartments, was undecorated; the lower part, where the shop's interior opened directly onto the street, was decorated with marble and Doric columns.

Indeed, the Doric column summarised everything that Loos thought essential in a public building: it was bare and unornamented, it was classical and therefore spoke a universal language, and it was traditionally associated with strength and power. This must explain why he decided not only to add Doric columns to the building in Chicago, which he intended to be a landmark like St Peter's in Rome or the 'leaning tower' of Pisa, but to turn it into a Doric column itself, eliminating every distinction between object and ornament. But in doing so he revealed that his non-ornamental asceticism was a form of primitivism after all, an attempt to return to the 'pure forms' of the earliest type of classical construction, and, moreover, a classicism that was justified by a specific vision of political order.

The Doric Revival

In the Western tradition, primitivism is often seen as the opposite of classicism. But the quest for origins and for a lost simplicity does not necessarily lead to non-Western or non-classical sources of inspiration. Classicism has its own primitivism. And this is a primitivism which appeals immediately to ascetic ambitions, to visions of strength, purity and harmony. In his last, unfinished work, *The Preference for the Primitive*, E.H. Gombrich ignores the Greek revival of the late eighteenth century,[32] even though this was as much a return to a supposed original simplicity. A second Greek revival became a further source of inspiration in the early twentieth century.

To understand the range of meanings the Doric column had acquired by that time, we must make a short excursion into the history of neo-classicism. In his treatise on architecture, written in the first century B.C., Vitruvius described the Doric order, the first and oldest of the three classical orders, as strong and severe, and associated it with warlike, heroic and usually masculine gods and demi-gods.[33] It was the order most suitable for temples dedicated to Mars, Hercules or Minerva. The architectural treatises of the Renaissance and the Baroque followed Vitruvius closely in this respect, maintaining the gender associations which had been accorded to the orders, sometimes even exchanging Minerva for Jupiter, thus making the Doric an exclusively male order.

The three orders were later adapted to Christian requirements. Whereas the Ionic order was thought to be fit for churches dedicated to holy virgins, the Doric order was more appropriate in churches dedicated to the steadfastness of the holy martyrs. As far as non-religious buildings were concerned, the Doric order was preferable in buildings which suggested serious and important thoughts, such as military fortifications, gates and gatehouses, treasure houses, arsenals, prisons, tombs and funerary monuments. Vitruvius seems to have been of the opinion, however, that in all the orders, including the Doric, the shaft of the column had to rest on a base. The Doric order distinguished itself mainly by its more sturdy proportions and its undecorated capital, and was depicted and applied in this way from the Renaissance until the middle of the eighteenth century.

Around 1750, however, scholars suddenly realised that the columns in the original Greek Doric temples were even more squat in proportion than the Vitruvians had assumed, and that they rested flatly on the plinth, without the addition of a base. This discovery was mainly discussed in connection with the Greek temple complex in Paestum, ancient Posidonia, in southern Italy, which had gradually became one of the southern-most destinations of the Grand Tour. Of course the Doric temples in Paestum were no recent archaeological find. They had always been more or less accessible, but it was only after 1750 that travellers and architectural writers began to comment on them.

This was the beginning of the neo-classicist movement, which is usually labelled the Greek or Doric Revival.[34] In the later eighteenth century, Greek Doric columns suddenly came into fashion and were used for all kinds of monumental buildings. Although its prominence was an indication of a preference for greater austerity in all aspects of design, the Doric remained a style best suited for all grave and serious matters. Thus far the precepts of Vitruvius and his more recent followers still held good. Most of the buildings in the Doric style planned or erected in the later eighteenth century in England, France, Germany and Scandinavia, where the Doric was especially favoured, were still buildings of the kind recommended in the older treatises: custom houses, barracks, dockyard gates, prisons.

Nevertheless, it is clear that the meaning of the orders in the eighteenth century shifted from the standardised allegorical conception in the Vitruvian tradition to a more flexible and much more complex symbolic interpretation. The eighteenth-century fascination for the Doric reflected a wide range of intellectual concerns. It could be perceived as the most rational style, because it seemed to be the most simple and transparent form of architecture. But it also appealed to feelings of nostalgia, for with its elementary, straight lines it could be seen as a reference to an earlier, unspoiled and egalitarian society.

For those in power, it suggested the stability of the state and of the existing political order. For those in opposition, it suggested a radical break with the *ancien régime*. The asceticism implied in the return towards a severe and sober style was an obvious reaction against the frivolity of the rococo. This attitude went hand-in-hand with a rejection of court culture and everything associated with it, from social hypocrisy and artificiality to political absolutism.

Both interpretations of the Doric order seem to have been at work in Loos's design for the office of the *Chicago Tribune*. The project expressed, in no uncertain terms, his rejection of the ornamental style of art nouveau, which, much to his regret, was revived in the art deco of the 1920s. In this respect his attitude paralleled the rejection of the rococo in eighteenth-century neo-classicism. As a political statement, the design for the Tribune Tower symbolised both republicanism and social stability and was particularly appropriate for the United States, which developed its political symbolism at the time when neo-classicism was the most advanced modern movement in the arts.

In the American context, the Doric column came to represent republican virtues such as simplicity, honesty, strength, determination and will-power. For this reason, most of the monuments dedicated to the memory of George Washington are in the Doric style. It may well be that Loos was aware of this tradition of Doric virtues.[35] But his Doric column was also a symbol of order, of a newly found or newly hoped-for stability, certainty and progress after the moral confusions of the *fin de siècle* and the disasters of the First World War.

Of course, Loos was not the only one to associate the Doric style with visions of a new age of reason, order, clarity and strength. There is a profound irony in the fact that some of the artists of the Wiener Secession, his declared enemies in the struggle against ornamentation, had begun their career with similar ideas. Josef Maria Olbrich visited the Doric ruins at Paestum in 1894, and wrote enthusiastic letters about them to Josef Hoffmann. When Olbrich's masterpiece, the exhibition hall and headquarters for the Wiener Secession, was opened to the public in 1898, it was often compared to a Doric temple, because of its tapering shape and bare white walls, crowned only by a golden laurel wreath.[36]

Competition and emulation, the wish to outdo his predecessors by making an even stronger statement, may also have played a part in Loos's design. But in both cases the use of the Doric order heralded a new world of clear, robust outlines; of energy, simplicity and strong social cohesion. These designs announced a future in which the individual would be happy to exchange the pursuit of private pleasure for a life in service of a glorious community.

Was this appeal to asceticism anything more than a kind of magic, a conjuring trick to facilitate the transition to a modern, urban, bureaucratic and collectivist society? The neo-Greek movement in the late eighteenth century, which partly coincided with the French Revolution, harboured a secret admiration for ancient Sparta and the Spartan way of life. The image of Sparta implied a total dedication to the fatherland, and the ideal of a thoroughly healthy, unintellectual society, dedicated to martial exercise, in which life was lived in close male companionship under open skies.[37] The Doric style was supposed to have originated in Sparta, whose inhabitants descended from the war-like and ascetic Doric tribes. The Dorians dedicated themselves to the cult of Apollo, the sun god. His world was a world of clear, hard, sharp and rational outlines.

German literature of the early twentieth century – but not only German literature – frequently invokes an atmosphere and a style of life associated with Sparta and the Doric style. Examples run from R.M. Rilke's earnest admonition to 'change one's life', in his poem on the archaic torso of Apollo written in 1908, to the strange celebration of National Socialism published by Gottfried

Benn in 1934, in the guise of a description of life in ancient Sparta.[38] Le Corbusier's vision of air and light, health and exercise, among elementary architectural forms was not completely dissimilar when he, after a long period of deep contempt for academic classicism, rediscovered the *moralité Dorique* on a trip to Greece.[39]

A Classicist Utopia

There is no way of knowing how Loos would have reacted to the temptation of totalitarianism. He was very ill during the last years of his life, and died in 1933 in an asylum, completely deaf and no longer in control of his mind.

His Doric design for the Chicago Tribune Tower remained a unique moment in his career. As I have tried to show, it was a project with several layers of meaning. In the first place, it was a symbol of the power of modern democratic society. Perhaps it was also a symbol of the lost potential of the now-defunct Habsburg Empire. But in its wilful anti-ornamentalism, Loos's Doric column was not only an expression of the strength and power of modern social and political organisation, it was also an invocation of a new idea of empire, a magical gesture to install a new radiant Apollo-like order after the catastrophe of the war.[40]

Why should such a forward-looking building use the architectural language of classicism? Because, Loos would answer, classicism was one of the few really universal elements in Western civilisation. Two years after submitting the Chicago project, he stressed this idea in a short text which acted as a footnote to 'Ornament and Crime'. 'Classical education', he said, 'created, despite the differences of languages and frontiers, a common Western culture; to abandon it would be to destroy this last common ground'. And somewhat further on: 'Classical ornament brings order into the shaping of our objects of everyday use, orders us and our forms, and creates, despite ethnographic and linguistic differences, a common fund of forms and aesthetic concepts. And it brings order into our lives'.[41]

Loos was right when he asserted that he had always been true to his principles: architecture should express universal values; excessive ornamentation can only express individual sentiments; therefore a strict asceticism of form is necessary to find the way back to a style which represents the general values of the modern age. But as far as classical culture still embodies universal aspirations, stylistic asceticism may imply a return to classical architecture, if only in its purest, Doric form. Loos was a radical, but in no way a revolutionary.[42] As with so many prominent figures of the modernist movement, there was a strong conservative element in his thought. His ascetic modernism was rooted in classical aesthetic ideals.

However much Loos wanted to do away with the formalities and hypocrisy of the nineteenth century, and however much he thought of his architecture as an expression of a modern, universally accessible culture, in the end the stress was always placed on order. For him, asceticism in architecture meant a return to the order and strength of the Greek city-state. The modern individual, at least as they were represented by the architect, should become like a classical column themselves, strong, self-restrained, severe, solid, and looking down with a mild and universal sympathy on everything going on around them. Loos explained this elitist point of view – including a mixture of power, order, magic and distinction – eloquently in 'Ornament and Crime':

> I preach the aristocrat, that is to say, that person who stands at the highest point of humanity and who nevertheless has the profoundest understanding of the aspirations and needs of those from below. The African, who according to a certain rhythm weaves ornaments in his textiles, which only become visible when they are taken off; the Persian, who works his tapestry with his fingers; the Slovak country woman, who embroiders her lace; the old lady, who makes wonderful needle-work of glass beads and silk; such people he understands well enough. The aristo-crat lets them do what they are doing; he knows that to them, the hours they spend on their work are sacred. A revolutionary would go and tell them: 'All of this is nonsense', just as he would tear an old woman from the wayside cross, and tell her: 'There is no God.' But an aristocrat, even if he is an atheist, raises his hat, when he passes a church.[43]

In the same manner, we must now raise our hats to Adolf Loos.

Notes

1. A. Briggs, 'The 1890s. Past, Present and Future in Headlines', in A. Briggs (ed.), *Fins de Siècle: How Centuries End, 1400–2000* (New Haven, 1996), 170–71.
2. V.L. Wimbush and R. Valantasis (eds), *Asceticism* (New York, 1995) discusses ascetic practices in a great variety of cultures.
3. For the social and ideological context of art nouveau, see, e.g., the wide-ranging collection of essays edited by K. Buchholz and R. Latocha, *Die Lebensreform: Entwürfe zur Neugestaltung von Leben und Kunst*, 2 vols. (Darmstadt, 2001).
4. C. Schorske, *Fin de Siècle Vienna: Politics and Culture* (New York, 1981) has rightly become famous for its interpretation of Viennese culture around 1900 as a rebellion against the liberal optimism of the older generation, and as an attempt to blur the boundaries between the public and the private. This may have been true for a small but very conspicuous group of artists and intellectuals, but on the whole much of the older liberal rationalism and optimism remained in place. See

A. Janik and S. Toulmin, *Wittgenstein's Vienna* (New York, 1973) and many more recent studies.

5. The complex publishing history of the essay is outlined in B. Rukschcio, 'Ornament und Mythos', in A. Pfabigan (ed.), *Ornament und Askese im Zeitgeist des Wien der Jahrhundertwende* (Vienna, 1985), 57–68. In A. Loos, *Trotzdem* (Innsbruck, 1931), 78–89, the essay is dated 1908. This date is generally retained, even as a date of publication. See also A. Loos, *Sämtliche Schriften, I*, ed. F. Glück (Vienna, 1962), 276–88. However, it seems not to have been written before 1909, and was first read to an audience in Vienna in January 1910.

6. Until that time, Loos was probably better known as a journalist, who specialised in fashion and design. The standard biography is B. Rukschcio and R. Schachel, *Adolf Loos: Leben und Werk* (Salzburg, 1982). Among the many short introductions to his work, K. Lustenberger, *Adolf Loos* (Zurich, 1994) is the most comprehensive. J. Stewart, *Fashioning Vienna: Adolf Loos's Cultural Criticism* (London, 2000), studies Loos's writings (without reference to his architecture) from a Marxist point of view.

7. F.S. Connelly, *The Sleep of Reason: Primitivism in Modern European Art and Aesthetics* (University Park, 1995), 23, 27; D. Schafter, *The Order of Ornament, the Structure of Style: Theoretical Foundations of Modern Art and Architecture* (Cambridge, 2003), 23; D. Brett, *Rethinking Decoration: Pleasure and Ideology in the Visual Arts* (Cambridge, 2005), 194–96.

8. D. Schafter, *The Order of Ornament*, 118.

9. A. Loos, 'Ornament und Verbrechen', in A. Loos, *Sämtliche Schriften, I*, 277. Several English versions of this essay exist, none of them completely satisfactory (see also note 43). In a version in A. Loos, *Ornament and Crime: Selected Essays*, ed. A. Opel, trans. M. Mitchell (Riverside, 1998), this paragraph is left out altogether, without explanation.

10. A. Loos, 'Ornament und Verbrechen', *Sämtliche Schriften, I*, 288.

11. For the idea of the inside and outside as a box and a decorated screen, see W. Oechslin, *Otto Wagner, Adolf Loos and the Road to Modern Architecture*, trans. L. Widder (Cambridge, 2002). See also D. Schafter, *The Order of Ornament*, 186–87. The theatrical aspect of Loos's interiors, with the man in the house overseeing the scene, is stressed in B. Colomina, *Privacy and Publicity: Modern Architecture as Mass Media* (Cambridge MA, 1994), 234–81.

12. A. Loos, 'Ornament und Verbrechen', *Sämtliche Schriften, I*, 277.

13. A. Pfabigan (ed.), *Ornament und Askese im Zeitgeist des Wien der Jahrhundertwende*, Vienna, 1985.

14. C. Schorske, 'Abschied von der Öffentlichkeit. Kulturkritik und Modernismus in der Wiener Architectur', in A. Pfabigan, *Ornament und Askese im Zeitgeist des Wien der Jahrhundertwende* (Vienna, 1985), 47–56.

15. B. Rukschcio, 'Ornament und Mythos', 57–68.

16. A. Loos, 'Ornament und Verbrechen', *Sämtliche Schriften, I*, 280. The true ascetic in Loos's circle was the philosopher Ludwig Wittgenstein, who followed his advice to the letter, and designed a house for his sister without any ornament.

17. J. Rykwert, 'Adolf Loos: the New Vision', in J. Rykwert, *The Necessity of Artifice* (London, 1982), 66–73, was one of the first to see sensuality (the touch of the

material surface) as the dominant motif in Loos's architecture. See also D. Schafter, *The Order of Ornament*, 185–89; L. Topp, *Architecture and Truth in Fin de Siècle Vienna* (Cambridge, 2004); A. Alofsin, *When Buildings Speak: Architecture as Language in the Habsburg Empire and its Aftermath, 1867–1933* (Chicago, 2006), 120. In the opinion of Oechslin, *Otto Wagner*, 112–18, Loos remains an isolated figure. For the shifting appreciation of Loos's work, see also Colomina, *Privacy and Publicity*, 279.

18. F.R. Ankersmit, *Sublime Historical Experience* (Stanford, 2005), 290. For a similar conclusion, see J. Trilling, *The Language of Ornament* (London, 2001), 190–93.

19. A. Loos, 'Ornament und Verbrechen', *Sämtliche Schriften*, I, 288.

20. On the racist aspects of Loos's polemic, see J. Stewart, *Fashioning Vienna*, 69–70.

21. Other congenial spirits were the expressionist poet Georg Trakl and the composer Arnold Schönberg, then in his expressionist phase.

22. L. Topp, *Architecture and Truth*, 132–33.

23. Ibid., 154.

24. K. Solomonson, *The Chicago Tribune Tower Competition: Skyscraper Design and Cultural Change in the 1920s* (Cambridge, 2001).

25. Ibid., 118–23.

26. Ibid., 118.

27. F.R. Ankersmit, *Sublime Historical Experience*, 306.

28. B. Rukschcio and R. Schachel, *Adolf Loos*, 563–64.

29. J. Stewart, *Fashioning Vienna*, 44–51. In 1908, Loos designed an 'American Bar' in the Kärtner Durchgang in Vienna, which has recently been restored.

30. B. Rukschcio and R. Schachel, *Adolf Loos*, 562.

31. See also D. Schafter, *The Order of Ornament*, 187.

32. E.H. Gombrich, *The Preference for the Primitive: Episodes in the History of Western Taste and Art* (London, 2002).

33. For the symbolism of the classical orders, see E. Forssman, *Dorisch, Jonisch, Korinthisch: Studien über den Gebrauch der Säulenordnungen in der Architektur des 16.–18. Jahrhunderts* (Stockholm, 1961); J. Onians, *Bearers of Meaning: The Classical Orders in Antiquity, the Middle Ages, and the Renaissance* (Princeton, 1988); J. Rykwert, *The Dancing Column: On Order in Architecture* (Cambridge MA, 1996).

34. N. Pevsner, 'The Doric Revival' [1948], in N. Pevsner, *Studies in Art, Architecture and Design, Vol. 1* (London, 1968), 197–212; R. Rosenblum, *Transformations in Late-eighteenth-century Art* (Princeton, 1967), 140–45; J. Raspi Serra (ed.), *Paestum and the Doric Revival 1750–1830* (New York, 1986).

35. D. Wiebenson, 'From Palladianism to Greek Revival Architecture in America', in J. Raspi Serra (ed.), *Paestum and the Doric Revival 1750–1830* (New York, 1986), 181.

36. L. Topp, *Architecture and Truth*, 36, 53–54.

37. E. Rawson, *The Spartan Tradition in European Thought* (Oxford, 1969).

38. G. Benn, 'Dorische Welt. Eine Untersuchung über die Beziehung von Kunst und Macht' [1934], in G. Benn, *Essays, Reden, Vorträge* (Wiesbaden, 1959), 262–94.

39. W. Oechslin, *Otto Wagner*, 132. A. Tzonis and L. Lefaivre's *Classical Architecture: The Poetics of Order* (Cambridge MA, 1986) once more takes up the idea of

modern architecture as a continuation of the Greek Doric temple, and therefore stands in a long line of myth-making.

40. T.J. Heinisch, *Destruktionen zur Säule: Nach einem Projekt von Adolf Loos* (Berlin, 1981), 31, makes Loos's Chicago Tribune Tower design into a symbol of the unfulfilled potential of twentieth-century social democracy. The project certainly tries to unite the conflicting aristocratic and democratic tendencies in Loos's work. Cf. J. Stewart, *Fashioning Vienna*, 82–83, 97.

41. A. Loos, 'Ornament und Erziehung' [1924], *Sämtliche Schriften*, I, 391–98, quotation p.397. A similar and earlier declaration of adherence to classicism is Loos's 'Architektur' [1909], *Sämtliche Schriften*, I, 302–18.

42. After much hard work, J. Stewart, *Fashioning Vienna*, 168–69, arrives at the conclusion that Loos was 'surprisingly bourgeois'.

43. A. Loos, 'Ornament und Verbrechen', *Sämtliche Schriften*, I, 286. August Sarnitz, *Adolf Loos 1870–1933: Architect, Cultural Critic, Dandy* (Cologne, 2003), contains yet another English version of 'Ornament and Crime'. Here, 'atheist' (in the last sentence of the quotation) is changed to 'aesthete', which totally obscures the point Loos is making.

References

Alofsin, A. 2006. *When Buildings Speak: Architecture as Language in the Habsburg Empire and its Aftermath, 1867–1933*, Chicago.

Ankersmit, F.R. 2005. *Sublime Historical Experience*, Stanford.

Benn, G. 1959. 'Dorische Welt: Eine Untersuchung über die Beziehung von Kunst und Macht' [1934], in G. Benn, *Essays, Reden, Vorträge*, Wiesbaden, pp.262–94.

Brett, D. 2005. *Rethinking Decoration: Pleasure and Ideology in the Visual Arts*, Cambridge.

Briggs, A. 1996. 'The 1890s: Past, Present and Future in Headlines', in A. Briggs (ed.), *Fins de Siècle: How Centuries End, 1400–2000*, New Haven, pp.157–95.

Buchholz, K., and R. Latocha. 2001. *Die Lebensreform: Entwürfe zur Neugestaltung von Leben und Kunst*, 2 vols, Darmstadt.

Colomina, B. 1994. *Privacy and Publicity: Modern Architecture as Mass Media*, Cambridge MA.

Connelly, F.S. 1995. *The Sleep of Reason: Primitivism in Modern European Art and Aesthetics*, University Park.

Forssman, E. 1961. *Dorisch, Jonisch, Korinthisch: Studien über den Gebrauch der Säulenordnungen in der Architektur des 16.-18. Jahrhunderts*, Stockholm.

Gombrich, E.H. 2002. *The Preference for the Primitive: Episodes in the History of Western Taste and Art*, London.

Heinisch, T.J. 1981. *Destruktionen zur Säule: Nach einem Projekt von Adolf Loos*, Berlin.

Janik, A., and S. Toulmin. 1973. *Wittgenstein's Vienna*, New York.

Loos, A. 1931. *Trotzdem*, Innsbruck.

——— 1962. *Sämtliche Schriften*, I, ed. F. Glück, Vienna.

———— 1998. *Ornament and Crime: Selected Essays*, ed. A. Opel, trans. M. Mitchell, Riverside.

Lustenberger, K. 1994. *Adolf Loos*, Zurich.

Oechslin, W. 2002[1994]. *Otto Wagner, Adolf Loos and the Road to Modern Architecture*, trans. L. Widder, Cambridge.

Onians, J. 1988. *Bearers of Meaning: The Classical Orders in Antiquity, the Middle Ages, and the Renaissance*, Princeton.

Pevsner, N. 1968. 'The Doric Revival' [1948], in N. Pevsner, *Studies in Art, Architecture and Design, Vol. 1*, London, pp.197–212.

Pfabigan, A. (ed.) 1985. *Ornament und Askese im Zeitgeist des Wien der Jahrhundertwende*, Vienna.

Raspi Serra, J. (ed.) 1986. *Paestum and the Doric Revival 1750–1830*, New York.

Rawson, E. 1969. *The Spartan Tradition in European Thought*, Oxford.

Rosenblum, R. 1967. *Transformations in Late-eighteenth-century Art*, Princeton.

Rukschcio, B. 1985. 'Ornament und Mythos', in A. Pfabigan (ed.), *Ornament und Askese im Zeitgeist des Wien der Jahrhundertwende*, Vienna, pp.57–68.

Rukschcio, B., and R. Schachel. 1982. *Adolf Loos: Leben und Werk*, Salzburg.

Rykwert, J. 1982. 'Adolf Loos: the New Vision', in J. Rykwert, *The Necessity of Artifice*, London, pp.66–73

———— 1996. *The Dancing Column: On Order in Architecture*, Cambridge MA.

Sarnitz, A. 2003. *Adolf Loos 1870–1933: Architect, Cultural Critic, Dandy*, Cologne.

Schafter, D. 2003. *The Order of Ornament, the Structure of Style: Theoretical Foundations of Modern Art and Architecture*, Cambridge.

Schorske, C. 1981. *Fin de Siècle Vienna: Politics and Culture*, New York.

———— 1985. 'Abschied von der Öffentlichkeit. Kulturkritik und Modernismus in der Wiener Architectur', in A. Pfabigan (ed.), *Ornament und Askese im Zeitgeist des Wien der Jahrhundertwende*, Vienna, pp.47–56.

Solomonson, K. 2001. *The Chicago Tribune Tower Competition: Skyscraper Design and Cultural Change in the 1920s*, Cambridge.

Stewart, J. 2000. *Fashioning Vienna: Adolf Loos's Cultural Criticism*, London.

Topp, L. 2004. *Architecture and Truth in Fin de Siècle Vienna*, Cambridge.

Trilling, J. 2001. *The Language of Ornament*, London.

Tzonis, A., and L. Lefaivre. 1986. *Classical Architecture: The Poetics of Order*, Cambridge MA.

Wiebenson, D. 1986. 'From Palladianism to Greek Revival Architecture in America', in J. Raspi Serra (ed.), *Paestum and the Doric Revival 1750–1830*, New York, pp.176–81.

Wimbush, V.L., and R. Valantasis (eds). 1995. *Asceticism*, New York.

7

Disguised Asceticism: The Promotion of Austerity in Interior Design during the Interwar Period in Flanders, Belgium

Sofie De Caigny

In drawings produced in an issue of 1929, *De Boerin*, the magazine of the Belgian Association of Farming Women (Belgische Boerinnenbond) tried to direct its readers towards a more austere and less ornamented bedroom. In the text that accompanied the drawings, the author stated that it was not important whether one preferred an iron or a wooden bed, as long as there was 'no excess garnishing, no lie, no swaggering'. Austerity was closely linked to authenticity and readers were warned not to imitate expensive types of wood, but to keep with the natural colours of cheaper timbers. The ideal was 'not a showpiece bed, but a solid, strong, simple bed wherein the children of your children will be sleeping as comfortably as you!'[1]

The Belgian Association of Farming Women was not the only organisation to promote austere interiors after the First World War. As in other European countries, domestic science schools, home economics manuals,[2] commercial women's magazines, various exhibitions on popular housing, commercial furniture companies and the female branches of social organisations, as intermediary level between the individual and the state and with divergent socio-political ideologies, all engaged in the crusade for interior decoration according to ascetic values. In most countries, central organisations such as the Women's Housing Sub-committee in Great Britain,[3] the Salon des Arts Ménagers in France,[4] or the Dutch Association of Housewives (Nederlandse Vereniging van Huisvrouwen)[5] played a key role in distributing new ideas on interior design after the First World War.

In some countries, like Belgium, strong divisions along socio-political lines and cultural differences between regions prevented national institutes like the Higher Institute for Agricultural Domestic Sciences (Hoger Instituut voor Landbouwhuishoudkunde) and the National Centre for the Study of Domestic Sciences (Nationaal Studiecentrum voor de Huishoudkunde) from dominating the debate on new types of interior design. They had to co-operate with intermediary social organisations, which were the most important disseminators of domestic advice during the interwar period.

In this search for the meaning of austerity in interior design and its relationship to the concept of 'modern asceticism', I will examine the discourses developed by the main social organisations that addressed the rural and working classes in Flanders during the interwar period.[6] Their female branches in particular – the Belgian Association of Farming Women, a Catholic organisation with a large following in the countryside,[7] plus the Catholic Working-class Women (Katholieke Arbeidersvrouwen, KAV)[8] and the Socialist Visionary Women (Socialistische Vooruitziende Vrouwen, SVV),[9] both operating in urban districts – produced well thought out, detailed discourses on a more austere and less ornate form of home furnishing.

Austerity in Various Discourses on Interior Design in Interwar Flanders

The Belgian Association of Farming Women aimed to reduce the difference in comfort between rural and urban living conditions without losing the specific characteristics of rural homes. Its ideas on housing and interior design were strongly interwoven with other elements, such as comfort, health, education, marriage and Catholicism.[10] In this way, the Belgian Association of Farming Women closely related home culture with rural identity.

The first, most obvious reason why the Association wanted to persuade its members about the advantages of an austere interior was that this would improve hygiene, and consequently the occupants' physical health. In order to make it easier to clean the house regularly, the housewife had to get rid of all the superfluous decorative elements and choose furniture that was not overloaded with scrolls that would rapidly be transformed into dust traps. Austerity was equated with hygiene.[11] For example, tables had to be ascetic and white, symbolising purity, sobriety and hygiene. Simplicity not only had hygienic benefits, but was juxtaposed with pomp and circumstance as an aesthetic category with strong moral implications, the opposite of waste and falsity.[12] In order to stimulate honest beauty in the home, the Association stressed that objects and furniture were also there to catch the eye. Promoting simplicity was closely related to discussions about functionality and comfort: kitchens and living rooms ought not to be filled with cupboards 'full of odds and ends … Smooth panels, simple lines are also preferable in these rooms'.[13]

Figure 7.1 Washing table in *De Boerin*, 1929. © KADOC, Leuven, Belgium.

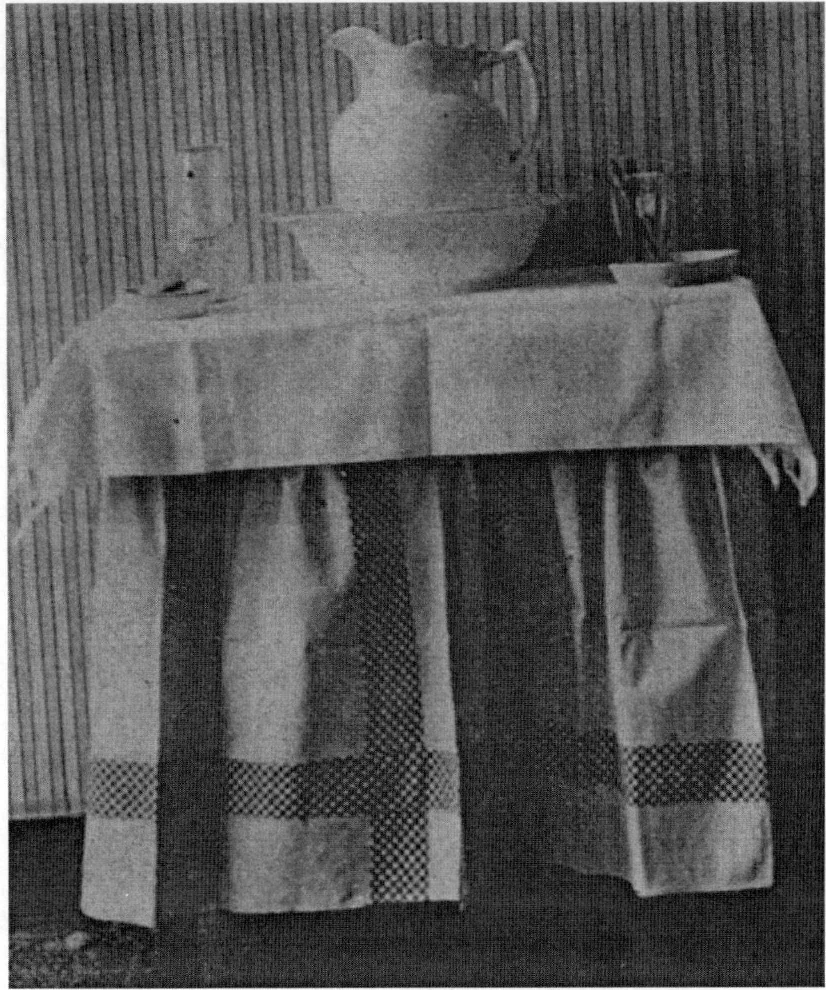

Figure 7.2 Washing table in *De Boerin*, 1929. © KADOC, Leuven, Belgium.

The Belgian Association of Farming Women communicated its ideas on home culture through its monthly magazine for members. In the articles about austerity, the Association juxtaposed 'bad' examples with 'good'. The texts accompanying the illustrations made it clear that it was not just about taste, but that living conditions influenced the occupants' religious, moral and political opinions. Apart from its magazine, the Association also helped to organise model farms to show innovations in interior design, domestic comfort and agricultural equipment.[14]

Figure 7.3 Washing table in *De Boerin*, 1929. © KADOC, Leuven, Belgium.

During the interwar period, model farms were constructed at the International Exhibitions in Liège (1930) and Brussels (1935) and at the International Water Exhibition in Liège (1939).[15] Visitors were guided through the rooms of ideal farmhouses, filled with the newest and most efficient furniture. The organising committees seemed to have been aware that these were still far beyond the reach of most of its target group, but hoped that these farmhouses would stimulate the visitors to install similarly austere furniture in their own homes.

Housing was also a permanent item on the agenda of the Catholic Working-Class Women (KAV) during the interwar period. This stemmed from a dual concern: on the one hand, the need to improve hygiene, functionality and comfort (including water distribution and electricity) of working-class housing; and on the other, for the full-time housewife to raise the cognitive standards of furnishing a house. In discussing interior design, the KAV stressed the need for plain, simple interiors, as was well illustrated in the design of bedrooms: 'No musty curtains, no heavy wallpapers, these are old fashioned sources of infection … The housewife cleans the bedroom every day, which is an easy job when the room is not filled with unnecessary stuff. So, no extra compacts, flacons, statues in the bedroom!'[16]

The writing mirrored that of the Belgian Association of Farming Women by closely interweaving the advantages of hygiene with those of functionality – austerity helped the housewife in her duty to keep the home clean – and aesthetics. Only simple and practical furniture would have a permanent value: 'One has to think of decoration in terms of simplicity, beauty and functionality'.[17]

The KAV promoted its ideas on interior design through three different media. Firstly, its members' magazine – its most important means of communication. Secondly, local branches of the association held a number of small exhibitions to inspire visitors to imitate the design and placing of furniture in their own homes. Thirdly, local delegates organised courses and classes on housekeeping and interior design.[18] The KAV's continuous efforts to improve and reorient the daily living habits of its members resulted in a travelling exhibition, 'We're Building a New Home', visited by over 38,000 people in 1939.[19]

The Socialist Visionary Women (SVV) and some magazines of the Socialist Centre for the Professional Education (Socialistische Centrale voor Arbeidsopvoeding) also gave austerity a central role in home decoration.[20] Their magazines similarly showed 'good' and 'bad' examples of furniture, accompanied by explicit educational texts. Like their Catholic counterparts, these stressed the idea that socialist houses ought to be freed of superfluous decoration in order to become more hygienic and functional.

The educational programme of the SVV, in particular, paid considerable attention to simplifying home interiors and rationalising household practices in order to relieve women from domestic work and create more possibilities for them to work outside the home. In socialist discourse, most arguments related class identity closely with sobriety. Socialist women had to be 'pioneers' in adopting the new austere forms of interior design since they were supposed to be important advocates of 'a new culture that was young and had a future'.[21] This statement encapsulates the conviction that nineteenth-century bourgeois culture was in decline, a belief the socialists shared with other modernist progressive ideologies.

Bourgeois concepts of beauty were attacked on the basis that the highest aesthetic category was simplicity created for functionality. 'Decoration just for decoration is always based on an incorrect logic and consequently is of an incorrect taste, so its conception is barbaric'.[22] In contrast to decent working-class homes, bourgeois homes were not adapted to their occupants' real needs.

Their only function was to show off, which socialist experts in interior design strongly rejected on functional, aesthetic and ethical grounds.[23] The moral dimension followed from the notion of authenticity. People had to learn that imitating historical styles was old fashioned, could not be beautiful, and was the opposite of truth.

These examples of the various intermediary organisations' domestic advice show that most of them developed very similar arguments on sobriety: all stressed the material and moral advantages of an austere interior. The mate-

Figure 7.4 Interior design in the socialist magazine *Opgang*, 1931, 40–41. © AMSAB-Instituut voor Sociale Geschiedenis, Gent, Belgium.

rial advantages of plain interiors were expressed in terms of hygiene, health, comfort, functionality, economics, solidity, beauty and thrift. The moral values they represented were linked to authenticity, soundness, modesty and dignity. In parallel with the moral implications, an austere interior would have a liberating effect on its inhabitants. All of these intermediary organisations were convinced that austerity and asceticism in their members' houses would raise them to a higher moral and physical level. It was important that they internalised ascetic interior design in order to become better human beings.

Figure 7.5 Interior design in the socialist magazine *Opgang*, 1931, 40–41. © AMSAB-Instituut voor Sociale Geschiedenis, Antwerp, Belgium.

This tendency to a sober interior and its formative effects was inspired by two cultural traditions that gained momentum in interwar Europe: home economics and modernist architecture. Austerity as a key value in housing was one of the most important objectives of domestic advisory literature that was published in the United States from the middle of the nineteenth century and became widely available, including in translation, in Europe in the 1920s.[24] The publications of some European experts on home decoration and household practices, like Paulette Bernège and Erna Meyer, also reached a wide international readership.[25] Whereas the US literature mainly addressed middle-class women, its European counterparts also focused on farming and working-class homes. However, this focus towards new target groups did not produce fundamental shifts in the emphasis on austerity as objective for popular interiors. Although the language that was used to argue for austerity evolved from simple concerns about hygiene and health into well-developed scientific arguments, the content of the message remained basically the same.

These experts in domestic science received unexpected support from modernist architects, including Adolf Loos (see the previous chapter), who started to address popular housing as an important field of work after the First World War. During the interwar period, concepts like rationality, functionality, economics and social reform became equally as important in architecture as aesthetics, monumentality and representation.[26] Central to the discourse and practices of modernist architects was the rejection of ornamentation and the encouragement of abstinence in daily life and home culture.

These architects developed three complementary arguments to support their conviction that asceticism was crucial when taking the current socio-economic and cultural circumstances into account. Firstly, architecture had to be defined in terms of transparency, hygiene, openness, purity and functionality.[27] This meant that form had to follow function, that the aesthetic of a building had to reflect its constructive logic, and the use of materials and constructive elements had to be 'true'. It is in this context that Ernst May stated that asceticism was needed to achieve the essence of things.[28] This line of argument aimed at liberating human beings from their (excessive) material concerns.

Secondly, socio-economic and political arguments stressed that architecture should reflect social justice and equality.[29] Every citizen, it was said, has the right to decent housing that meets contemporary needs. For this to be possible, the cost of proper housing had to be reduced, and ornamentation dispensed with – the social emancipation of the masses played a central role in this argument.

A third line of argument saw the lack of ornament as the logical response to the uprooted and fragmented modern way of life.[30] If architecture and housing wanted to be authentic, they had to show up the conflicting structures of modern society. According to this reasoning, ornamentation was rejected as an empty instrument of display, which was condemned as a nineteenth-century bourgeois relic that had no place in modern society.

The modernists' arguments for an ascetic architecture all reflected an ethical and an aesthetic concern, and they were applied in both ideology and material culture.[31] By embracing the unstable, discontinuous, progressive and revolutionary characteristics of modernity, the modernists defended a radical social renewal.[32] As a logical consequence, modernist interior design broke with prewar traditions, used new materials like glass and steel, and experimented with new forms. Sobriety was only a first step that radical modernists like Hannes Meyer recommended to come to terms with an ever-changing, complex and anonymous society. They believed that authentic modern interior design also had to redefine domesticity in terms of 'transience and instability rather than permanence and rootedness'.[33]

Domestic advisers, mostly women, and modern architects, mostly men, were aware that their objectives were very similar.[34] In many countries their collaboration resulted in revolutionary kitchens, built-in furniture and popular housing design. During the interwar period, a mutually influential dynamic developed between modernist architects and experts in domestic science and much of the popular media started to spread the ideal of austerity in housing. As a result, austerity became a dominant value in normative discussions about interior design.

Popular Resistance against Modern Asceticism in the Home

Unfortunately, it is difficult to know what visitors' actual opinions were about the Belgian Association of Farming Women's model farms, about the KAV's exhibition on interior design or about the furniture that was published in their members' magazines. Based on the historical evidence that she found on the situation in the United States, Sarah Leavitt concludes that a great part of the public disliked the austere furniture on show because they did not find it very 'homely'.[35]

Reading the repeated domestic advice of the governing bodies of Flemish intermediary social organisations gave me the impression that their efforts were probably not very successful. In their attempt to implement the ascetic ideal, domestic scientists, the media and modernist architects discovered that practices in interior design were resistant to change. The explanation for this probably lay in the political and social-economic developments in most Western European countries during the 1920s and 1930s. Male universal suffrage was introduced in most countries after the First World War and fuelled the hope of the masses that they might acquire the respectability and standard of living of bourgeois families. More and more working-class and rural families could indeed participate in consumer culture for the first time in history when the Roaring Twenties reached Europe from America in the second half of the decade. Better education, fashion and modern entertainment (especially cinema) came within the reach of the masses. Exemplifying Norbert Elias's explanation of the progress of civilisation, these social groups liked to show their increasing income and progress up the social ladder by buying objects to decorate their homes. In doing so, they imitated nineteenth-century bourgeois houses. Most people thought of austere interiors as furniture for poor people.

To overcome the resistance to more sober interiors, and to inform people about the inherent moral and material advantages of voluntary austerity, Flemish social organisations designed a specific strategy to promote the ascetic ideal. First of all, the designs they created were fairly traditional compared to the radical ascetic interiors of some modernist architects.[36] The two, very different forms of material outcome that emerged illustrate the divergent attitudes towards modernity taken by intermediary social actors and modernist architects. In contrast to the radical position of modernist architects, social organisations and the media advocated an 'integrative modernity': they were not opposed to modernity, but tried to control the way the public would handle it.[37] From this perspective, asceticism as a formative value could be used for the physical and mental well-being of society. It was thus possible to offer a model of austerity in dwelling culture that was adjusted to the organisation's ideology. Asceticism could be used to control modernity in its members' daily lives and was promoted as an instrument to stimulate the positive aspects of 'being modern'.

Catholic organisations, in particular, combined traditional interpretations of domesticity and family life with modern ideas of hygiene and sobriety. They selected 'good' aspects of modernity, such as health care, and passed them to their members. The situation was somewhat different for the socialist organisations that supported progress and modernization as a means of social emancipation for the working class. Consequently, their examples of what they saw as good, contemporary design reflected this more progressive perspective.

A second strategy that the intermediary social organisations adopted to overcome the difficulties of implementation closely linked the ascetic ideal with class identity and disguised it by an idiosyncratic definition of *gezelligheid*, the Dutch word for 'cosiness' or *Gemütlichkeit*. In the ideology of the KAV, class identity had to be visible in housekeeping and the appropriate decoration of the home.[38] In concrete terms, this meant that a Christian working-class woman had to be the central figure of the household, had to have fixed washing and cleaning days, and had to get up early to prepare coffee for her husband and those of her children who left the house for the factory every morning. In other words, she organised the family rituals of daily life according to her class identity. By doing so, she would bind the family members to the home. Material culture could help her in this process of homemaking.

The KAV explained carefully how a Christian working-class fireplace had to be decorated, which cushions were appropriate on the chairs in the 'living-kitchen', and where fresh flowers should be placed.[39] The Catholic working-class movement explicitly stated that the working-class home should not imitate a bourgeois or middle-class home.[40] The parlour, a symbol of nineteenth-century bourgeois culture, had no function in a working-class house since it was inefficient, unhealthy and immoral for families to live in small kitchens while the parlour was only used to receive occasional visitors.

Austerity played a key role in the development of a kind of Flemish popular interior design that distinguished itself from the 'exaggerated and unreasonable bourgeois boasting in possessions, not in correspondence with the actual democratic spirit'.[41] Thus, in defining the close relationship between class identity and interior design, the Catholic working-class movement's governing body attacked remnants of the bourgeois, stuffy interior and pleaded for austerity.

This assault on the bourgeois home was also one of the main focal points of the modernists' struggle for an austere dwelling culture. The most radical modernists of the Weimar period attacked the bourgeois idea of domesticity and did away with its most important character, namely the idea of a cosy interior.[42] Only a classless society could represent authentic cosiness, and there would be no need to clothe it.[43] This rejection of what had traditionally been understood as cosiness had strong implications. After all, cutting all ties to representative material objects led to the ideal of the 'naked' or ascetic house, in which the experience of a new and better life would emerge.

Although some parallels existed between the modernists and the Catholic working-class movement's plea to do away with bourgeois interior design, the Catholic working-class movement did not want to do away with the concept of cosiness. On the contrary, according to its female branch, the KAV, an austere interior would lead to cosiness! Cosiness was indeed the central concept in the KAV's marketing strategy of austerity. This seemingly paradoxical statement can be understood by examining the two meanings of cosiness in KAV discourse. On the one hand, cosiness had a conceptual meaning of 'togetherness', including 'a caring housewife', 'Catholicism and feelings of safety'. On the other, cosiness needed a material dimension to create an appropriate framework for this conceptual meaning. Austere and thus authentic cosy interiors would generate physical well-being because bodies could freely move in them without being hindered by excessive decoration and furniture.[44] The combination of the conceptual and material dimension came down to values like order, purity, functionality and simplicity. It seems as if the KAV governing body was disguising austerity by introducing this new notion of cosiness in an attempt to convince its members of its advantages.

Figure 7.6 Material culture of 'cosiness' in the women's magazine *Vrouwenbeweging*, 24(6), 1937, 7. © KADOC, Leuven, Belgium.

Figure 7.7 Mental significance of 'cosiness' in *Vrouwenbeweging*, 22(12), 1935, 4. © KADOC, Leuven, Belgium.

The situation seemed to have been somewhat different for other social organisations. As illustrated above, socialist discourse focused more explicitly on the anti-bourgeois character of its dwelling ideology then did that of its Catholic counterparts. In fact, the socialists' entire political, cultural and socio-economic ideology was far more opposed to bourgeois culture than that of the Catholic working-class movement. The ideology of the Catholic socio-political bloc mirrored a peaceful class-based society, whereas the ideology of the socialist bloc was rooted in class struggle.[45] Thus, when the socialist governing body argued that interior design had to be closely linked to class identity, all remnants of bourgeois culture had to be rooted out. Therefore, 'the "home" of the workman cannot be what it used to be. Austere beauty must rule in it'.[46]

At first glance, in contrast to the strategy of the Catholic working-class movement, cosiness does not seem to have been a central instrument in the socialist marketing of austerity in the home. Did 'cosiness' sound too bourgeois to the ears of socialists? It is striking that socialist discourse avoided the use of the word *gezelligheid* (cosiness), and instead substituted the English word 'home' (rather than the equivalent Dutch word, *thuis*, which was only used sporadically). A 'home' was a house that met all the requirements of its occupants' daily living practices,[47] it was functional and was rationally equipped,[48] and it was a symbol of welfare and happiness.[49] Although the word 'cosiness' was not used, there was great similarity between the KAV's notion of cosiness and the socialist idea of 'home'. However, the concrete material examples given by the socialists often corresponded more to the modernist designs than did Catholic examples.

Whereas the socialist and Catholic working-class movements defined class identity by focusing on the differences between themselves and the bourgeoisie, the Belgian Farmers' Association and its female branch accentuated differences between the countryside and the city in marking out its identity. Consequently, the Belgian Association of Farming Women did not attack the bourgeois notion of cosiness. In fact, cosiness in terms of clothing, furnishing and decoration was a central and structuring topic of the Association's ideology of 'good living'. 'Someone who appreciates cosiness will find it most rewarding to give his house, and everything surrounding it, a nice appearance. The choice of the curtains, the place of the flowers on the windowsill and the planting of a climber can perform miracles to the most ponderous houses and the most naked façades'.[50]

As this example demonstrates, a sensory analogy was constructed in which 'cosy', 'clothed' and 'warm' were the opposites of 'uncomfortable', 'naked' and 'cold'. Besides, since it was the woman's duty to create a cosy interior for her husband and children, the notion of cosiness went far beyond the merely material. Cosiness was a way to introduce a family atmosphere into rural life and culture.

Nevertheless, women were warned that they should not overdo cosiness: moderation was the watchword. Meeting the requirements of cosiness could indeed run counter to the demands of cleanliness and sobriety. To overcome this paradox the governing body of the Association of Farming Women marked out different spheres in the house. The place where people had to wash themselves and the bedrooms must be as austere and clean as possible.[51] In contrast to this, the living-kitchen ought to be cosy and nicely decorated with flowers, wallpaper and paintings.

Figure 7.8 A farmer's model kitchen in *De Boerin,* 1928, 30. © KADOC, Leuven, Belgium.

Modern Asceticism as an Emancipating or Restricting Value?

Both modernist architects and domestic scientists hoped to improve the living conditions of the working classes and the rural population with their plea for austere interiors. But it was hard to convince these social groups of the advantages. If they had the economic means to change their interiors, people seemed to prefer decorated interiors in which they could express their newly acquired purchasing power. In order to get more control over this development, both socialist and Catholic working-class organisations started to market the austere ideal. The socialists disguised austerity by covering it up with the concept of 'home', while the Catholic organisations substituted the notion of 'cosiness' for it. Whereas expensive Wilhelmine sanatoria tried to sell their unpleasant ascetic practices under the palliative umbrella of luxurious residence (see the chapter by Michael Hau, this volume), the advisors of working-class and farming people sold austere interiors as a new form of cosiness. Both wrapped their own modern ascetic ideals, for the so-called common good, in a pragmatic, attractive frame.

However, surveys of the actual living conditions of working-class families revealed that many dwellings during the interwar period were over-populated and unhealthy, often lacking water and sanitation.[52] Moreover, most families had no furniture except for some old, inherited, worn-out pieces,[53] and the problem of the masses living in slums was a recurring central issue in social debates during the interwar years in Flanders.[54] The data clearly suggest that not all working-class and rural families enjoyed increased purchasing power in the 1920s, particularly taking into account the general economic crisis of the Great Depression, when a large number of families were hit by high unemployment.[55] Therefore, one might question what was excessive in popular dwelling culture.

Nevertheless, most of the social organisations' governing bodies fulminated against superfluous elements in their members' homes. They tried to control their members' slow economic emancipation and hoped to persuade them to buy more austere furniture. Firstly, because the women of the governing bodies believed that a higher level of austerity would make housekeeping easier. These women, who followed the recent trends in housing matters, operated

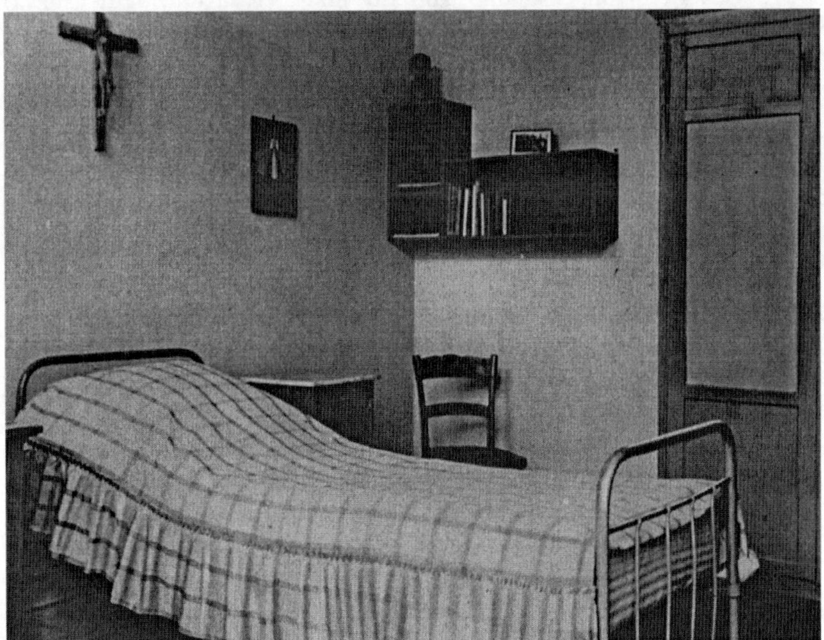

Figure 7.9 The ideal bedroom for a girl in *De Boerin, Jubilee Issue 1911–1936*.
© KADOC, Leuven, Belgium.

at a professional level between the daily struggle of most of their members and the advice of domestic science experts, architects, politicians and entrepreneurs.[56] Their position at the top of influential social organisations gave them opportunities to take part in workshops, to visit international housing projects and exhibitions, and to read international literature regarding recent developments in architecture and domestic science.[57] This convinced them that more sober interiors would liberate their members from domestic drudgery. Moreover, they believed that their mission was to liberate their members by teaching them how to reduce the workload of housekeeping.

Secondly, the leading bodies of intermediary organisations appealed to their members to introduce a more ascetic material culture into their homes because they classified the objects and furniture their members were buying as pure kitsch, objects that were appropriate to the bourgeois home rather than authentic designs for the urban working classes and rural population.[58] They disapproved of their members' spontaneous taste and outlined what should be the appropriate content and appearance of decent working-class culture.

Indeed, as the analysis of the marketing of austerity reveals, austerity was promoted as a means of liberation and social emancipation, but also as an instrument of class identity and a means of dissociating the working-class and urban population from bourgeois culture. The relation between this class-bound way of applying austerity and social emancipation was very ambiguous. Both ways of understanding austerity limited each other. After all, a farmer had to stay a farmer, just as a worker had to remain a worker, and this had to be visible in the material culture of the home. At the same time, the cultural elite and avant-garde of the interwar period adopted new ascetic values in interior design on a large scale. The way in which the aforementioned social organisations promoted these ascetic values in the furniture of farming and working-class houses can therefore also be read as an offensive in the process of emancipation and civilisation.[59]

The paradox lies in the difference between asceticism as an explicit individual choice – an option among other options – of someone who could materially fulfil all his or her needs on the one hand, and the forced asceticism of less well-to-do social groups on the other. A key factor in this dichotomy was that the governing bodies of these social organisations were composed of women who, whilst they did not necessarily come from well-off backgrounds, had received training and a broader education than those they were appealing to and had the power to impose values and norms upon them. In the domain of interior design, these women, supported by male architects, promoted ascetic values in the homes of their target group, hoping to consolidate a strong connection between social identity and home culture. Paradoxically, in contrast to the emancipating task these organisations assigned themselves, the fairly haughty way they had of defining and imposing what they considered appropriate in matters of taste veiled a conservative belief in social and gender inequality.

Notes

This article originated from a research project entitled 'His Work, Her Home: Research into the Translation into Social Terms of Architectural Views on Domestic Life in Flanders, 1920–1970', supported by the Research Foundation Flanders, and headed by professors Leen Van Molle, Hilde Heynen, Patrick Pasture and Veerle Draulans.

1. Matant, 'De Slaapkamer', *De Boerin* 5 (1929), 103.
2. Examples include: the provincial exhibition of cheap dwellings in Ghent, 1929 – see N. Poulain, 'Provinciale tentoonstelling "De goedkope woning", Gent 1929', *Interbellum* 18,3 (1998), 6–15, 18,4 (1998), 6–12; the provincial exhibition of ornamental arts and modern industries in La Louvière, 1930 – see P. Werrie, 'Exposition Provinciale des arts décoratifs et industriels modernes', *Habitation à Bon marché* 10,7 (1930), 121–23; and the Catholic Working-Class Women's exhibition 'Wij bouwen een Nieuwen Thuis', 1939 – see S. De Caigny, '"We're Building a New Home!" The Significance of the Domestic Sphere among Working-class Women in Flanders during the Interwar Years', *Home Cultures* 21 (2005), 1–24.
3. D.S. Ryan, *The Ideal Home through the Twentieth Century* (London, 1997); D.S. Ryan, '"All the World and Her Husband": the Daily Mail ideal home exhibition 1908–39', in M.M. Andrews and M.M. Talbot (eds), *All the World and Her Husband: Women in Twentieth-century Consumer Culture* (London, 2000), 10–22.
4. M. Segalen, 'The Salon des Arts Ménagers, 1923–1983: A French Effort to Instil the Virtues of Home and Norms of Good Taste', *Journal of Design History* 7 (1994), 267–75.
5. R. Oldenziel and C. Bouw, 'Huisvrouwen, hun strategieën en apparaten 1898–1998', in R. Oldenziel and C. Bouw (eds), *Schoon Genoeg! Huisvrouwen en huishoudtechnologie in Nederland 1898–1998* (Nijmegen, 1998), 9–29.
6. There could be considerable differences between the Walloon provinces of Belgium. The development of social movements was, for example, quite different in Flanders where Catholic organisations were always more powerful in the twentieth century, while socialist organisations had more members in the French-speaking part of Belgium. This article focuses mainly on the Flemish situation. See also S. Hellemans, *Strijd om de moderniteit* (Leuven, 1990).
7. In 1919, the Association had a membership of around 20,000; in 1940 it had risen to 120,000.
8. The KAV was established in 1920 and its membership had risen to 125,000 by 1940. See R. Christens and A. De Decker, *Vormingswerk in vrouwenhanden: De geschiedenis van de KAV voor de Tweede Wereldoorlog (1920–1940)* (Leuven, 1988).
9. After the introduction of universal suffrage for men in Belgium in 1917, most socialist organisations started to grow fast. The socialist women's organisation already had over 40,000 members by the beginning of the 1920s. More detailed figures of the membership of the later interwar years are difficult to reconstruct since most archives of the SVV have been lost. See D. De Weerdt, *De dochters van Marianne* (Antwerp, 1997).

10. S. De Caigny and W. Vanderstede, 'Spiegel van het Hemelhuis: De wissel-werking tussen woonideaal en sociale rollen bij de Belgische Boerinnenbond (1907–1940)', *Tijdschrift voor Sociale en Economische Geschiedenis* 2,1 (2005), 3–29. Note that Catholicism is the dominant form of Christianity in Belgium; the two terms are used as synonyms in this text.

11. S. De Caigny, '"White Cells": Norms and Practices of Sanitary Installations in Houses during the Interwar Period in Flanders', unpublished paper presented at the Joint Doctoral Seminar, Theory and History of Architecture, Louvain-la-Neuve, 4 November 2004.

12. M.L., 'Ons Huis', *De Boerin* 10 (1919), 145.

13. Matant, 'Over keukenkasten', *De Boerin* 1 (1928), 7–8.

14. Prewar examples were the model farm at Liège in 1905, the Provincial Agricultural Exhibition in Brussels in 1907, the 'Pavilion of the Farmer's Wife' at the International Exhibition in Brussels in 1910, and 'The Modern Village' that was constructed at the World Exhibition in Ghent in 1913. See P. De Vuyst and E. Tibaut, *Het moderne dorp op de wereldtentoonstelling te Gent 1913* (Brussels, 1913).

15. F. Graftiau, *La ferme moderne démonstrative: applications mécaniques et électriques, procédés et méthodes rationnelles d'exploitation* (Louvain, 1930); J. Giele, *De betoog-hoeve: Tentoonstelling Brussel* (Leuven, 1935); J. Giele, *La ferme démonstrative: maison rurale, bâtiments d'exploitation, jardins, l'amélioration de la vie rurale* (Louvain, 1939).

16. Martha, 'Gezondheidsleer: Onze slaapkamer', *Vrouwenbeweging* 4 (1925), 57–58.

17. 'Onze levende thuis', *Vrouwenbeweging* 1 (1930), 9.

18. KAV/KADOC/L – 2.10.55: Modelvoordrachten 1920-1959, Lecture 1927–1928 "Oost West, 't Huis Best", Paaswerking 1938 "Wij bouwen onzen haard"; KAV/KADOC/L – 2.10.55/17: Lecture 1938 "Wij bouwen een nieuwen thuis"; KAV/KADOC/L – 2.10.45: 1939 "Woningactie"; CSVW/KADOC/L – 95: "Over vrouwenadel".

19. De Caigny, '"We're Building a New Home!"', 2.

20. As most of the archives of the Socialist Visionary Women are lost and as its magazine focused more on household practices than on furniture design, I have also used publications of the Socialist Centre for Education of Workmen to reconstruct the socialist ideology of interior design and furniture. See: P. Van den Eeckhout and P. Creve, 'De socialistische sociaal-culturele organisaties voor volwassenen', in P. Van den Eeckhout and G. Vanthemsche (eds), *Bronnen voor de studie van het hedendaagse België, 19de-20ste eeuw* (Brussels, 2001), 967.

21. 'Goede smaak in verband met de Huisinrichting', *Opgang* 2 (1931), 40.

22 O. Van de Casyne, 'De stemmige woning', *Arbeid en Kennis* 1 (1924), 69.

23. J.K., 'Een praatje over bouwkunst', *Arbeid en Kennis* 1 (1924), 113.

24. I. Cieraad, 'Het huishouden tussen droom en daad, over de toekomst van de keuken', in Oldenziel and Bouw, *Schoon Genoeg! Huisvrouwen en huishoudtechnologie in Nederland 1898–1998* (Nijmegen, 1998), 31–57.

25. See, e.g., P. Bernège, *De la méthode ménagère* (Paris, 1928); E. Meyer, *Der Neue Haushalt* (Stuttgart, 1926).

26. H. Heynen, 'Plekken van het dagelijkse leven: Over vrouwen in de architectuur-kritiek', *Archis* 4 (2000), 60.

27. K. Van Herck, '"Only Where Comfort Ends, Does Humanity Begin": On the "Coldness" of Avant-garde Architecture in the Weimar Period', in H. Heynen and G. Baydar (eds), *Negotiating Domesticity: Spatial Productions of Gender in Modern Architecture* (London, 2005), 125.

28. H. Heynen, *Architectuur en de kritiek van de moderniteit* (Nijmegen, 2001), 72.

29. L. De Cauter, 'Authenticiteit', in H. Heynen et al. (eds), *Dat is architectuur* (Rotterdam, 2001), 683.

30. H. Heynen, *Architectuur en de kritiek van de moderniteit*, 138.

31. B. Verschaffel, '"Architectuur is (als) een gebaar": Over het "echte" als architectu-raal criterium', in H. Heynen (ed.), *Wonen tussen gemeenplaats en poëzie: Opstellen over stad en architectuur* (Rotterdam, 1993), 76.

32. H. Heynen, 'Modernity and Domesticity: Tensions and Contradictions', in H. Heynen and G. Baydar (eds), *Negotiating Domesticity: Spatial Productions of Gender in Modern Architecture* (London, 2005), 1.

33. H. Heynen and K. Van Herck, 'Introduction', *Journal of Architecture* 7 (2002), 224.

34. S. Leavitt, *From Catharine Beecher to Martha Stewart: A Cultural History of Domestic Advice* (Chapel Hill, 2002), 99; S. Stage and V. Vicenti (eds), *Rethinking Home Economics: Women and the History of a Profession* (London, 1997); G. Lees-Maffei (ed.), *Domestic Design Advice, Journal of Design History* 16,1 (2003), special issue.

35. S. Leavitt, *From Catharine Beecher*, 97.

36. This ambiguity is very similar to the situation of Das Neue Frankfurt, where the fairly traditional but austere designs of Kramer were contemporary with more modernist designs of, for example, Marcel Breuer. See H. Hirdina, *Neues Bauen, Neues Gestalten: Das Neue Frankfurt, Die neue Stadt. Eine Zeitschrift zwichen 1926 und 1933* (Berlin, 1984), 40–41, 185.

37. S. Hellemans, *Strijd om de moderniteit*, 125.

38. My analysis of the ideology of dwelling culture of the Catholic working-class movement is based on a reading of the archives and periodicals of its female branch, the KAV, and on the periodical of the League of Owner-occupiers, the most active section of the General Christian Workers' Union in terms of com-munication on home culture.

39. The living-kitchen was the most common space in popular Flemish houses. It was the room with the fireplace that served as both living room and kitchen at the time. See S. De Caigny, '"We're Building a New Home!"', 10–13.

40. 'Wij bouwen een nieuwen thuis', *Vrouwenbeweging* 25,5 (1938), 6–7.

41. J.L., 'Een gezellige woning heeft haar socialen terugslag op de bewoners', *Onze Woning* 7 (1933), 4–5.

42. K. Van Herck, '"Only Where Comfort Ends, Does Humanity Begin"', 125.

43. The translation of the Dutch word *gezelligheid* into English is fairly problematic since it has a material and social component that refers to the etymology of the word *gezelschap*, signifying 'company'. As 'cosiness' is used here as the translation of *gezel-ligheid*, I want to stress both the material and the mental significance of the word.

44. S. De Caigny, '"We're Building a New Home!"', 13–15.

45. S. Hellemans, *Strijd om de moderniteit*, 1–50.

46. A. Gautier-Finck, 'De meubelskunst', *Arbeid en Kennis* 1 (1924), 72. The English word 'home' was used, and put between quotation marks in the original Dutch: *Het "home" van den werkman mag niet zijn wat het vroeger was. Eenvoudige demokratische schoonheid moet er heerschen.*

47. Ibid., 70.

48. V., 'Het stemmige huis', *Arbeid en Kennis* 1 (1925), 169–72.

49. Van de Casyne, 'De stemmige woning', *Arbeid en Kennis* 1 (1924), 68.

50. M. Lemaire, 'Ons huis', *De Boerin* 1 (1920), 6.

51. Most farmhouses in Flanders were not equipped with a bathroom during the interwar years. People washed themselves near the water pump or, as was recommended by the Association of Farming Women but hardly practised, by means of washing tables in bedrooms. See S. De Caigny, '"White Cells"'.

52. The information is hard to reconstruct, but data from 1961 show that only 22.2 per cent of the homes had a bathroom or shower (hot water), 12.2 per cent had central heating, while 22.75 per cent could only warm one room. See Werkgroep alternatieve ekonomie-Leuven, *Ongezond Verbeterbaar: Ekonomische en sociale aspekten van het wonen in België* (Leuven, 1977).

53. 'Vijfde Algemeen Congres der Christelijke Sociale Vrouwenwerken', *Vrouwenbeweging* 25,7 (1938), 114–19.

54. The National League against Slums was founded in 1927. The League functioned as a central organ where political groups, social organisations and housing companies discussed various solutions for the slums.

55. G. Vanthemsche, *Le chômage en Belgique de 1929 à 1940: son histoire, son actualité* (Brussels, 1994).

56. Interview with Liesje Moelants and Régine Katrysse, Kraainem, 12 July 2004, conducted by S. De Caigny and E. De Vos. Both Moelants and Katrysse were active in the governing body of the KAV from the 1930s until the 1970s.

57. Socialist authors visited Rotterdam – see A. Van den Brempt, 'De Arbeiderswoning', *Ontwikkeling en Uitspanning* 2 (1921), 167–68; the Netherlands – see 'De socialistische arbeidersvrouwen op studiereis door Nederland', *Stem der Vrouw* 27,6 (1937), 6; Russia – see S. Blieck, 'Sovjet-Rusland: De Positie der Vrouw', *Stem der Vrouw* 16,2 (1926); Vienna – see 'Een bezoek aan Weenen', *Stem der Vrouw* 26,12 (1936); Strasbourg, Colmar and Mulhouse – see M. De Keyzer, 'Op Studiereis: Straatsburg, Colmar, Mulehouse', *Stem der Vrouw* 28,7 (1938), 6–7. Catholic authors visited the exhibition of Das Neue Frankfurt in 1929 – see H. Heynen and A. Van Caudenberg, 'The Rational Kitchen in the Interwar Period in Belgium: Discourses and Realities', *Home Cultures* 1 (2004), 23–50.

58. 'Dit is de moderne Vlaamsche trant', *Vrouwenbeweging* 25,4 (1938), 5; Martha, 'De schouw onzer keuken', *Vrouwenbeweging* 25,4 (1938), 19.

59. A. de Regt is one author that explicitly underscribes this vision. See A. de Regt, *Arbeidersgezinnen en beschavingsarbeid: Ontwikkelingen in Nederland, 1870–1940. Een historisch-sociologische studie* (Amsterdam, 1984), 136–42.

References

Published Sources

Bernège, P. 1928. *De la méthode ménagère*, Paris.

Christens, R., and A. De Decker. 1988. *Vormingswerk in vrouwenhanden: De geschiedenis van de KAV voor de Tweede Wereldoorlog (1920–1940)*, Leuven.

Cieraad, I. 1998. 'Het huishouden tussen droom en daad, over de toekomst van de keuken', in R. Oldenziel and C. Bouw (eds), *Schoon Genoeg! Huisvrouwen en huishoudtechnologie in Nederland 1898–1998*, Nijmegen, pp.31–57.

De Caigny, S. 2004. '"White Cells": Norms and Practices of Sanitary Installations in Houses during the Interwar Period in Flanders', unpublished paper presented at the Joint Doctoral Seminar, Theory and History of Architecture, Louvain-la-Neuve, 4 November.

——— 2005. '"We're Building a New Home!" The Significance of the Domestic Sphere among Working-class Women in Flanders during the Interwar Years', *Home Cultures* 2(1): 1–24.

De Caigny, S., and W. Vanderstede. 2005. 'Spiegel van het Hemelhuis: De wisselwerking tussen woonideaal en sociale rollen bij de Belgische Boerinnenbond (1907–1940)', *Tijdschrift voor Sociale en Economische Geschiedenis* 2(1): 3–29.

De Cauter, L. 2001. 'Authenticiteit', in H. Heynen et al. (eds), *Dat is architectuur*, Rotterdam, pp.681–86.

De Regt, A. 1984. *Arbeidersgezinnen en beschavingsarbeid: Ontwikkelingen in Nederland, 1870–1940: Een historisch-sociologische studie*, Amsterdam.

De Vuyst, P., and E. Tibaut. 1913. *Het moderne dorp op de wereldtentoonstelling te Gent 1913*, Brussels.

De Weerdt, D. 1997. *De dochters van Marianne*, Antwerp.

Giele, J. 1935. *De betooghoeve: Tentoonstelling Brussel*, Leuven.

——— 1939. *La ferme démonstrative: maison rurale, bâtiments d'exploitation, jardins, l'amélioration de la vie rurale*, Louvain.

Graftiau, F. 1930. *La Ferme moderne démonstrative: applications mécaniques et électriques, procédés et méthodes rationnelles d'exploitation*, Louvain.

Hellemans, S. 1990. *Strijd om de moderniteit*, Leuven.

Heynen, H. 2000. 'Plekken van het dagelijkse leven: Over vrouwen in de architectuurkritiek', *Archis* 4: 58–64.

——— 2001. *Architectuur en de kritiek van de moderniteit*, Nijmegen.

——— 2005. 'Modernity and Domesticity: Tensions and Contradictions', in H. Heynen and G. Baydar (eds), *Negotiating Domesticity: Spatial Productions of Gender in Modern Architecture*, London, pp.1–30.

Heynen, H., and A. Van Caudenberg. 2004. 'The Rational Kitchen in the Interwar Period in Belgium: Discourses and Realities', *Home Cultures* 1: 23–50.

Heynen, H., and K. Van Herck. 2002. 'Introduction', *Journal of Architecture* 7: 221–28.

Hirdina, H. 1984. *Neues Bauen, Neues Gestalten: Das Neue Frankfurt, Die neue Stadt. Eine Zeitschrift zwichen 1926 und 1933*, Berlin.

Leavitt, S. 2002. *From Catharine Beecher to Martha Stewart: A Cultural History of Domestic Advice*, Chapel Hill.

Lees-Maffei, G. (ed.) 2003. *Domestic Design Advice. Journal of Design History* 16(1), special issue.

Meyer, E. 1926. *Der Neue Haushalt*, Stuttgart.

Oldenziel, R., and C. Bouw. 1998. 'Huisvrouwen, hun strategieën en apparaten 1898–1998', in R. Oldenziel and C. Bouw (eds), *Schoon Genoeg! Huisvrouwen en huishoudtechnologie in Nederland 1898–1998*, Nijmegen, pp.9–29.

Poulain, N. 1998. 'Provinciale tentoonstelling "De goedkope woning", Gent 1929', *Interbellum* 18(3): 6–15; 18(4): 6–12.

Ryan, D.S. 1997. *The Ideal Home through the Twentieth Century*, London.

——— 2000. '"All the World and Her Husband": The Daily Mail Ideal Home Exhibition 1908–39', in M.M. Andrews and M.M. Talbot (eds), *All the World and Her Husband: Women in Twentieth-century Consumer Culture*, London, pp.10–22.

Segalen, M. 1994. 'The Salon des Arts Ménagers, 1923–1983: A French Effort to Instil the Virtues of Home and Norms of Good Taste', *Journal of Design History* 7: 267–75.

Stage, S., and V. Vicenti (eds). 1997. *Rethinking Home Economics: Women and the History of a Profession*, London.

Van den Brempt, A. 1921. 'De Arbeiderswoning', *Ontwikkeling en Uitspanning* 2: 167–68.

Van den Eeckhout, P., and P. Creve. 2001. 'De socialistische sociaal-culturele organisaties voor volwassenen', in P. Van den Eeckhout and G. Vanthemsche (eds), *Bronnen voor de studie van het hedendaagse België, 19de-20ste eeuw*, Brussels, pp.966–71.

Van Herck, K. 2005. '"Only Where Comfort Ends, Does Humanity Begin": On the "Coldness" of Avant-garde Architecture in the Weimar Period', in H. Heynen and G. Baydar (eds), *Negotiating Domesticity: Spatial Productions of Gender in Modern Architecture*, London, pp.123–44.

Vanthemsche, G. 1994. *Le chômage en Belgique de 1929 à 1940: son histoire, son actualité*, Brussels.

Verschaffel, B. 1993. '"Architectuur is (als) een gebaar": Over het "echte" als architecturaal criterium', in H. Heynen (ed.), *Wonen tussen gemeenplaats en poëzie: Opstellen over stad en architectuur*, Rotterdam, pp.67–79.

Werkgroep alternatieve ekonomie-Leuven. 1977. *Ongezond verbeterbaar: Ekonomische en sociale aspekten van het wonen in België*, Leuven.

Werrie, P. 1930. 'Exposition Provinciale des arts décoratifs et industriels modernes', *Habitation à Bon marché* 10(7): 121–23.

Periodicals

Arbeid en Kennis, 1924–1925.
De Boerin, 1919–1938.
Ontwikkeling en Uitspanning, 1921.
Onze Woning, 1933.

Opgang, 1931.
Stem der Vrouw, 1926–1937.
Vrouwenbeweging, 1925–1938.

Archives

KAV/KADOC/L – Katholieke Arbeidersvrouwen archive, KADOC-K.U.Leuven, Leuven
CSVW/KADOC/L – Christelijke Sociale Vrouwenwerken archive, KADOC-K.U.Leuven, Leuven

Part IV
The Lonely Passions of Science

Wilhelm Prager (director) and Nicholas Kaufmann (scriptwriter) 'Wege zu Kraft und Schönheit' (1924). © Friedrich-Wilhelm-Murnau-Stiftung, Wiesbaden, Germany.

8

The Revelation of a Modern Saint: Marie Curie's Scientific Asceticism and the Culture of Professionalised Science

Kaat Wils

'According to my statistics, I worked in November on average five hours, fifty one minutes and thirty-six seconds per day (Sundays included)'. The Belgian student of physics and mathematics George Sarton made this calculation in 1906 at the bottom of a letter to a friend, and added: 'It's not enough'.[1] In the years to come, Sarton's work discipline as a history of science professor at Harvard would improve, and he became famous for his seemingly endless capacity for work. If we can trust the description of his work routine by his daughter, the poet and novelist May Sarton, his early desire to regulate and systematise his daily life was persistent. Sarton himself, however, would read his own career not in terms of discipline and order, but in terms of passion. His double project of organising the history of science into a scientific discipline and, in doing so, enabling the creation of a new philosophy of science in the shape of a 'new humanism', was ambitious.[2] 'I was not crazy, but seemed to be, because I was overwhelmingly dominated by two passions, a passion for science and another equally ardent one for the humanities', he explained in 1955, three years into retirement after a forty-two year run as editor of the scholarly journal *Isis*, based in Wondelghem near Ghent, Belgium.[3]

The combination of a devotion to science and the cultivation of a disciplined lifestyle marked Sarton's personal life and crossed into his professional career as well. When reviewing a series of biographical and autobiographical publications on Marie and Pierre Curie for *Isis* in 1938, he heralded 'their rationalism, their passionate love of truth and of science, their indifference to money and fame, their innate austerity'. His selection of photographs of both scientists supported this image of frugality. The moral stature of the

Figure 8.1 Marie Curie. © Taken from G. Sarton, 'Review of Eve Curie, *Madame Curie*; Marie Curie, *Pierre Curie*; Claudius Regaud, *Marie Skłodowska-Curie*', *Isis* 28, 1938, 480–484.

Curies was comparable to that of Faraday and Darwin, Sarton added, concluding: 'I will expect my Harvard and Radcliffe students to read and ruminate the lives of Pierre and Marie Curie; it may awaken in them, if it be there, the love of truth and the love of science'. This recommendation was not commonly made in scientific circles at the time, he suggested, and he noted that many French scientists disliked Marie Curie; they said she was cold and dry. Further evidence of this negative judgement was provided in a footnote.[4]

Modern Science and Asceticism

The moral characteristics that Sarton attributed to Marie Curie, and which seemed to irritate many of her colleagues, had a respectable history. Sarton's laudatory description echoed an ancient trope from Greek antiquity that had been attributed to authentic lovers of truth. The Greek truth-seeker or philosopher was someone who attained truth by denying the demands of the stomach and, more generally, the body. In early Christian culture as well, the attainment of spiritual knowledge was linked to a disengagement from the world, or more specifically to a disembodied mind. In the Middle Ages, heroic abstinence became for holy men and women a condition and a sign of entitlement to spiritual knowledge, while it was increasingly considered to be a potential threat for the institutions of Christianity. Dietary advice remained central to humanist and early modern scientific culture. Prudent moderation and temperance were recommended for those who wished to live a healthy and productive life in society. This reinterpretation of older literature continued, however, to offer ways of understanding the austere dietetics of the otherworldly intellectual. The concept of scholarly melancholy added to the idea that dedication to truth was bodily inscribed. The figures of Robert Boyle and, later, Isaac Newton became culturally powerful examples of bodily disengagement; their stories were eagerly retold up to the twentieth century. Humoral understandings of the female constitution as colder than the male's could provide a basis for explaining women's absence in intellectual enterprises. The few women who participated in philosophical inquiries were prone to suffer from a high degree of bodily heat.[5]

Whereas this reading by Steven Shapin of the link between ideals of knowledge and asceticism focuses on bodily abstinence as a road to truth, the first major historiographical contribution in this field associated a broader concept of asceticism with a more specific sort of knowledge. As early as 1938, the year in which he wrote about Marie Curie, Sarton published in his new journal *Osiris* a monograph by his student Robert K. Merton in which the birth of modern science in seventeenth-century England was correlated with the Puritan culture of asceticism. Following Max Weber's thesis on the birth of capitalism, this culture was related to intramundane rather than monastic asceticism. The systematic labour of studying natural phenomena, Merton argued, was within this culture not only considered a way to be diligent in one's calling – success in one's profession being the hallmark of salvation – but also a means to preserve the faculties of the mind and to remain far from worldly temptations. Science was in this process sanctified. The study of natural phenomena was not only seen as an effective means for promoting the glory of God but also a way to enlarge man's dominion over nature, which again increased the religiously assigned value of the new knowledge.[6]

The theological logic that made this sanctification of science possible would soon be threatened by the very scientific spirit it had fostered, Merton argued. Science, however, did not necessarily become less sanctified throughout this process. Nineteenth-century scientism avidly created the idea of an unbridgeable opposition between science and religion, but at the same time it reinforced the religious discourse that accompanied the scientific enterprise. Even in cultural contexts where the topos of the conflict between science and religion did not imply a harsh and polemical clash between the heralds of naturalist and agnostic science on the one hand, and protectors of traditional knowledge and education on the other, the scientific enterprise was easily read in religious terms. In the United States, for example, the metaphor of science as a temple and scientists as priests who guarded the shrine of science was frequently used. According to David Hollinger, this tendency should be linked to the relative autonomy of nineteenth-century self-regulating communities of scientists. The more detached from their fellow citizens that scientists became, the more necessary it became that they were subject to an ethical code intrinsic to their practice.[7]

Within these new scientific communities of the late nineteenth century, Rebecca Herzig has recently argued, the concept of self-sacrifice (a term that appeared in the English language as late as the nineteenth century) became an important element of identity for the scientist. The capacity to deliberately offer one's own body for the sake of science functioned as a form of distinction. Suffering could only be ennobling for people who were truly in possession of their selves: the suffering of slaves, for instance, was debasing rather than ennobling. Evolutionary ideas were used in this context to stress that progress required pain, and to map sensibility to pain onto capacity for self-possession. The principles of Darwinism were also invoked to underscore the necessity for the individual to submit to a larger collective. The idea that science could function as such a collectivity, worthy of bodily sacrifice, was new. Whereas the word 'science' had previously evoked a mental faculty, the word now came to refer to a collective and impersonal body. The ongoing processes of institutionalisation, professionalisation and internationalisation transformed science into an abstract collectivity with its own imperatives. Just as the nation became in this period an 'imagined community', science acquired a new autonomy and authority. And just as one had to be willing to die for one's country, one had to be ready to suffer for science.[8]

The representation of the scientist as scientist, rather than as philosopher or savant in the humanist and classical tradition, was a relatively new phenomenon as well. The genre had been gradually developed in, among other things, the eighteenth-century French academy, and in particular through the *laudatio* of its deceased members. The qualities which were attributed to these scholars (such as perseverance, modesty and honesty) referred to stoic ideals of learning, but gradually were adopted for the praxis of the natural sciences. Scientists were no longer just a new type of philosopher. They wanted to represent an autonomous field and hoped, certainly from the second half of the nineteenth century, to radiate a great moral authority.[9]

Both Hollinger and Herzig have rightly paid attention to the overbearingly masculine conception of this modern scientific vocation. The modern scientist, who was in full possession of his own self and was hence able to subject himself to the discipline of science, could only be a white man. The Baconian ideal of science as an active and masculine enterprise seems to have grown in importance from the end of the eighteenth century onwards. In this period, for example, a war was waged against a style that was all too poetic and 'feminine' in science, a style that was connected with the aristocratic and 'effeminate' salon. Men no longer employed a female pseudonym, for example, when writing about science for a female audience, nor did their texts encourage women to engage in science themselves.[10] The cultural process whereby science became inextricably bound up with notions of masculinity saw its definitive embedding through the budding culture of remembrance which characterised science from the late eighteenth century. This culture was not limited to scientific communities such as the academies. Within the new and very successful field of the popularisation of the sciences as well, much attention was given to the personality of the 'great' scientist who, seemingly by himself, albeit through necessary personal sacrifices, made an important scientific discovery. Gradually, in the representation of the history of science, fixed associations arose between one heroic man, one scientific discovery, and one nation – such as Isaac Newton, gravity, and Britain.[11]

Obviously, women had never been at the centre of learning. The informal character of early modern scientific networks had enabled women's participation, although their access to the academies had for example remained extremely limited. As science in the nineteenth century professionalised, women's exclusion became more a public and official matter. Women continued to participate in science as wives, daughters or nieces of scientists, but the core of scientific activities now lay in institutions such as academies and universities, to which women had no access. As science moved away from the home, only certain scientific disciplines, botany being the most well-known, continued to find a partial dwelling in the domestic sphere, by now characterised as 'feminine'. When the first 'exceptional' women were allowed to enter academia in the late nineteenth century, it was not just their career which had difficulties developing. Their portrayal and canonisation equally implied a complex dialogue with a masculine scientific culture. Ideals of asceticism seemed to facilitate as well as complicate this process. That was at least the case for 'the mother' of modern female scientists, Marie Curie.

The Silence of the Laboratory

The 'ascetic' life of Marie Curie started in 1891, when she was still Marya Skłodowska. That year she arrived as a poor, 24-year-old Polish student in Paris. She registered at the Sorbonne for a degree in mathematics and physics, because the university of her home city, Warsaw, did not admit women. The hard-working Marya obtained brilliant results and was encouraged via a small research grant to continue doing research. A Polish professor introduced her to the laboratory of the 35-year-old Pierre Curie, a physicist who in those days already enjoyed considerable standing in his profession, but who had not yet gained institutional recognition. Very soon there was a close bond between the two. After some hesitation on Marie's part, they were married in 1895.[12]

It was shortly after the birth of their first daughter, Irène, that Marie and Pierre began collaborating intensively. During her (unpaid) doctoral research on the luminous radiation of uranium, which had recently been discovered by the French scientist Henri Becquerel, Marie concluded that there had to be chemical elements which produced more radiation than uranium. Pierre decided to join in the research and left his own study of crystals and magnetism behind. This common quest led to the isolation in 1898 of two new elements: polonium and radium. Thereafter, analysis of radium and radioactivity would remain the core of both their research careers. In 1903 it led to the award of Marie's Ph.D. by the Sorbonne. That same year, together with Pierre and Henri Becquerel, she also received the Nobel Prize for Physics – becoming the first woman laureate – although it had originally looked as though only the two men were eligible for the prize.

The effect of the Nobel Prize on Pierre and Marie Curie's careers was considerable. Pierre was offered a chair at the Sorbonne, though he had applied in vain for a post at the same university twice before. For the first time Marie obtained a paid research post in the small laboratory associated with Pierre's professorship. After Pierre's sudden death in an accident in 1906, his professorship and the lead role in the laboratory were assigned to Marie. She thereby became the first woman lecturer, and later also the first woman professor at the Sorbonne.

Marie's academic position was, however, not self-evident and Pierre's shadow followed her. This became clear in 1910 when an argument arose about her candidacy for the Academy of Science. To many, among them female authors, the membership of a woman of this prestigious and masculine institution was impossible. Marie was accused of merely profiting from Pierre's success, and was not elected. Reproaches for her assumed vanity and shamelessness were voiced against her in the press, and these were echoed more strongly a year later when her relationship with the married physicist Paul Langevin became public. The cold, masculine Polish woman scientist was said to have destroyed a French family, and nationalist and anti-feminist sides reacted. There had, therefore, been some hesitancy over awarding the Nobel Prize for Chemistry to Marie Curie that same year.[13]

Marie's moral authority in France and elsewhere grew during the First World War, when she directed the organisation of a system of cars with built-in Röntgen apparatuses to assist with operations on wounded soldiers at the front. Another, even more important catalyst in this process was her trip to the United States in 1921, at the invitation of Marie Meloney, a woman who had been raising funds to support her scientific work. It was on the advice of this woman that soon afterwards she wrote a short autobiography for the American market and a biography of Pierre, which were published both in France and the United States.[14] Marie's self-portrait would become canonised through the biography which her daughter Eve published in 1937. The book appeared four years after Marie died of leukaemia, presumably caused by over-exposure to radioactive substances. It was an immensely popular book, and was reprinted eighty-eight times during its first two years in print.[15] Most of the subsequent biographies of Marie would remain indebted to the romantic storylines of Eve's portrait.

Figure 8.2 Pierre and Marie Curie in the laboratory, 1898.
© ACJC-musée Curie, Paris, France.

In Marie's self-portrait as well, romance was present, but this seemed subordinate to the position and meaning of the laboratory. It is this position that I will explore so as to analyse the specificity of late nineteenth and early twentieth-century scientific asceticism. Marie's autobiography starts in Poland, where her father, an enthusiastic science student, did not gain access to a laboratory. It ends with her dream of building a new laboratory outside Paris, in memory of Pierre. In between is a life in which happiness is closely linked to living in the laboratory. Pierre and Marie installed their rudimentary laboratory in an old and disused storage room. There they made their great discoveries, and it was there, Marie told and retold, that they had felt really happy, passing 'the best and happiest years of our life, devoting our entire days to our work'.[16] The seriousness of the place could only result in chaste and serious love, so it seemed. The Curies' 'first encounters, in the midst of the vapours of the laboratory, surrounded by alembics, retorts, the instruments of physics, are a far cry from the flirtations … which go on in our salons', a contemporary newspaper reported when the news of the first Nobel Prize spread.[17] By reporting in this way, a clear distinction was made between, on the one hand, the intellectual tradition which went back to the eighteenth-century 'promiscuous' salon, and, on the other hand, a new 'ascetic' and scientific attitude which was to be found in a new location, the laboratory. The diary which Marie kept after the death of Pierre testifies to the central role which this laboratory played in her personal life. Two weeks after his fatal accident, she started her diary with the following words: 'My dear Pierre whom I won't see again here, I want to talk to you in the silence of this laboratory. I had never thought of having to live here without you'. In subsequent entries of the diary, the laboratory remains the site most intimately linked to her grief, but offering at the same time her only possibility of emotional survival.[18]

In her published descriptions of laboratories as sacred places and as the temples of the future where progress is realised, Marie also joined a popular discourse on science which was, among others, developed by Claude Bernard, whose work she had avidly read in her pre-student years as a governess in Poland.[19] In his famous *Introduction to the Study of Experimental Medicine* (1856), Bernard described the laboratory as the place where the scientist retreats in order to try to understand the phenomena which has been observed in nature.[20] The most important characteristic which Marie as well as Pierre attributed to the laboratory in their lyric – private as well as published – descriptions of their *hangar*, was its quietness, 'its atmosphere of peace and reflection' (*paix et recueillement*), the only visitors being scientist friends with whom scientifically fruitful conversations were held.[21]

By praising the solitary aspect of laboratory life, the Curies echoed the old view that social withdrawal is a precondition of access to universal truths. They also echoed a concern for privacy that had been strong since laboratories

Figure 8.3 The hangar in which Pierre and Marie Curie established their laboratory, around 1900. © ACJC-musée Curie, Paris, France.

were created in the seventeenth century. Since many of these early laboratories were to be found in the basement of the house of a scientist or patron, whilst also open to a select group of guests who could attend experiments, the border between private and public had never been clear.[22] Idealisations of the laboratory as a bucolic and pastoral refuge from worldly labours remained in any case vivid in the eighteenth century.[23] In the nineteenth century, the country-house laboratory played a similar role: it helped sustain a universe in which material technology and spiritual value could temporarily be reconciled.[24] It was probably this type of reconciliation which Marie – a harsh critic of unhealthy life in the city, and a passionate lover of nature and its healing capacities – was thinking of, when dreaming about a large laboratory as an annex to a country house, in the south of France or, more realistically, in the outskirts of Paris.[25]

Pierre and Marie's work in the laboratory seemed to parallel an old discourse on scientific asceticism in still another way. Scientific work was physically exhausting and at times unpleasant. 'Truth is not easy to seize; there exists no easy road for arriving at it; to draw near to it requires work, patience, exactness, time and funds', the Protestant Swiss anatomist and theorist of science Albrecht von Haller had argued in the middle of the eighteenth century, developing Francis Bacon's pronouncements on experimental research. For von Haller, this was a clear statement against the speculations of Descartes and other would-be scientists who did not follow 'the tedious path of experiment' or who did not expose themselves to the 'pains that are inseparable from reality'.[26] Whereas von Haller's religiously inspired asceticism prevented him from expanding too much on the pleasures of his work – enthusiasm having a negative connotation within early modern Protestant culture – intellectual passion and suffering were intrinsically linked for the Curies, and this in a seemingly less problematic manner.[27] Reflecting on the years of arduous labour which finally led to the separation of the new element radium, Marie concluded: 'All that can be said now is that the constant progress of our work held us absorbed in a passionate research, while the difficulties were ever increasing'.[28] Physical injuries counted among these difficulties. In 1903, Pierre told a journalist in discussing his skin lesions: 'I am happy after all with my injury. My wife is as pleased as I … You see, these are the little accidents of the laboratory: they shouldn't frighten people who live their lives among alembics and retorts'.[29] Pierre probably never realised that the permanent exhaustion from which he would soon suffer and which would, to his continual frustration, prevent him from doing serious new research, was probably due to the effects of exposure to radioactivity. In Marie's biography of Pierre the emphasis shifted gradually to the sacrifices which accompanied a scientific calling: the prematurely deceased Pierre became a martyr to science. By writing in this vein, Marie joined, probably unconsciously, a discourse of martyrdom which was particularly successful within the new science of radiology, the status of which was enhanced through the authority of bodily injury and even death.[30]

The indifference to fame and honours which Pierre had always demonstrated, and which fitted in well with family traditions and his choice of a career as a civil servant, was also part of this martyrdom, which, again, had remarkable historical roots. Whereas the deeply religious von Haller had rebuked himself in his diary for the sins of pride and ambition, the agnostic Pierre seemed to have more worldly motivations for this attitude. As early as the 1890s, he explained his attitude as a way of creating liberty to work on his own, 'at my leisure'.[31] His more general publicity-shyness went together with a global choice for social and bodily asceticism. It was a choice which Marie herself had also made during her years as a poor, foreign student. This asceticism became the couple's explicit and extensively documented lifestyle. In Marie's public writings, for example, relaxation during holidays was presented as an instrumental, necessary relieving of the mind from the tensions of scientific work.[32] And this was certainly not just a publicity campaign. In her correspondence with her daughter Irène, similar mechanisms were at work.[33] Nevertheless, the ideal of asceticism as a necessary condition of being a true scientist was a powerful trope with an autonomous reality. Just as the power of representations of Newton as the most ascetic scientist in history is not diminished by the knowledge that food deliveries to his London household in a single week included one goose, two turkeys, two rabbits and one chicken, the picture of the daily, and of course not always ascetic life of the Curies derived from reading the letters and accounts of Marie does not lessen the cultural strength of this image.[34]

The Limits of Female Asceticism

The image of the ascetic scientist nevertheless seemed to have its weaknesses as well. Or rather, it seemed to offer at times a problematic narrative to host Curie's personal experiences and life narrative. The representation of modern science as a process of hard and physical labour could have a different meaning for a woman who collaborated with her husband. Just as manual labour had occupied an ambiguous position in monastic ascetic ideology, scientific asceticism could not do without a hierarchy between activities of the body and the mind.[35] In popular representations of the couple, Marie was easily reduced to 'the doer', whereas Pierre was portrayed as 'the thinker'. While Pierre was thinking, Marie patiently stirred the pots of boiling fluids from which radium was to be isolated, or so it was said in the press of the day.[36] It was an image that referred to a real division of labour between both scientists, yet which at the same time also magnified the differences between them both. In the period preceding the discovery of radium, at the end of 1898, the collaboration had been so intense that it was impossible to say who had contributed what. This began to change from 1899, when Marie undertook the particularly laborious chemical process of isolating radium, temporarily in closest collaboration with Pierre – as the lab notebooks from this period testify. Only from 1900 was a differentiation in the research initiated. Pierre directed his research systematically towards the characteristics of radioactivity, while Marie pursued the chemical side. She thereby used the precision scale designed and built by Pierre. In other words, neither had a monopoly on the title 'doer' or 'thinker'.[37]

On an existential level, Marie collided with the boundaries of the scientific asceticism she avidly promoted herself. The laboratory might have been a real haven for her, but it was also the object of tensions between husband and wife. Pierre felt that Marie ought to be in the laboratory more often. Marie regretted that Pierre spent so little time with his family. On the morning of Pierre's fatal accident, he had asked whether he could expect Marie at the laboratory. Marie had told him that she could not say and urged him not to pester her with the question. Eventually she decided to spend the day with their children, who had a holiday.[38] It was, indeed, Marie who was responsible for the organisation of the household and childcare. It was Marie who made notes in cookery books, designed and sewed the children's clothes, decorated the Christmas tree and organised parties for the children.[39] Because Pierre's health was shaky, she tried to spare him as much as possible when he was at home. Although they had many conversations about the children's education, and they were of the same mind in this area, Pierre wrote revealingly about Marie and 'her children' in his correspondence.[40]

If ideals of scientific asceticism were almost by definition beyond reach for a woman with children, they seemed to be more easily attainable for unmarried or widowed women. Like many of the other 'first female students' in Europe and the United States, Marie had always observed an extremely sober dress code as a student.[41] This choice was almost certainly due to her poor financial situation, but it was also an efficient strategy to ensure that she would be taken as seriously as possible in her intellectual ambitions. After the death of Pierre, and certainly after the smear campaign against her so-called 'adulterous attitude' in the Langevin affair, Marie kept her sober and dark clothing, resembling a nun's habit, according to some.[42] This strategy of asceticism was, however, not self-evident either. As Ludmilla Jordanova has argued, the depiction of a woman scientist always involved a monitoring of femininity: a woman who was depicted as appropriately feminine seemed less threatening than she otherwise might have done.[43] Marie's opponents in the daily press depicted her systematically as an all too male woman who deliberately pretended to be unpretentious – the ultimate sign of unsurpassed pride, according to the obituary notice on Curie in the French newspaper *Le Journal*.[44] The incompatibility between ideals of scientific asceticism and public expectations about feminine behaviour also became acutely apparent during Marie's media-hyped American trip. The only known photographs of a smiling Marie Curie are those taken of her during this trip, posing arm in arm with President Harding in front of the White House. Presumably she felt obliged to smile, just as she had been strongly encouraged to wear a coquettish outfit.[45]

Gender was, however, not the only factor which complicated Curie's adherence to a narrative of asceticism. The whole American fundraising campaign makes it clear how Marie was ready to perform to public expectations so as to guarantee financial support. Being a multiple Nobel Prize winner, she was materially far better off than most of her French colleagues. She nevertheless participated to a certain extent in the construction of the poverty myth which her American fundraiser needed.[46] Both Pierre's biography and her autobiography were written in this vein. In both texts, complaints about the lack of financial support for scientific research were aired in a personal mode. Asceticism had become a professional strategy. Pictures of the *hangar* could be instrumentalised for this mission.[47]

The conditions for Marie Curie's scientific work had of course dramatically changed since her years in the *hangar*. In the years after Pierre's death, she succeeded in expanding the laboratory staff considerably. The university soon financed the construction of a new laboratory according to her needs

Figure 8.4 Marie Curie and Warren G. Harding, 1921. © History of Science Collections, University of Oklahoma Libraries, Oklahoma, USA.

and specifications. It formed part of a broader Radium Institute, where the medical applications of radioactivity were studied as well. After the First World War Marie expanded her laboratory further. The presence there of many women as well as foreigners was striking. As laboratory director, life was extremely busy and many of Marie's tasks had hardly any links with scientific research. Time had to be devoted, for instance, to trying to convince the inspector of the Paris Academy of the need for repairs to the broken heating, to negotiating university regulations on the admission of cars to the site of the Radium Institute, or to supporting her chauffeur's application for social housing.[48] If some people described the atmosphere of Curie's laboratory as that of a religious convent, this probably testifies in the first place to the attractiveness of nineteenth-century sacralised conceptions of science.[49] Marie Curie herself was busy travelling around the world and actively participating in the Commission on Intellectual Co-operation of the League of Nations. As the vice-president of this commission, she worked on the development of guidelines for international scholarships in science. In the texts she wrote in this context, the laboratory was no longer a place of solitary refuge, but a busy centre where an efficient division of labour had to reign in order to be able to live up to the needs of increasing specialisation. Asceticism was not at stake, but fair pay for young researchers was. The rhetoric used to support these actions could still refer to older notions of science. The protection of scientific vocations was a sacred duty for every society, Curie stated in a memorandum.[50] In her daily life, however, the scientist had become an administrator and an expert rather than a unworldly seeker of sacred knowledge.

This last image retained some of its popularity. Four years after Marie's death, George Sarton recommended the biographies of the Curies by saying that 'their lives should be read in the same spirit as people read the lives of the saints'.[51] From a commercial viewpoint, however, too much asceticism was dull, especially when a woman was involved. The successful 1943 Hollywood film *Madame Curie*, starring Greer Garson, was less a story about asceticism than a chaste (and thoroughly gendered) love story. It was not a domestic quarrel about Marie's presence in the laboratory which preceded Pierre's tragic accident in the film, but the purchase of a beautiful pair of earrings for Marie. This utterly un-ascetic message did not prevent a contemporary critic from reading the film as 'the revelation of a modern saint'.[52] Modern Western culture remained under the spell of scientific asceticism, albeit seeing it as a primarily male feature.

Notes

1. George Sarton to Irénée van der Ghinst, 16 December 1906 – Royal Library, Brussels (RL/B), MS III 786.3. On this correspondence, see H. Elkhadem, 'George Sarton: ses années de formation et ses réalisations académiques à travers sa correspondance avec Irénée van der Ghinst', *Mededelingen van de Koninklijke Academie voor Wetenschappen, Letteren en Schone Kunsten van België. Klasse der Wetenschappen* 47 (1985), 103–25.

2. E. Garfield, 'The Life and Career of George Sarton: The Father of the History of Science', *Journal of the History of the Behavioral Sciences* 21 (1985), 107–17. On Sarton's scholarly passions, see L. Pyenson, *The Passion of George Sarton: A Modern Marriage and Its Discipline* (Philadelphia, 2007).

3. Ibid., 115.

4. G. Sarton, 'Review of Eve Curie, *Madame Curie*; Marie Curie, *Pierre Curie*; Claudius Regaud, *Marie Skłodowska-Curie*', *Isis* 28 (1938), 481, 484.

5. S. Shapin, 'The Philosopher and the Chicken: On the Dietetics of Disembodied Knowledge', in C. Lawrence and S. Shapin, *Science Incarnate. Historical Embodiments of Natural Knowledge* (Chicago, 1998), 21–50.

6. R.K. Merton, *Science, Technology and Society in Seventeenth-Century England* (New York, 1970)[1938], 55–79.

7. D.A. Hollinger, 'Inquiry and Uplift: Late Nineteenth-Century American Academics and the Moral Efficacy of Scientific Practice', in T.L. Haskell (ed.), *The Authority of Experts: Studies in History and Theory* (Bloomington, 1984), 142–56.

8. R.M. Herzig, *Suffering for Science: Reason and Sacrifice in Modern America* (New Brunswick, 2005), 17–46. On the ideal of science as a vocation, familiar to a priestly vocation (and on its disappearance in the twentieth century), see also Steven Shapin, *The Scientific Life: A Moral History of a Late Modern Vocation* (Chicago, 2008), 21–46.

9. C.B. Paul, *Science and Immortality: The Eloges of the Paris Academy of Sciences (1699–1791)* (Berkeley, 1980), 1–12, 99–109.

10. L. Schiebinger, *The Mind Has No Sex? Women in the Origins of Modern Science* (Cambridge, 1989), 150–59, 237–41.

11. L. Jordanova, 'Science and Nationhood: Cultures of Imagined Communities', in G. Cubitt (ed.), *Imagining Nations* (Manchester, 1998), 192–211.

12. The best biography of Marie Curie is S. Quinn, *Marie Curie: A Life* (New York, 1995). See also more recent works: B. Goldsmith, *Obsessive Genius: The Inner World of Marie Curie* (New York and London, 2005); M.B. Ogilvie, *Marie Curie: A Biography* (Westport, 2004); G. Noordenbos, *Marie & Irène Curie. De eerste vrouwelijke Nobelprijswinnaars* (Delft, 2003).

13. Quinn, *Marie Curie*, 277–331.

14. M. Curie, *Pierre Curie: With the Autobiographical Notes of Marie Curie*, trans. C. Kellogg and V. Kellogg (New York, 1963), hereafter Curie, *Autobiographical Notes*; M. Curie, *Pierre Curie: Avec une étude des 'Carnets de laboratoire' par Irène Joliot-Curie* (Paris, 1955), hereafter Curie, *Pierre Curie*.

15. E. Curie, *Madame Curie* (Paris, 1938).

16. Curie, *Pierre Curie*, 65, 84; Curie, *Autobiographical Notes*, 92 (quotation).

17. *Le Matin*, 20 December 1903, quoted in Quinn, *Marie Curie*, 195.

18. Diary 30 April 1906, Archives Marie Curie, Bibliothèque Nationale, Paris (MC/BN/P), Nouvelles Acquisitions Françaises, no. 18517.

19. Curie, *Pierre Curie*, 96; Quinn, *Marie Curie*, 82.

20. C. Bernard, *Introduction à l'étude de la médecine expérimentale*, ed. L. Binet (Paris, 1966), 237.

21. Curie, *Pierre Curie*, 67.

22. S. Shapin, 'The House of Experiment in Seventeenth-century England', *Isis* 79 (1988), 373–404; D.N. Livingstone, *Putting Science in its Place. Geographies of Scientific Knowledge* (Chicago, 2003), 21–29.

23. G. Weisz, 'The Self-Made Mandarin: The *Eloges* of the French Academy of Medicine, 1824–1847', *History of Science* 26 (1988), 27.

24. S. Schaffer, 'Making Space for Science: Physics Laboratories and the Victorian Country House', in C. Smith and J. Agar (eds), *Making Space for Science: Territorial Themes in the Shaping of Knowledge* (Basingstoke, 1998), 173–80.

25. Marie Curie to Marie Mattingly Meloney, 9 March 1921 – MC/BN/P, Nouvelles Acquisitions Françaises, no. 18457.

26. O. Sonntag, 'The Motivations of the Scientist: The Self-image of Albrecht von Haller', *Isis* 64 (1974), 346.

27. On the theological critique of the new experimental philosophy as reflecting enthusiasm and fanaticism, see M. Heyd, *'Be Sober and Reasonable': The Critique of Enthusiasm in the Seventeenth and Early Eighteenth Centuries* (Leiden, 1995), 144–64.

28. Curie, *Autobiographical notes*, 90.

29. Quinn, *Marie Curie*, 416.

30. Herzig, *Suffering for Science*, 85–99.

31. Quinn, *Marie Curie*, 106.

32. Curie, *Autobiographical Notes*, 87.

33. Marie to Irène Curie, 19 July 1922, in Z. Ziegler (ed.), *Marie et Irène Curie: Correspondance. Choix de lettres (1905–1934)* (Paris, 1974), 233.

34. Shapin, 'The Philosopher and the Chicken', 44; Marie Curie to Marie Mattingly Meloney, 15 December 1921 and Cahier de Dépense 1913 – MC/BN/P, Nouvelles Acquisitions Françaises, no. 18457 and 18496.

35. I.F. Silber, 'Monasticism and the "Protestant Ethic": Asceticism, Rationality and Wealth in the Medieval West', *British Journal of Sociology* 44 (1993), 110–11.

36. See, e.g., A. Beaunier, 'Pierre Curie', *Eloges*, (Paris, 1909), 119, quoted in E. Gubin, 'Marie Curie et le radium: l'information et la légende en Belgique', in *Marie Skłodowska Curie et la Belgique* (Brussels, 1990), 123.

37. On the reciprocal character of this collaboration, see H.M. Pycior, 'Marie Curie's "Anti-natural Path": Time only for Science and Family', in P.G. Abir-Am and D. Outram (eds), *Uneasy Careers and Intimate Lives. Women in Science, 1789–1979* (New Brunswick, 1987), 191–214; H.M. Pycior, 'Pierre Curie and "His Eminent Collaborator Mme Curie": Complementary Partners', in H.M. Pycior, N.G. Slack and P.G. Abir-Am, *Creative Couples in the Sciences* (New

Brunswick, 1996), 39–56; L. Barbo, *Pierre Curie 1859–1906: Le rêve scientifique* (Paris, 1999), 171–98.

38. Quinn, *Marie Curie*, 235.

39. Curie, *Madame Curie*, 134, 135, 145, 188.

40. Pierre Curie to Georges Gouy, 22 January 1904 and 7 November 1905 – MC/BN/P, Nouvelles Acquisitions Françaises, no. 18515.

41. See, e.g., R. Putnam (ed.), *Life and Letters of Mary Putnam Jacobi* (New York and London, 1925), 69, 127, 134, 144, 166, 182.

42. Quinn, *Marie Curie*, 250.

43. L. Jordanova, *Defining Features: Scientific and Medical Portraits 1660–2000* (London, 2000), 108–15.

44. P.O. Enquist, *Blanche en Marie,* trans. C. Polet (Amsterdam, 2005), 191, 222.

45. E. Curie, *Madame Curie*, 259.

46. Quinn, *Marie Curie*, 386–87.

47. See, e.g., Conference Notes Chicago June 1921 – MC/BN/P, Nouvelles Acquisitions Françaises, no. 18394.

48. Letters by Marie Curie 25 May 1918, 9 June 1931, 6 January 1933, 27 June 1933 – Archives du Laboratoire Curie de l'Institut du Radium, Musée Curie, Paris (LC/MC/P), I, no. 2229, 1782, 2018, 2441.

49. Quinn, *Marie Curie*, 405.

50. Mémorandum de Mme Curie, membre de la Commission sur la Question des Bourses Internationales, pour l'Avancement des Sciences et le Développement des Laboratoires, Geneva, 16 June 1926 – MC/BN/P, Nouvelles Acquisitions Françaises, no. 18441.

51. Sarton, 'Review', 484.

52. T.H. Crawford, 'Glowing Dishes: Radium, Marie Curie, and Hollywood', *Biography* 23 (2000), 71–84; A. Elena, 'Skirts in the Lab: *Madame Curie* and the Image of the Woman Scientist in the Feature Film', *Public Understanding of Science* 6, 1997, 269–78 (quotation 275).

References

Published Sources

Barbo, L. 1999. *Pierre Curie 1859–1906: Le rêve scientifique*, Paris.

Bernard, C. 1966[1856]. *Introduction à l'étude de la médecine expérimentale*, ed. L. Binet, Paris.

Crawford, T.H. 2000. 'Glowing Dishes: Radium, Marie Curie, and Hollywood', *Biography* 23: 71–84.

Curie, E. 1938[1937]. *Madame Curie*, Paris.

Curie, M. 1955[1923]. *Pierre Curie: Avec une étude des 'Carnets de laboratoire' par Irène Joliot-Curie*, Paris.

——— 1963[1923]. *Pierre Curie: With the Autobiographical Notes of Marie Curie*, trans. C. Kellogg and V. Kellogg, New York.

Elena, A. 1997. 'Skirts in the Lab: *Madame Curie* and the Image of the Woman Scientist in the Feature Film', *Public Understanding of Science* 6: 269–78.

Elkhadem, H. 1985. 'George Sarton: ses années de formation et ses réalisations académiques à travers sa correspondance avec Irénée van der Ghinst', *Mededelingen van de Koninklijke Academie voor Wetenschappen, Letteren en Schone Kunsten van België. Klasse der Wetenschappen* 47: 103–25.

Enquist, P.O. 2005. *Blanche en Marie*, trans. C. Polet, Amsterdam.

Garfield, E. 1985. 'The Life and Career of George Sarton: The Father of the History of Science', *Journal of the History of the Behavioral Sciences* 21: 107–17.

Goldsmith, B. 2005. *Obsessive Genius: The Inner World of Marie Curie*, New York and London.

Gubin, E. 1990. 'Marie Curie et le radium: l'information et la légende en Belgique', in *Marie Skłodowska Curie et la Belgique*, Brussels, pp.111–29.

Herzig, R.M. 2005. *Suffering for Science: Reason and Sacrifice in Modern America*, New Brunswick.

Heyd, M. 1995. *'Be Sober and Reasonable': The Critique of Enthusiasm in the Seventeenth and Early Eighteenth Centuries*, Leiden.

Hollinger, D.A. 1984. 'Inquiry and Uplift: Late Nineteenth-Century American Academics and the Moral Efficacy of Scientific Practice', in T.L. Haskell (ed.), *The Authority of Experts: Studies in History and Theory*, Bloomington, pp.142–56.

Jordanova, L. 1998. 'Science and Nationhood: Cultures of Imagined Communities', in G. Cubitt (ed.), *Imagining Nations*, Manchester, pp.192–211.

——— 2000. *Defining Features: Scientific and Medical Portraits 1660–2000*, London.

Livingstone, D.N. 2003. *Putting Science in its Place: Geographies of Scientific Knowledge*, Chicago.

Merton, R.K. 1970. *Science, Technology and Society in Seventeenth-century England*, New York.

Noordenbos, G. 2003. *Marie & Irène Curie: De eerste vrouwelijke Nobelprijswinnaars*, Delft.

Ogilvie, M.B. 2004. *Marie Curie: A Biography*, Westport.

Paul, C.B. 1980. *Science and Immortality: The Eloges of the Paris Academy of Sciences (1699–1791)*, Berkeley.

Putnam, R. (ed.) 1925. *Life and Letters of Mary Putnam Jacobi*, New York and London.

Pycior, H.M. 1987. 'Marie Curie's "Anti-natural Path": Time only for Science and Family', in P.G. Abir-Am and D. Outram (eds), *Uneasy Careers and Intimate Lives: Women in Science, 1789–1979*, New Brunswick, pp.191–214.

——— 1996. 'Pierre Curie and "His Eminent Collaborator Mme Curie": Complementary Partners', in H.M. Pycior, N.G. Slack and P.G. Abir-Am, *Creative Couples in the Sciences*, New Brunswick, pp.39–56.

Pyenson, L. 2007. *The Passion of George Sarton: A Modern Marriage and Its Discipline*, Philadelphia.

Quinn, S. 1995. *Marie Curie: A Life*, New York.

Sarton, G. 1938. 'Review of Eve Curie, *Madame Curie*; Marie Curie, *Pierre Curie*; Claudius Regaud, *Marie Skłodowska-Curie*', *Isis* 28: 480–84.

Schaffer, S. 1998. 'Making Space for Science: Physics Laboratories and the Victorian Country House', in C. Smith and J. Agar (eds), *Making Space for Science: Territorial Themes in the Shaping of Knowledge*, Basingstoke, pp.173–80.

Schiebinger, L. 1989. *The Mind Has No Sex? Women in the Origins of Modern Science*, Cambridge.

Shapin, S. 1988. 'The House of Experiment in Seventeenth-century England', *Isis* 79: 373–404.

———— 1998. 'The Philosopher and the Chicken: On the Dietetics of Disembodied Knowledge', in C. Lawrence and S. Shapin, *Science Incarnate: Historical Embodiments of Natural Knowledge*, Chicago, pp.21–50.

———— 2008. *The Scientific Life: A Moral History of a Late Modern Vocation*, Chicago.

Silber, I.F. 1993. 'Monasticism and the "Protestant Ethic": Asceticism, Rationality and Wealth in the Medieval West', *British Journal of Sociology* 44: 103–23.

Sonntag, O. 1974. 'The Motivations of the Scientist: The Self-image of Albrecht von Haller', *Isis* 64: 336-351.

Weisz, G. 1988. 'The Self-made Mandarin: The *Eloges* of the French Academy of Medicine, 1824–1847', *History of Science* 26: 13–40.

Ziegler, Z. (ed.) 1974. *Marie et Irène Curie: Correspondance. Choix de lettres (1905–1934)*, Paris.

Archives

LC/MC/P – Archives du Laboratoire Curie de l'Institut du Radium, Musée Curie, Paris.

MC/BN/P – Archives Marie Curie, Bibliothèque Nationale, Paris

RL/B – Royal Library, Brussels.

9

Ludwig Wittgenstein, the *Tractatus* and the Linguistic Turn in Modern Asceticism

Klaas van Berkel

'Whereof one cannot speak, thereof one must be silent'.[1] With this sentence the Austrian philosopher Ludwig Wittgenstein concluded his provocative *Tractatus Logico-Philosophicus* (1922), and this proposition has become perhaps the most quoted statement in the history of modern philosophy.[2] First of all, one should abstain from making 'positive' remarks about metaphysics and ethics since propositions of this nature always contain elements that have no reference to the facts and are therefore in a technical sense senseless. Even to demonstrate that metaphysics is senseless would result in nonsense. Thus, even though the *Tractatus* was meant to demonstrate the utter untenability of metaphysics, in the end the book itself must also be recognised as being strictly 'senseless' (*unsinnig* in German). The propositions it contains should be abandoned as soon as their true character has been revealed. The reader, in Wittgenstein's no less famous comparison, must throw away the ladder after they have climbed up it.[3] They must surmount the propositions in the book and then they will see the world correctly.[4] What remains is silence.

Hundreds of books and thousands of articles have been devoted to the famous and curiously self-defeating point of view taken by Wittgenstein in the concluding propositions of his *Tractatus*. Although the book was meant to put an end to all philosophical discussion, in fact it initiated a new spate of philosophical comments, elucidations, criticisms and defences of metaphysics. In this chapter, however, it is not my intention to add another interpretation to the growing number of philosophical commentaries on the *Tractatus* and its much-quoted final sentence. Being a cultural historian and not a philosopher, I am more interested in a cultural interpretation of Wittgenstein's urgent call to refrain from further debating philosophical questions.

Many scholars have come forward with such a cultural interpretation, highlighting the way in which Wittgenstein's effort to determine the limits of language and thought relates to his criticism of modern culture.[5] However, this has hardly ever resulted in Wittgenstein's philosophy being interpreted as part of the ascetic movement that was on the rise in Europe at the turn of the twentieth century.[6] The fact that Wittgenstein's final sentence in the *Tractatus* is often paraphrased in terms of 'refraining from' and 'abstaining from' strongly suggests that it is indeed possible to get a deeper understanding of Wittgenstein's place in the history of modern culture by interpreting his philosophy as the expression of an ascetic who wanted to make a point by keeping silent. By doing so, by writing the *Tractatus* Wittgenstein added a completely new dimension to the history of modern asceticism.

I will therefore not be dealing with the question of whether Wittgenstein was right in stating that metaphysics is nonsense. Nor will I be discussing the question of whether his philosophy of language – even though he dismissed it himself some years later – still has any value for us today. Instead, I will discuss the way in which the *Tractatus* was an expression of asceticism, a philosophical or more precisely a linguistic form of asceticism that had not been expressed before.

A Wonderful Life

Nothing in his family background indicated that Ludwig Wittgenstein would ever be associated with asceticism.[7] Ludwig Wittgenstein, who was born in Vienna on 26 April 1889, was the youngest son of a wealthy engineer and industrialist, Karl Wittgenstein, one of the richest men in Austria. In 1898, having accumulated a fortune, Karl retired from business, resigning from the boards of the steel companies he presided over and transferring all of his securities into foreign equities. (It later turned out that by doing so Wittgenstein *père* protected his family fortune from the rampant inflation that would hit Austria after the First World War.)

Mainly though Karl's wife Leopoldine, née Kalmus, who was extremely musical, the Wittgenstein house became one of the cultural centres in the capital of the Austro-Hungarian Empire. Composers Johannes Brahms and Gustav Mahler were regular visitors, and later Maurice Ravel and Richard Strauss were among those who wrote one-handed piano concertos for Ludwig's brother Paul, a concert pianist who lost an arm during the First World War.

Young Ludwig was educated at home and afterwards, from 1903 to 1906, attended a provincial *Realschule* in Linz, where his exact contemporary Adolf Hitler had become a pupil a few years earlier. He was less musical than some of his sisters and brothers, but his mechanical skills were out of the ordinary. In addition, at a very young age, he was very interested in moral and religious issues (Wittgenstein was raised as a Roman Catholic, but already at an early age had distanced himself from any official religion).

After leaving Linz, Wittgenstein went to Berlin, where he studied at the Technische Hochschule in Charlottenburg from 1906 to 1908. From there, he went to Manchester University to study aeronautical engineering until 1911. Yet, instead of becoming an engineer, he became more and more intrigued with mathematics and particularly with the philosophical foundations of mathematics. Stimulated by reading Gottlob Frege's *Grundgesetze der Mathematik* (1893–1903) and Bertrand Russell's *Principles of Mathematics* (1903), he decided to leave Manchester and go to Cambridge to attend Russell's lectures. The British philosopher did not know what to make of his new student. 'My German engineer, I think he is a fool. He thinks nothing empirical is knowable – I asked him to admit that there was not a rhinoceros in the room, but he wouldn't', Russell wrote to his mistress, Lady Ottoline Morrell. And somewhat later:

> My German is hesitating between philosophy and aviation; he asked me today whether I thought he was utterly hopeless at philosophy, and I told him I didn't know but I thought not. I asked him to bring me something written to help me to judge. He has money, and is quite passionately interested in philosophy, but he feels he ought not to give his life to it unless he is some good.[8]

In the end, Russell came to like him and introduced him to other philosophers in Cambridge. Nevertheless, Wittgenstein did not like the intellectual atmosphere at the university and instead preferred remote, rural places. With a friend, David Pinsent, he visited Iceland in 1912 and Norway in 1913. He came back from Norway with the idea of moving there permanently 'to live', as Pinsent recorded him saying, 'entirely alone and by himself – a hermit's life – and do nothing but work in Logic'.[9] He thought that a place like that would be more suited to him than Cambridge, where all kinds of interruptions and distractions were a constant hindrance. Russell tells what happened then:

> Then my Austrian, Wittgenstein, burst in like a whirlwind, just back from Norway, and determined to return there at once to live in complete solitude until he has solved *all* the problems of logic. I said it would be dark, and he said he hated daylight. I said it would be lonely, and he said he prostituted his mind talking to intelligent people. I said he was mad, and he said God preserve him from sanity.[10]

So Wittgenstein went to Norway, first staying in the village of Skjolden, by the side of the Sognefjord north of Bergen, and later on, in the spring of 1914, building himself a little house or hut outside the village. Here, in the seclusion (*in der Einsamkeit*) of his cabin, he intended to finish the book that was eventually to become the *Tractatus*.[11]

When war broke out in August 1914, Wittgenstein was at home in Vienna. As a volunteer he enlisted in the Austrian army, despite being exempt from service because of a double rupture. He served on the Vistula River as a mechanic, went to Olmütz in Moravia for officer training, and again ended up at the Eastern front in 1916. In those years he read – among others – Tolstoy, Dostoevsky and Nietzsche, and friends noticed how deeply interested he had become in religious issues – even though he confessed to not believing in God.

In the spring of 1918 Wittgenstein was transferred to the Tyrol section of the southern front, where he was decorated for bravery (he sought out particularly dangerous places, partly in order to test his fearlessness). When the front collapsed in October, most of the soldiers and officers, including Wittgenstein, were taken prisoner by the Italians. He was sent to a prisoner-of-war camp in Monte Cassino, where he stayed until August 1919.

On his release, Wittgenstein had become a different man, changed for good by the war. The experience of the war had almost given him a new identity. His attitude to possessions and his way of life, which had already been strange before the war, became very eccentric.

On the death of his father in 1913 Wittgenstein inherited a substantial fortune and lived the life of a millionaire's son. When he and Pinsent had travelled to Iceland and Norway – first class, of course – Wittgenstein paid all his friend's expenses, and whereas Pinsent brought with him only one suitcase, Wittgenstein came to the station with no fewer than three. On another occasion, so it is reported, when he wanted to go to Liverpool and was told that there were no trains scheduled, he promptly set about trying to hire a private train, which was still possible in those days, provided you had enough money. He did not succeed, and so he hired a taxi to take him to where he wanted to go. Wittgenstein also seems to have been rather scrupulous in his choice of ties.

After the war all this changed. Within a month of his return from Italy, he gave all of his inheritance to his only surviving brother, Paul, and two of his sisters, reasoning that since they were already rich, more money would not spoil them. He also moved out of the large family house and took lodging elsewhere in Vienna. From then on he lived a life of complete simplicity, rarely if ever wearing ties again (even when going to the opera).[12]

The reasons for this change of personal outlook have puzzled biographers. Some relate this drastic change to Wittgenstein's reading of Tolstoy's *The Gospels in Brief* (1883). At the beginning of the war, while stationed in Galicia, he laid hands on Tolstoy's book and was profoundly moved by it. He read it over and over again and carried it with him wherever he went. His comrades used to call him 'the man with the gospels'. Tolstoy's selfless spirituality made a deep and lasting impression on him and caused in him something like a religious conversion.

Another possible explanation for his change of lifestyle is that the austerity and simplicity of army life simply proved congenial to him. Of course, before the war Wittgenstein had already manifested a predilection for the simple life, as for instance testified by his plans to move permanently to Norway. His experiences in the army may have simply reinforced this inclination. In any case, Wittgenstein's letters and recorded conversations show that he was now much concerned with his own sinfulness, even to the point of spiritual self-mortification.[13]

Throughout the war, Wittgenstein had been working on his *Tractatus*, which he finished while on leave in August 1918, shortly before returning to the front. According to Wittgenstein, this work provided the answer to all philosophical problems, but it was not easy to find a publisher willing to print the book, even with the help of Russell. Several publishers turned it down, until it was at last published in German in the final issue of Wilhelm Ostwald's journal *Annalen der Naturphilosophie* in 1921, with a poorly translated introduction by Russell and with many typographical and editorial errors. The following year, Wittgenstein's friends in Cambridge were finally able to persuade a London publisher to publish a parallel German/English edition, entitled *Tractatus Logico-Philosophicus* (the Latin title, quite erroneously alluding to Spinoza, was suggested by the philosopher G.E. Moore). F.P. Ramsay and C.K. Ogden translated the book, and Russell again provided an introduction.[14]

By the time the book was published, Wittgenstein and Russell had, however, parted ways. Before the war, the initial friendship had already lost some of its intensity, but when Wittgenstein and Russell met again after the war, they realised how far they had grown apart. The war had made Russell a socialist and had convinced him of the urgent need to change the way the world was governed. He subordinated questions of personal morality to the overriding public concern of making the world a safer place. To Wittgenstein, however, personal morality was all that mattered. When Wittgenstein and Russell met again in The Hague in December 1919, Russell was shocked by the mystical and religious tendencies he saw in Wittgenstein: 'I had felt in his book a flavour of mysticism, but was astonished when I found that he has become a complete mystic. He reads people like Kierkegaard and Angelus Silesius and he seriously contemplates becoming a monk'.[15] Now that he had solved all problems in philosophy and had shown – or so he believed – there was nothing more to say, Wittgenstein wanted to withdraw from academia and start a new life.

The reference to Kierkegaard and especially to Angelus Silesius is a very interesting one, of which not many authors have taken notice. Yet, as Max Black indicated in his *Companion to Wittgenstein's 'Tractatus'* (1964), there are some interesting parallels between the final sentences of the *Tractatus* and some of the epigrams of the seventeenth-century German mystic who called himself Angelus Silesius.[16] In fact, his real name was Johannes Scheffler, the son of a Polish nobleman, who, because of his Lutheran confession, had moved to Breslau (currently Wroclaw) in Silesia. Scheffler was born in Breslau in 1624, and studied medicine in Germany, the Netherlands and Italy before settling as a medical doctor in his native country.

During his studies at Leiden University he had already become a mystic and a follower of Jacob Böhme. After his return to Silesia he converted to Roman Catholicism, adopted the name Angelus Silesius as a nom de plume, and became a prolific writer against the Protestants, though he remained faithful to the mysticism of the Protestant authors whose works he had studied during his journeys abroad. His most famous work is the *Cherubinischer Wandersmann* (1657), which is not a straightforward apologetic text but a collection of mystic and pietistic epigrams. It first appeared in Vienna and a second edition was published in 1675, two years before his death.[17] It is not known when and where Wittgenstein got to know the book, but the parallels are indeed remarkable. In the *Cherubinischer Wandersmann* Silesius extols the virtue of silence: *Schweig, Allerliebster, schweig: kannst du nur gänzlich schwei- gen, / So wird dir Gott mehr Gut's, als du begehrst, erzeigen* (Be silent, most beloved, be silent: if you are able to be completely silent, / God will show you more good things than you desire).

The similarities are particularly striking in another epigram, entitled *Mit Schweigen wirds gesprochen* ('With silence it is said'), in which Silesius counsels those who wish to talk about things that are beyond the grasp of man to first refrain from talking: *Mensch, so du willst das Sein der Ewigkeit aussprechen, / So musst du dich zuvor des Redens ganz entbrechen* (Friend, if you want to express the Being of eternity, / You must first completely refrain from talking). It is tempting to think that Wittgenstein knew about these epigrams and imitated them in some way in his *Tractatus,* especially in its conclusion. However, as mentioned above, there are no indications as to where and under what cir- cumstances Wittgenstein read Silesius. So any definite statement about the connection between the asceticism of Wittgenstein's *Tractatus* and the mysti- cism of the *Cherubinischer Wandersmann* would be pure speculation.[18]

To return to Wittgenstein's life, he indeed took some steps to become a monk after his conversation with Russell, but nothing came of it and in the end he decided on a different, though in a sense, related calling: that of a primary school teacher. After a one-year course in primary school teaching in Vienna, he graduated in 1920 and became a schoolteacher in the tiny village of Trattenbach, in the mountains near Semmering (Lower Austria). Although Wittgenstein was a very energetic schoolteacher, the parents and their children did not like the lonesome man with his quaint habits and he therefore regularly moved village schools. In one of these villages he was visited by Ramsay (one of the translators of the *Tractatus*), whose description of the circumstances under which Wittgenstein lived was not meant to be very positive: 'He is very poor, at least he lives very economically. He has one *tiny* room whitewashed, containing a bed, washstand, small table and one hard chair and that is all there is room for. His evening meal which I shared last night is rather unpleasant coarse bread, butter and cocoa'.[19] In 1926, however, Wittgenstein struck a boy in his class two or three times and the boy collapsed. Wittgenstein was accused of using undue force, and although acquitted of misconduct he decided to quit his job and go back to Vienna, deeply depressed. He then took a job as a gardener at a monastery outside the Austrian capital and again contemplated becoming a monk (as he had on his release from the camp in Monte Cassino).

Wittgenstein was saved from total despair by becoming involved in the design and construction of a house for one of his sisters, Margarethe, or Gretl. Paul Engelmann was the official architect, but Wittgenstein left his mark on the mansion. Every detail of the house received his painstaking attention: radiators, for instance, had to be exactly positioned in order not to disturb the symmetry of the rooms. Some Wittgenstein scholars have compared the beauty of this unornamented house (influenced by the modern style of Adolf Loos) to the logical beauty of the *Tractatus*. And indeed, in some of his notes on *Culture and Value*, Wittgenstein compared architecture and the philosophy of language: good architecture expresses a thought and is a type of language.[20]

While working on his sister's house, Wittgenstein slowly resumed contact with the academic world. Margarethe introduced him to the Vienna philosopher Moritz Schlick, one of the founders of the Vienna Circle, a group of philosophers who were very much enthralled by Wittgenstein's *Tractatus*.

Inspired by contacts like these, Wittgenstein returned to philosophy, realising that the *Tractatus* had not solved all problems in philosophy after all. He returned to Cambridge in 1929, where he submitted the *Tractatus* for his Ph.D. examination. At the same time, however, he set about working on a completely different kind of philosophy of language, that of ordinary language, which culminated in the posthumous publication of *Philosophical Investigations* (1953), following his death on 29 April 1951 from cancer. While at Cambridge Wittgenstein became a British citizen and remained connected to the university for the rest of his life. To one of his friends who visited him on his deathbed, and who announced the arrival of some other friends, Wittgenstein said: 'Tell them that I've had a wonderful life'.

The Repertoire of Asceticism

As a philosopher who lived the life of an ascetic, Wittgenstein was not unique. One immediately thinks of the Greek philosopher Diogenes the Cynic, who lived in Athens in the fourth century BC. Many stories are told about the strange behaviour of Diogenes and from these one can safely conclude that he was indeed an ascetic. Most of these stories have come down to us in the *Lives of Eminent Philosophers* by Diogenes Laertius (third century BC).[21] Diogenes Laertius tells us, for example, how Diogenes the Cynic searched Athens with a lighted lamp in broad daylight, looking, as he said to those who questioned him, for a good man. Another story illustrates his complete disregard for the powerful. When Alexander the Great visited Diogenes and offered him anything he wanted, the philosopher answered that he wished only that Alexander would step aside in order not to block the sun. The best-known story about Diogenes is, of course, that he lived in a tube.

Notwithstanding these stories about his eccentricity, Diogenes was a serious philosopher. As a disciple of the philosopher Antisthenes, who taught that only virtue brought happiness, Diogenes exceeded his master in his contempt for possessions, the conveniences of ordinary life, and everything that might hinder the pursuit of happiness. His mission was to call people back to a simple, more natural way of life, which meant for him a life of poverty, sleeping in public buildings and begging for food.

He advocated self-sufficiency, or the ability to find in oneself all that one needs for happiness. He also practised 'shamelessness', which implied the disregard for those conventions curbing human freedom. Therefore, he despised marriage and had nothing but contempt for those who professed to be loyal to their city. Finally, he taught that moral excellence could be obtained by methodical training or asceticism. After having told numerous stories about Diogenes the Cynic, Diogenes Laertius formulated what in his view was the gist of the Athenian philosopher's teaching:

> Nothing in life, he maintained, has any chance of succeeding without strenuous practice (*askèsis*); and this is capable of overcoming anything. Accordingly, instead of useless toils men should choose such as nature recommends, whereby they might have lived happily. Yet such is their madness that they choose to be miserable. For even the despising of pleasure is itself most pleasurable, when we are habituated to it; and just as those accustomed to a life of pleasure feel disgust when they pass over to the opposite experience, so those whose training has been of the opposite kind derive more pleasure from despising pleasure than from the pleasures themselves.[22]

The resemblance between Diogenes the Cynic and Wittgenstein is obvious. Although spending some time in a hut is not as demanding as living in a tube, and giving away your inheritance is not the same as giving away your drinking bowl, both philosophers seem to have thought that dispensing with bodily comforts and unnecessary possessions was beneficial to philosophical thinking. But does this make Wittgenstein an ascetic? Or was he just an eccentric who for a while behaved like an ascetic? After all, as a student of Russell, Wittgenstein did not act like any of the other students. 'My German friend threatens to be an infliction', Russell wrote to Lady Ottoline Morrell, his lover, 'he came back with me after my lecture and argued till dinnertime obstinate and perverse, but I think not stupid'.[23]

On a November day in 1912, immediately after having watched a boat race with Russell and some fellow students, Wittgensstein 'suddenly stood still and explained that the way we had spent the afternoon was so vile that we ought not to live, or at least he ought not, that nothing is tolerable except producing great works or enjoying those of others, that he has accomplished nothing and never will, etc. – all this with a force that really knocks one down'. Added to this is the story already mentioned of Wittgenstein's intention to hire a private train to get to Liverpool. Would it not be possible to classify Wittgenstein as a lifelong eccentric who during a restricted period of his life chose asceticism to express his eccentric state of mind?

What, after all, is asceticism? Asceticism can be defined as, 'a voluntary, sustained, and at least partially systematic program of self-discipline and self-denial in which immediate, sensual, or profane gratifications are renounced in order to attain a higher spiritual state or a more thorough absorption in the sacred'.[24] Some may find this definition to be too strict. Others might argue that it excludes all kinds of practices in non-Western societies which we are inclined to call ascetic, but which strictly speaking are not because they are not voluntary. For example, in preparation for ritual activities of a particular sacred nature – such as initiation, marriage, or sacrifice – participants rid themselves of impurity by engaging in often austere acts of self-denial. But practices like sexual continence or fasting that go with these initiation rituals are voluntary ordeals and they are strictly temporary, usually lasting for days or weeks, not years.

On the other hand, the above definition is fairly adequate for the Middle Ages and the modern period. Hermits in the days of the early Church, monks in medieval monasteries, and self-proclaimed saints like Ignatius of Loyola or Theresa of Sevilla fit the picture of people who on a voluntary basis and for a long period of time carried out a programme of self-discipline and self-denial.

The varieties of asceticism are endless. They fall into two categories: negative asceticism, the self-denial of bodily or mental pleasures or at least abandoning the comforts of normal life; and positive asceticism, the infliction of pain or the introduction of a strict discipline that is conducive to a higher state of mind.

Sexual continence and celibacy have also been commonplace in almost all ascetic movements: sexuality was seen as one of the strongest forces of corruption, so to deny oneself the pleasures of the flesh was therefore regarded as an essential step towards reaching a higher goal. One of the reasons that Christian ascetics left the cities, opting instead for a hermit's life in the desert, was to avoid stimulating their sexual appetite in the cities – a decision that could not protect them from being constantly occupied and threatened by 'demons' in the guise of beautiful and lustful women.

Abdication of worldly goods is another fundamental principle of the ascetic way of life. In order to follow Christ, who was portrayed as an ascetic himself, monks were supposed to live a life of sometimes extreme poverty. In Christian monasticism this ideal was enacted in its most drastic form by Alexander Akoimetos, who died in Mesopotamia around AD 430. Centuries before St Francis of Assisi, Alexander betrothed himself to poverty and through his disciples expanded his influence in Eastern Christian communities. These monks lived from alms, taking no more than they strictly needed.

Abstaining from certain types of food or fasting in general is also very common. Almost all religious movements have prescribed fasting or related practices. Jews are not allowed to eat pork; Roman Catholics (and some Protestants) fast during a period of forty days before Easter, while for Muslims the most important period of fasting is the Ramadan. These ordinary fasting cycles, however, did not satisfy the needs of the ascetics, who therefore created their own traditions. In the early Church, the Manichaean monks, in particular, won general admiration for the intensity of their fasting achievements. Christian authors write about their ruthless and unrelenting fasting, in which only some Syrian monks could offer them any competition. These Syrian ascetic virtuosi even tried abstaining from sleep, trying everything they could to make it as troublesome as possible and reduce the amount they slept.

It is not a great step from reducing sleep to inflicting pain. In both cases the body is tormented in order to reach a higher state of mind. Undergoing physically exhausting or painful exercises was rather popular among the ascetics. Once again the Syrian monks were very inventive in devising all kinds of self-torture – they sometimes tied ropes around their bellies and were hung up in awkward positions, while others were tied to standing posts. A highly regarded custom involved the use of iron devices, such as girdles or chains, placed around the loins, neck, hands, and feet, and often hidden under garments. Pain-producing forms of asceticism include self-mutilation, particularly castration, and flagellation by whipping, which even became a mass movement in Italy and Germany during the Middle Ages and is still practiced today, both among Roman Catholics and Muslims.

Yet it is not only the body that the ascetics believe should be disciplined, chastised and even tormented – there are also psychological forms of asceticism. Social isolation, ranging from restrictions on contact with other human beings to solitary confinement in the wilderness, on a cliff or in the desert, is in itself a form of self-imposed psychological warfare. The early Christian Church also developed techniques of pain-producing introspection. Theologians counselled monks that meditation on guilt, sin, death and punishment – that is the pre-enactment of appearing before the Eternal Judge – should be carried out with as much passion as possible. Clearing the mind of everything that could distract from paying attention to spiritual matters was a necessary step towards reaching higher perfection. As such, techniques of meditation and self-discipline are inherent in all religions – as they are also in the secular spiritual movements that have taken the place of religion over the course of the last two centuries.

Was Wittgenstein an Ascetic?

From this brief survey of the repertoires of asceticism it should be clear that it is perhaps taking it too far to call Wittgenstein an ascetic. His attitude towards sexuality is unclear; some think that his homosexuality troubled him, but the indications that he felt guilt-ridden by it are at best inconclusive.[25] He gave away his inheritance to his brother and sisters and lived a sober life thereafter, but he was not poor. Whenever he needed money to travel, there were always others who were glad to give it to him, and which he was happy to accept.

As far as his eating habits are concerned, Wittgenstein preferred a simple meal, but he does not seem to have despised certain types of food or to have practised fasting. In accounts of his life, self-inflicted pain is never mentioned, and if he was psychologically tormented this was due to his character more than from any act of will. All in all, the biographical information is insufficient to classify Wittgenstein as an ascetic.

Even Wittgenstein's involvement with the design and construction of his sister Margarethe's house in Vienna should not be interpreted as a sign of asceticism as easily as has sometimes been the case. Wittgenstein indeed preferred simplicity and condemned the use of ornamentation, but simplicity could also be very expensive. In building the house, no expense was spared and Wittgenstein insisted on the best materials; if corrections or alternations were deemed necessary, orders were given immediately, regardless of the cost. A preference for simplicity and an aversion to ornamentation as such therefore do not have to be seen as signs of asceticism.[26] In this sense, Wittgenstein stands apart from the whole history of asceticism, in which simplicity is the opposite of luxury.

It is not his life that qualifies Wittgenstein for a place in the history of Western asceticism, it is his philosophy – at least the philosophy of the *Tractatus*. If there is one temptation Wittgenstein fought against, it was the temptation to say things that could only be shown. He believed that neither the body nor the mind could lead people astray and prevent them from reaching their true destination; rather, it was language that does so.

Therefore in the *Tractatus* Wittgenstein tried to show what one can say and by implication what cannot be said and can only be shown. 'The limits of my language mean the limits of my world', as Wittgenstein famously says. Since language only consists of propositions picturing matters of fact, propositions that pretend to deal with other matters, including ethics and metaphysics, are technically nonsense. This does not mean that nothing of any importance exists outside what can be said in language; on the contrary, religion and ethics were of the utmost importance to Wittgenstein.

The truth, however, is that nothing meaningful can be said about religion and ethics. Propositions cannot express anything higher or deeper than facts and therefore meaningful ethical propositions are impossible: 'Hence also there can be no ethical propositions. Propositions cannot express anything higher'.[27]

The conclusion to be drawn from this is that ethics, important though it is, cannot be expressed in language: 'It is clear that ethics cannot be expressed. Ethics is trancendental'.[28] Ethics is not something to be talked about, but something to put into practice. To lead an ethical life (or to be very religious) therefore presupposes refraining from talking about it; abstaining from talking about ethics is a prerequisite of being truly ethical.[29]

Wittgenstein's philosophy marks the linguistic turn in modern philosophy, the transition from a philosophy dealing with thought and knowledge to a philosophy dealing with language and logic. In the Preface to the *Tractatus*, where Wittgenstein addresses the problem of drawing the limits of thought, including ethics, and states that we should do this indirectly by drawing the limits 'of the expression of thought', we see the linguistic turn actually being taken.[30] In the new approach to philosophy, language provides the key to any understanding of reality. I contend, at least in Wittgenstein's case, that asceticism played a fundamental part in this transition.

What interests us here is Wittgenstein's place in the history of asceticism. His philosophy of language, as expressed in the *Tractatus*, is fundamentally ascetic; a more radical type of asceticism is hardly conceivable. The ascetic who denies himself the possibility of communicating (in language) about his views has withdrawn from social life in the most radical sense. By predicating this ascetic view of life on a philosophy of language, Wittgenstein added a completely new dimension to the history of asceticism in the West. A new, linguistic dimension of asceticism manifested itself in the world. Wittgenstein was an ascetic primarily because of his philosophy of language, and because the life he was living around the time of the publication of the *Tractatus* was meant to be a demonstration of the conclusions drawn from his essentially ascetic philosophy of language, his life can be interpreted as ascetic too.

Notes

1. L. Wittgenstein, *Tractatus Logico-Philosophicus* (London, 1922), §7. The German original reads as follows: *Wovon man nicht sprechen kann, darüber muss man schweigen.* See also note 14.
2. *Tractatus Logico-Philosophicus*, §6.53.
3. Wittgenstein later also used a different metaphor: Philosophy is like a map showing you the way out of a wood. Once you have succeeded in leaving the wood, the map is no longer necessary. See J.C. Klagge and A. Nordmann (eds), *Ludwig Wittgenstein, Public and Private Occasions* (Lanham, 2003), 387.
4. *Tractatus Logico-Philosophicus*, §6.54.
5. See esp. A. Janik and S. Toulmin, *Wittgenstein's Vienna*, 2nd edn (Chicago, 1996); A. Janik, *Wittgenstein's Vienna Revisited* (New Brunswick, 2001).
6. It would be incorrect to say that Wittgenstein scholars have completely overlooked the ascetic aspects of his life and philosophy. See esp. B. McGuinness, 'Asceticism and Ornament', in *Approaches to Wittgenstein: Collected Papers* (London and New York, 2002), 17–26. Yet even in this essay the theme of asceticism is hardly touched upon, and McGuinness deals more with Wittgenstein's ideas about ornament than with the ascetic nature of his philosophy. Neither is asceticism a theme in his biography of Wittgenstein: B. McGuinness, *Wittgenstein, A Life: Young Ludwig 1889–1921* (London, 1988). Nor is it in recent introductions to the *Tractatus*, e.g.: H.J. Glock, *A Wittgenstein Dictionary* (Oxford, 1996); H. Sluga and D.G. Stern (eds), *The Cambridge Companion to Wittgenstein* (Cambridge, 1996); E. Friedlander, *Signs of Sense: Reading Wittgenstein's Tractatus* (Cambridge MA, 2001); A. Nordmann, *Wittgenstein's Tractatus: An Introduction* (Cambridge, 2005); M. McGinn, *Elucidating the Tractatus: Wittgenstein's Early Philosophy of Logic and Language* (Oxford, 2006); P. Frascolla, *Understanding Wittgenstein's Tractatus* (London, 2007).
7. For biographical information, see McGuinness, *Wittgenstein, A Life*; R. Monk, *Ludwig Wittgenstein: The Duty of Genius* (New York, 1990).
8. M. Nedo and M. Ranchetti (eds), *Wittgenstein. Sein Leben in Bildern und Texten* (Frankfurt am Main, 1983), 74. Also cited in McGuinness, *Wittgenstein, A Life*, 89, 92; and in Monk, *Ludwig Wittgenstein*, 39–40.
9. As quoted in Monk, *Ludwig Wittgenstein*, 89.
10. As quoted in McGuinness, *Wittgenstein: A Life*, 184, original emphasis.
11. McGuinness gives a description of the cabin: 'The little house had a wonderful view across the lake and the fjord to the south-west and itself looked cheerful enough in the summer when overgrown with creepers and surrounded by greenery. But it would take the temperament of a hermit or even a stylite to live there through a winter' (McGuinness, *Wittgenstein: A Life*, 202).

12. Monk, *Ludwig Wittgenstein*, 58; A.C. Grayling, *Wittgenstein* (Oxford, 1988), 5.

13. Grayling, *Wittgenstein*, 5.

14. In 1961, McGuinness and D.F. Pears published a new translation ('smoother and perhaps more philosophical', as McGuinees claimed) of the *Tractatus*, which was subsequenty revised in 1971. In this new translation, the final proposition reads as follows: 'What we cannot speak about we must pass over in silence'. Compare also D. Kolak's translation (Mountain View, 1998).

15. Russell to Lady Ottoline Morrell, 20 December 1919, as quoted in McGuinness, *Wittgenstein: A Life*, 279.

16. M. Black, *A Companion to Wittgenstein's 'Tractatus'* (Cambridge, 1964), 378. Neither McGuinness nor Monk mentions Silesius.

17. The full title reads: *Johannis Angeli Silesij Cherubinischer Wandersmann oder Geist-Reiche Sinn- und Schluss-Reime zur Göttlichen Beschaulichkeit anleitende. Von dem Urheber aufs neue übersehn, und mit dem Sechsten Buch vermehrt, den Liebhabern der geheimen Theologie und beschaulichen Lebens zur Geistlichen Ergötzlichkeit zum andernmahl herausgegeben*, (Glatz, 1675). On Silesius I consulted M.M. Böhm, *Angelus Silesius' Cherubinischer Wandersmann: A Modern Reading with Selected Translations* (New York, 1997), which contains English translations of the poems and provides a helpful bibliography of both primary and secondary sources.

18. Another interesting epigram is the final one in the sixth book of the *Cherubinischer Wandersmann*, entitled *Beschluss* ('Conclusion'): *Freund, es ist auch genug. Im Fall du mehr willst lessen, / So geh und werde selbst die Schrift und selbst das Wesen* (Friend, it is enough. In case you desire to read more, / Go and become the script and essence yourself). This is exactly what Wittgenstein decided to do after finishing the *Tractatus*: to become the script and the essence himself.

19. Ramsey to his mother, Puchberg, Austria, 20 September 1923. As cited in Nedo and Ranchetti, *Wittgenstein*, 188, original emphasis.

20. L. Wittgenstein, *Culture and Value*, ed. G.H. von Wright in collab. with Heikki Nyman, transl. Peter Winch (Chicago, 1980),16, 22.

21. Diogenes Laertius, *Lives of Eminent Philosophers*, trans. R.D. Hicks, 2 vols (Harvard, 1931), 2: 22–84.

22. Ibid., 2: 71.

23. McGuinness, *Wittgenstein. A Life*, 88–89.

24. W.O. Kaelber, 'Asceticism', in M. Eliade (ed.), *The Encyclopedia of Religion, Vol. 1* (New York, 1987), 441–45.

25. M. Stokhof, *World and Life as One. Ethics and Ontology in Wittgenstein's Early Thought* (Stanford, 2002), 31–32, 297 n.50, commenting especially on A.W. Levi, 'The Biographical Sources of Wittgenstein's Ethics', *Telos* 38 (1978), 63–77. Levi had interpreted Wittgenstein's ethics as a flight from his homosexuality, 'an attempt', in Stokhof's words, 'to shield himself from any indictments from others on this point'. On Wittgenstein's homosexuality, see also Monk, *Ludwig Wittgenstein*, 581–86.

26. This is the point of McGuinness, 'Asceticism and Ornament'.

27. *Tractatus Logico-Philosophicus*, §6.42.

28. *Tractatus Logico-Philosophicus*, §6.421.

29. Compare with what Wittgenstein said to the writer and journalist Ludwig von Ficker: 'My work consists of two parts: the one presented here [in the *Tractatus*], plus all that I have not written. And it is precisely the second part that is the important one. My book draws limits to the ethical from the inside as it were and I am convinced that this is the only rigorous way of drawing those limits'. As quoted in McGuinness, 'Asceticism and Ornament', 25.
30. Stokhof, *World and Life as One*, 37.

References

Black, M. 1964. *A Companion to Wittgenstein's 'Tractatus'*, Cambridge.

Böhm, M.M. 1997. *Angelus Silesius' Cherubinischer Wandersmann: A Modern Reading with Selected Translations*, New York.

Frascolla, P. 2007. *Understanding Wittgenstein's Tractatus*, London.

Friedlander, E. 2001. *Signs of Sense: Reading Wittgenstein's Tractatus*, Cambridge MA.

Glock, H.J. 1996. *A Wittgenstein Dictionary*, Oxford.

Grayling, A.C. 1988. *Wittgenstein*, Oxford.

Janik, A. 2001. *Wittgenstein's Vienna Revisited*, New Brunswick.

Janik, A., and S. Toulmin. 1996. *Wittgenstein's Vienna*, 2nd edn, Chicago.

Kaelber, W.O. 1987. 'Asceticism', in M. Eliade (ed.), *The Encyclopedia of Religion, Vol. 1*, New York, pp.441–45.

Klagge, J.C., and A. Nordmann (eds). 2003. *Ludwig Wittgenstein, Public and Private Occasions*, Lanham.

Laertius, D. 1931. *Lives of Eminent Philosophers*, trans. R.D. Hicks, 2 vols, Harvard.

Levi, A.W. 1978. 'The Biographical Sources of Wittgenstein's Ethics', *Telos* 38: 63–77.

McGinn, M. 2006. *Elucidating the Tractatus: Wittgenstein's Early Philosophy of Logic and Language*, Oxford.

McGuinness, B. 1988. *Wittgenstein, A Life: Young Ludwig 1889–1921*, London.

——— 2002. 'Asceticism and Ornament', in *Approaches to Wittgenstein: Collected Papers*, London and New York, pp.17–26.

Monk, R. 1990. *Ludwig Wittgenstein: The Duty of Genius*, New York.

Nedo, M., and M. Ranchetti (eds). 1983. *Wittgenstein: Sein Leben in Bildern und Texten*, Frankfurt am Main.

Nordmann, A. 2005. *Wittgenstein's Tractatus: An Introduction*, Cambridge.

Sluga, H., and D.G. Stern (eds). 1996. *The Cambridge Companion to Wittgenstein*, Cambridge.

Stokhof, M. 2002. *World and Life as One: Ethics and Ontology in Wittgenstein's Early Thought*, Stanford.

Wittgenstein, L. 1922. *Tractatus Logico-Philosophicus*, trans. F.P. Ramsay and C.K. Ogden, London.

——— 1961. *Tractatus Logico-Philosophicus*, trans. B. McGuinness and D.F. Pears, London.

——— 1980. *Culture and Value*, ed. G.H. von Wright in collab. with Heikki Nyman, transl. Peter Winch, Chicago.

——— 1998. *Tractatus Logico-Philosophicus*, trans. D. Kolak, Mountain View.

Part V
Discipline in the Age of Affluence

Wilhelm Prager (director) and Nicholas Kaufmann (scriptwriter) 'Wege zu Kraft und Schönheit' (1924). © Friedrich-Wilhelm-Murnau-Stiftung, Wiesbaden, Germany.

10

Necessity into Virtue: The Culture of Postwar Reconstruction in Western Europe between Asceticism and Anti-Asceticism

Marnix Beyen

Once upon a time, there lived a brave couple in a small but cosy house in a small but cosy country called Belgium. Then the Second World War came, which pitilessly destroyed their dwelling. After the war, they successfully applied to the Belgian Ministry for Reconstruction for a loan which would enable them to rebuild their house. Nonetheless, they did all they could to keep the reconstruction of their house as cheap as possible by helping the builders themselves and choosing the least expensive materials. The Ministry for Reconstruction highly valued this attitude, which helped keep the price of raw materials low, and thus held reconstruction within the reach of those who needed it most, the poor. If not for this thrift, the ministry feared that only 'luxury damage' would be repaired. Therefore, in the monthly journal published by the ministry, the couple were offered as an example to the Belgian people in October 1946. 'They have installed themselves in their new house, without even suspecting that they offered their fellow-citizens a lesson. A lesson of firm stubbornness, without any doubt. But at the same time a lesson in citizenship and in intelligence'.[1]

That these lessons of citizenship were not taken to heart by all war-stricken Belgians became clear from a complaint that was uttered one year later by the famous architect Jules Ghobert, who was responsible for the reconstruction of housing in the considerably damaged region of the Ardennes. Ghobert was very severe about those citizens who neglected approved reconstruction plans and commissioned builders to rebuild their houses according to the citizens'

Figure 10.1 An anonymous Belgian couple in front of their dwelling under reconstruction shortly after the Second World War. © Taken from [Anonymous], 'Dit is in België gebeurd', *Wederopbouw* 4, 1946.

particular inclinations. By doing so, they not only spoiled the beauty of the region, but they also jeopardized its future prosperity, which would be totally dependant on tourism, and therefore on its regional charm.[2]

These two examples immediately show the complexity and the pervasiveness of the concept of 'postwar reconstruction'. If the economic reconstruction of the 'wealth of nations' was one of the main aims of postwar reconstruction in the long run, in the short term it had to do as much with the equal – or at least just – redistribution of scarce goods, and with the reshaping of the landscape. These social and spatial aspects of reconstruction, however, also made it by definition into a moral undertaking. Reconstruction was as much about the regeneration of national communities as about their material prosperity. This accounts for the fact that reconstruction discourse was, more often than not, very normative.

Time and again this normative aspect was made explicit in the discourse of those who cared about the reconstruction of their country. The German civil engineer Heinrich Cordt reiterated a very topical theme when, in a booklet of 1947 on the solution to the postwar housing problem, he expressed his conviction 'that without an ethical basis for all propositions, a healthy spirit will not tackle the problem of reconstruction from the right side'.[3] Or, to put it more simply in the words of the Belgian intellectual Pierre de Smet, 'The material rebirth of the country postulates its moral renewal'.[4]

In earlier literature on this issue, asceticism and discipline have been revealed as crucial components of what might be called the moral codes of reconstruction. Dutch historians in particular seem to have made that point. As early as 1980 Hans Blom concisely labeled the period between 1945 and 1950 in the Netherlands as 'the years of discipline and asceticism' – a formula that has been repeated endlessly ever since.[5] In Great Britain, the historian Ina Zweiniger-Bargielowska also considers austerity and the myth of 'common sacrifice' to be the central features of the reconstruction paradigm as it was upheld in the first place by the Labour Party.[6]

However, Zweiniger-Bargielowska points to the weakness of this austerity discourse, which contributed to Labour's electoral losses in the early 1950s.[7] The examples with which I started this chapter also show that postwar austerity discourse did not necessarily rely on positively valued ideals of asceticism. Rather, a central paradox seems to arise from them. On the one hand, welfare and comfort are ideals sought by citizens and promoted by the authorities. On the other hand, a certain dose of abstinence was required in order to obtain them. Asceticism, in other words, was not an aim in itself but a prerequisite for future material welfare. Some movements and intellectuals considered the postwar situation of scarcity as an occasion to promote more unconditional ideals of sobriety and abstinence. Their temporary success, however, seems to have rested on a misunderstanding. Without doubt, many of their adepts did expect rewards for their ascetic attitude, not in some afterlife but in a future as near as possible.

In that sense, the austerity ideals contained in postwar reconstruction discourse seem to have been fundamentally different from the ascetic ideals of the late nineteenth and early twentieth centuries. If these latter were fundamentally an offspring of a crisis of modernity, postwar austerity relied on the ultimate acceptance of that same modernity. As a sign of this difference, one could point to the fact that explicitly ascetic movements, either of a monastic or of a scientific nature, did not see a particular resurgence after the Second World War. On the contrary, the success of ascetic movements as diverse as Franciscanism and naturism before and after the First World War was not repeated after the Second World War.[8]

The tension between the seemingly contradictory ideals of consumption and sobriety formed one of the shaky bases of postwar reconstruction discourse. In this chapter I will try to show how this tension was articulated at the different levels of reconstruction to which I referred earlier: the economic, the social, the spatial and the moral levels. By focusing on the ways in which this tension was articulated, I hope to reveal the national and/or ideological

Figure 10.2 A view on postwar reconstruction projects in Belgium © Taken from J. Ghobert, 'L'Urbanisme et la Reconstruction en Ardenne', *Reconstruction Nationale. Edition spéciale hors-série de la Revue Militaire Belge*, [1948], 203.

differences that pervaded this apparently homogeneous discourse. Since every discourse on reconstruction is informed by images of the period preceding destruction, this contribution will inevitably also deal with memories of the Second World War. Whether one preferred the virtue of consumption or that of sobriety depended to a large degree on one's interpretation of the war experience. The common will to build a better future was hampered from the start by heterogeneous memories of the past.

Economic Reconstruction

The first challenge that had to be faced by European political élites was the rebuilding of economic infrastructure. All over Western Europe it was understood that only through conscious and systematic planning could an economy of scarcity be transformed into an economy of abundance.[9] Nevertheless, most economic commentators seemed to agree that, unlike the case of a Soviet-style planned economy, growth in production had to be paired with growth in consumption.[10] The American New Deal and Keynesian economics had been discovered and enthusiastically promoted by many of the European technicians and politicians who had made preparations for the postwar future of their occupied countries during exile in London. Jef Rens, the Belgian socialist activist who in 1941 was appointed head of the Commission for the Study of Postwar Problems, loudly praised American plans for postwar reconstruction. These plans, he revealed to the Belgian population through a radio broadcast, were aimed at giving every American citizen a stable 'basis of comfort and well-being'.[11] In nearly all of the documents he wrote on Belgian reconstruction, comfort and well-being figured as his primary concerns, because they would guarantee social and political harmony in liberated Belgium.

One of Rens's contacts in London was the French economist Jean Monnet, who would become the main architect of the postwar reconstruction and modernisation of France. For Monnet, too, the driving force behind the economic revival had to be the enhanced purchasing power of French citizens. For that reason, he pressed De Gaulle to set aside his feelings of national pride and accept foreign loans. If not, wartime austerity would last much longer and the French economy would miss a unique chance to modernise swiftly.[12]

If Monnet's ambition was to enhance the prosperity of the French, his own lifestyle and the working methods of his team were characterised by sobriety and abstinence. While his plan for the modernisation of France were drawn up at the Hôtel de Martignac in Paris in 1944, his only request was that there should be a small refectory. By this, he reasoned, the work of his team would not be interrupted by long lunch breaks. 'In Paris', he noted in his memoirs, 'this practice surprised people – and the frugality of our meals confused more than one minister and more than one unionist, but it will have largely contributed to the progress in our work and to mutual comprehension. I believe it has been an example to many'. His own office in a luxurious baroque room of the hotel was judged by him to be the 'opposite of the intellectual rigour we were deemed to incarnate' and in his collaborators he invariably valued most their qualities of austerity and simplicity.[13] In Monnet's discourse, therefore, while France and the French were always associated with abundance and consumption, he and his collaborators were associated with restraint from conspicuous consumption. He cherished the ideal of the administrator who ignores his own needs for the sake of the nation. It is probably not a complete coincidence that this kind of discourse was held first of all by those men who had spent the war

Figure 10.3 The Dutch prime minister Willem Drees in front of his private home. © Spaarnestad Foto, Haarlem, The Netherlands.

in exile and who had, therefore, not known the deprivations of the occupation. The discourse of self-sacrifice can easily be interpreted, then, as a form of compensation for their advantaged position during the war.

Yet, Monnet's behaviour cannot simply be interpreted in this psychological manner. It can also be fitted within a larger shift in administrative and political style that took place after the Second World War. Monnet's unpolitical way of administering the country was echoed in the type of leadership that came to the fore in some Western European countries in the same period. The Dutch historian Henk te Velde has recently pointed to the striking resemblances between the Dutch postwar prime minister Willem Drees and his British counterpart Clement Attlee, both of whom he considers to be typical politicians of reconstruction. Sobriety and puritanism appear to be quintessential aspects of the style of those two socialists. Both of them preferred to make use of public transport, both of them were extremely frugal – Drees was even a teetotaler – and both of them refused to adorn their plans for the future of their respective countries with stylistic virtuosities.[14] It seemed as if the needs of reconstruction promoted a return to Jeffersonian republicanism, in which public offices were considered to be 'burdens to those appointed to them, which it would be wrong to decline, though foreseen to bring with them intense labor, and great private loss'.[15] By doing so, they wanted to remain safe from the prewar reproach that the political class had let its own interests prevail over that of their own country.

But whereas eighteenth-century American republicans had situated general well-being most of all in the protection of civil liberties, the engineers of the postwar Welfare State aimed first and foremost at the 'abolition of want', to use the mantra that dominated the immensely influential British Beveridge Report of 1942. Enhancing the nation's prosperity, one of the guiding principles of Lord Beveridge, could only be successful if citizens enjoyed the necessary amount of social security.

And yet, if the self-image of the economic planners was one of unlimited generosity and self-denial, they did expect something in return for their labours. In one of the opening passages of the Beveridge Report, for example, it was stressed that 'Want is one only of five giants on the road of reconstruction and in some ways the easiest to attack. The others are Disease, Ignorance, Squalor and Idleness'.[16] All of the economic planners were conscious that their objectives could only be reached if the populations of their countries were willing to work. 'Indeed', the Belgian prime minister Achiel Van Acker declared in May 1945, at the celebration of the fiftieth anniversary of the Belgian Ministry of Work, 'Belgium, our beloved Fatherland, will not stand up from its material and moral ruin, unless all its children work with ardour, with self-denial'. In order to strengthen his claim, the prime minister strategically referred to the war:

It is not given to everyone to give his life for his country, by paying for its liberation with a glorious death on the battleground, in front of the firing squads, or in the prisons of the enemy. But it is given to everyone to fulfil the duties that are assigned to him in society ... Too many of our fellow citizens have lost the notion of those eternal truths, the respect owed to labour, the necessity to dedicate oneself to the duties assigned to each one of us.

If administrators and politicians were aware after the war that they had to set an example of civic selflessness, some of them at least believed that they could ask the same of their subjects.[17]

Social Deliberation as a Mutual Demand of Asceticism

Planning was to be the crucial mechanism of economic reconstruction, but consultation was needed to allow scarce resources to be divided in a just way. And whereas the discourse of planning was dominated by the relation between a generous and self-denying public servant on the one hand and the grateful and industrious citizen on the other, social deliberations supposed a higher degree of mutuality, and at least some measure of self-restraint from both sides. The preamble of the so-called Social Pact that laid the basis for postwar social relations in Belgium was dominated by a strongly moralising plea for mutual respect between employers and labour, respect which rested on the recognition of pre-existing power-relations: 'The workers', it was stated: 'respect the legitimate authority of the employers and invest their honour in conscientiously executing their work. The employers, on their side, respect the dignity of their workers and invest their honour in treating them with justice. They engage themselves not to do any harm to their liberty of association nor to the development of their organisations'.[18] Because of these lofty intentions, the pact would later be stamped as a 'great work of magnanimity'.[19] In this respect, wartime hardships and the fight against a common enemy were generally deemed to have served as an education in solidarity and disinterestedness. About the precise kind of sacrifices that were demanded from the workers – other than the sacrifice of revolutionary utopias – the document remained rather vague. That explicit demands for wage restraint did not figure in it was not so surprising, given the fact that the main objective it envisioned was 'to enhance continually the living conditions of the population'. But a form of social responsibility on the part of the trade unions was undoubtedly implied in the demand for respect.

Subsequent history would show that self-restraint was not the cardinal virtue of the Belgian trade unions, and that real wages would quickly rise.

An explanation for this phenomenon should probably be sought in the fact that Belgium, the first Western European country to do so, was able to leave the age of reconstruction behind to enter a new age of abundance.[20] Its industrial infrastructure had remained relatively intact, and the so-called Gutt Operation, aimed at the prevention of inflation, had created the perfect conditions for a quick redress of purchasing power. With the return of abundance, the main condition for some 'ascetic' behaviour had passed away.

Significantly, in countries that were much harder hit by the war, the politics of wage restraint did result in considerable successes. The economic 'miracles' of West Germany and the Netherlands, most notably, owed much to the fact that the trade unions refrained from demands for wage increases, even when, during the 1950s, profit margins persistently increased. While trying to solve this puzzle, the German economic historians Giersch, Paqué and Schmieding allow for 'an element of group rationality that may deserve the name of social responsibility', although they consider organisational weakness, political distraction, and expectational errors to be at least equally important factors. Moreover, even social responsibility would have decreased significantly when, from the late 1950s onwards, people became 'accustomed to the fact that growth was fast and that the most urgent social problems were being solved'.[21] In the Netherlands, wage restraint was even more outspoken.[22] It is very tempting to ascribe this fact to that same Calvinist spirit which, according to Max Weber, had already been responsible for the rise of capitalism, and which would now have contributed to its resurgence. And yet, even in the Netherlands of the postwar period, the workers' asceticism turned out largely to be dependent on the needs of reconstruction. Once Germany and the Netherlands had definitively entered the 'age of abundance', demands for wage increases became generalised too. As a broad social phenomenon, asceticism seems to have been accepted only in a very instrumental and conditional way. Self-denial for the sake of the general interest only seemed to work as long as promoting the general interest was considered to be crucial for the promotion of future personal interests.

The Reconstruction of Space

Reconstruction in the most direct sense meant 'rebuilding' what had been materially destroyed. The question that dominated all debates about this material and spatial reconstruction was whether the new should be a copy of the old, or whether destruction should be considered as a welcome opportunity to start again from scratch. In that sense, the Second World War gave a new poignancy to ongoing debates between traditionalists and modernists. In these debates, too, the topic of self-denial or asceticism played its role.

What the traditionalist and the modernist options had in common was in any case their rejection of laissez-faire and conspicuous individualism. Both for social and for aesthetic reasons it was unacceptable for everyone to rebuild their houses according to their own tastes. This would result in an enormous rise in prices, and, moreover, it would lead to anarchism in the urban and rural environment. Traditionalists as well as modernists therefore accepted a certain degree of standardisation and planning in the rebuilding of houses and cities, and thus expected a certain amount of self-restraint from citizens. This sacrifice was, however, demanded for very different reasons. In the traditionalist version, individual taste had to be subjected to the identity of the region. Modernists, meanwhile, considered standardisation to be a pathway to a better and more equal society. In that sense, their demand for self-restraint was more radical than that of the traditionalists. They demanded not only the sacrifice of aesthetic idiosyncrasies but also that of regional memories and identities. For this reason, the French historian Rémi Baudouï dubbed the modernist version of reconstruction 'the silence of memory'. The most notorious advocate of this strategy was the Swiss architect and town planner Le Corbusier, who praised the destruction of the city of Saint-Dié, because it had perfectly prepared the way for his work of urban renewal.[23] But the German planners and architects also welcomed the war's devastation as 'the bright side of the catastrophe of World War II', because it offered 'a unique opportunity to correct the failings of the urban blight produced by the industrial and population expansion of the second half of the nineteenth century'.[24]

If modernism made a huge advance during the period of reconstruction, it was not able to become the dominant architectural idiom. It suffices to compare two neighbouring ruined cities – such as Caen and Rouen – to see how local circumstances could determine the direction of reconstruction.[25] Apparently, national authorities were either unable or unwilling to opt radically for the modernist solution, probably because of the big sacrifice it would demand from their citizens. This was in any case clear in Belgium, where the Ministry of Reconstruction tried to combine standardisation with respect for regional traditions: 'The house of the fisherman of Ostend', said the journal of the ministry, 'will not be the same as that of the miner in Saint-Ghislain, or that of the farmer of the Ardennes'.[26] The architect who was responsible for the reconstruction of the Ardennes, the aforementioned Jules Ghobert, even stressed the need to allow a large degree of regional diversity within the Ardennes.[27]

At this level, too, modernist solutions were implemented most radically in countries where destruction had been the most far-reaching, and where the population was most willing to accept sacrifices. Nonetheless, even in the Netherlands and Germany, the past was not entirely shaken off. As Diefendorf asserts, the quest for identity in postwar Germany was so strong that planners and authorities could not afford to opt for radical discontinuity. In the reconstruction plans for Dutch towns and villages, too, some kind of tie with

Figure 10.4 A view of postwar reconstruction projects in Belgium © Taken from J. Ghobert, 'L'Urbanisme et la Reconstruction en Ardenne', *Reconstruction Nationale. Edition spéciale hors-série de la Revue Militaire Belge*, [1948], 203.

the past was always maintained, even in cities that had been totally destroyed. Ignoring memory and identity was something modernist intellectuals were able to do in their utopian worlds, but devastated societies were unable to do the same. This had already been the case following the First World War, and it would be confirmed after the Second.[28]

The Moral Reconstruction of Youth and Women

The Second World War had not only caused material damage. All over Western Europe, an acute panic arose with regard to the moral consequences of the war. Four, respectively five years of war or, in the German case, twelve years of Nazi regime, was said to have considerably lowered the moral standards of Western societies, and the ecstasy over the Liberation only made things worse. The youth was deemed to have been particularly vulnerable to these processes. The head of the Belgian section of the Red Cross, together with the Leuven jurist Van der Bruggen, analysed the problem in the following allegedly neutral terms, in an article written for an American audience:

> While malnutrition impaired the health of Belgian youth, general condi-
> tions of life in an occupied country resulted in a serious deterioration of
> morals … After liberation, the situation did not quickly improve. The
> first stage of liberation was itself a period of social disorganisation. Black
> market operations continued, although to a diminishing extent. Easy
> money could still be made. Enthusiasm and friendliness with the allied
> soldiers could not but result in a certain amount of sexual laxity.[29]

The recurring element in all these complaints was that quick and easy satisfaction of needs had taken the place of self-restraint and aspiration towards
higher goals. The dramatic increase in juvenile delinquency, which was noticed
Europe-wide, and the worrying predilection of youngsters for cinema-going
and for American products, appeared to be aspects of the same phenomenon.

In this respect, the postwar moral imperative seems to have been an intensified version of the cultural pessimism of the prewar years. In conservative
circles, this continuity was expressly stressed, so that the war appeared in their
discourse rather as a catalyst than as the actual cause of moral deterioration.[30]
Many of those intellectuals went even so far as to consider moral laxity as one
of the causes of the war, and warned that with the end of the war the real
problem had not been solved yet. On the contrary, the Liberation would only
enhance the temptations of superficial American-style consumerism. This
diagnosis was nearly always accompanied by cries for a return to genuinely
ascetic ideals. Within those sections of Western European societies that were
tightly organised along confessional lines, such cries could gain a considerable
success. A striking example can be found in the Dutch Catholic Labourers'
Movement, whose ideal self-image during the late 1940s was, according to the
Dutch historian Hans Righart, 'monastic, ascetic'.[31]

Yet, the moral panic not only served the needs of confessional community
building. In addition, pleas for a return to high moral standards were considered as a means to restore the national community. In this regard, 'civic
education' became a crucial concept, by means of which youth would be
taught once again that loyalty to the national community had to supersede the
search for pleasure and gain. As in the case of the material reconstruction of
the nation, there existed two different versions of this civic education, one of
which can be called romantic or traditionalist, the other one modern. In the
first version, civic duties had to be acquired in the first place by learning about
great examples of patriotism in the past and by fostering a strong attachment
to national traditions. The second, modern, version stressed much more the
need to make youth acquainted with present-day political institutions, not
only of their own country, but also of the rest of the world.[32] This last option,
which gradually became the dominant one, seems, just as were modernist
urban solutions, to have rested on the 'silence of memory': the past – or at

least the distant past – was seen as an inappropriate instrument for solving present-day problems. Therefore, it had to be left behind in the most resolute manner. References to the immediate past, and more specifically to the Second World War, could be useful within both versions of civic education. The threat that fascism had posed to democratic institutions made the defence of these institutions a more urgent need than ever. At the same time, those who had defended these institutions could easily be presented as heroes who fitted within a long tradition of national glory. The moral depravity which reigned in occupied society made their feats more venerable. For all the moral deterioration it had witnessed, the Second World War also offered abundant examples of – to use the words of the British Minister of Reconstruction, Lord Woolton – 'national devotion and subjugation of self-interest'.[33] The example set by these heroes was not only political, but also moral.

In most countries, remembrance of heroes of the resistance therefore formed a part of the program of civic education. Only in the Netherlands did the government decree that references to specific heroic deeds were to be banned in favour of a united memory of the resistance of the Dutch people as a whole. By doing so, Dutch authorities seemed to forsake a chance to impress ideals of heroic self-denial upon the country's citizens. On the other hand, one might interpret this policy as a plea for another, and maybe even higher form of asceticism: by abstaining from particular memories, the Dutch were also required to abstain from particular prides or from the political recuperation of memory. Only then, it was thought, could a genuine and disinterested devotion to the nation be achieved.[34]

While considering the postwar discourse on civic education as a road to moral regeneration, one is struck by the recurring theme of virility. Both conservative and progressive advocates of civic education stressed that it should aim at forming 'men', or even at making the nation virile.[35] With regard to France, the literary historian Michael Kelly has even detected in reconstruction discourse an attempt at restoring masculinity after the humiliation that it had experienced during the war.[36] In any case, in the postwar discourse of moral decay, women seem to have played an iconic role: women's sexual relations with German soldiers were ritually punished after the war, and their relations with Allied soldiers only seemed to confirm that they were to a large extent responsible for the weakening of the nation.[37] Stereotypical images of women as irrational consumers, and therefore as vehicles of Americanisation, were to interpreted along the same lines.[38] Nearly everywhere, processes of moral deterioration were seen as particularly threatening for women.[39] Ina Zweiniger-Bargielovska has even noted that the postwar Labour government in Great Britain placed the burden of the rationing system disproportionately on women, thereby suppressing alleged female frivolity.[40] 'Making the nation more virile' therefore meant promoting the virtues of self-control and abstinence. And that was what the nation, according to many, needed more than ever, now that it was threatened by abundance. Republican ideals of asceticism could in other words remain unambiguously intertwined with ideals of masculinity; the perceived lack of them with a surplus of femininity.

Conclusion

During the postwar years, many people were condemned to asceticism because of the sheer lack of resources. Intellectual and political elites discovered in this fact an occasion to promote asceticism as a virtue in itself. These ascetic ideals could be motivated both by traditionalist and by modernist ideals. However, most people in Western Europe seem to have accepted some degree of self-restraint only insofar as they hoped that by adopting it they would reach their goal, which was not self-denial but 'abolition of want'. In other words, discourses of sacrifice seemed to have had a chance at success only when direct need rendered this sacrifice meaningful. Or, as Jeffry Diefendorf has stated, 'It was during this period of general need that the willingness to share and sacrifice was greatest, not during the subsequent period of prosperity'.[41]

If we exclude the political and intellectual elites, therefore, the dominant feature of the culture of European reconstruction could be described as anti-ascetic rather than as ascetic. The immense popularity of cinema going in the postwar years probably had much to do with a longing for luxury in an age of shortages (as it had done already in the 1930s),[42] as did the breakthrough in France and Great Britain in 1947 of Christian Dior's voluptuous, nearly baroque 'new look' in fashion.[43] Likewise, the jazz rage of this period has recently been described as a movement of corporeal emancipation from the bourgeois values of self-restraint.[44] The success of Americanisation was probably due to a common longing within European societies for escape from cultural patterns dominated by asceticism. American culture was appropriated within and framed by this set of expectations, rather than being simply adopted wholesale. The cultural and political elites who hoped to revitalise ancient cultural patterns inevitably went against the grain.

This view leads me to revisit the famous thesis of Alan Milward concerning European reconstruction.[45] According to Milward, the entire discourse of acute economic and social crisis in Europe immediately after the war was forged by the US administration, which wanted to legitimise the Marshall Plan, its programme of economic aid to Europe. In reality, suggests Milward, the postwar economy of Western Europe was recovering relatively quickly even without American aid. In my view, the discourse of crisis might not simply have been the creation of the American administration, but also of the traditional European elites whose moralising pleas for austerity were rendered more credible by it. Hence, in a rather paradoxical way, they paved the way for an American support programme which helped to promote the very American cultural influences they wanted to keep at a distance.

In any case, once Marshall Plan aid, and with it the era of abundance, had arrived, it became clear that the ascetic ideals propounded by some had been built on quicksand. They would only come to the surface again once a new generation reached adulthood, a generation that had never known the hardships of war, and therefore could long for self-inflicted deprivations. But even the anti-consumerism of 1960s protest movements could not prevent their style of revolt resulting less in a new asceticism then in a generalisation of hedonism.

Notes

1. 'Dit is in België gebeurd', *Wederopbouw* 4 (1946), n.p. For an example of the fear that reconstruction of 'luxury damage' would be given priority, see the radio speech by the Minister of Reconstruction, Jean Terfve, 21 May 1946, reproduced in *Wederopbouw* 2 (1946), n.p.
2. J. Ghobert, 'L'urbanisme et la reconstruction en Ardenne', *Reconstruction Nationale, Revue Militaire Belge*, special issue, off-series (n.d.[1948]), 203–4.
3. H. Cordt, *Die Wiederaufbau, eine soziale Gemeinschaftsaufgabe* (Aachen, 1947), 7.
4. P. De Smet, 'La préparation des élites', *Reconstruction Nationale, Revue Militaire Belge*, special issue, off-series (n.d.[1948]), 68–70. A similar remark can also be found in the familial policy programme presented in 1947 by the Catholic labourer's organisation in Belgium: 'Ons familiaal programma: De bescherming en verdediging van het arbeidersgezin', *De Gids op Maatschappelijk Gebied* 38 (1947), 180–201.
5. J.C.H. Blom, 'Jaren van tucht en ascese:. Beschouwingen bij de stemming in herrijzend Nederland', *Bijdragen en Mededelingen betreffende de Geschiedenis der Nederlanden* 96 (1981), 300–31.
6. I. Zweiniger-Bargielowska, *Austerity in Britain: Rationing, Consumption and Controls, 1939–1945* (Oxford, 2000).
7. I. Zweiniger-Bargielowska, 'Rationing, Austerity and the Conservative Party Recovery after 1945', *Historical Journal* 37 (1994), 173–97.
8. On the cult of Franciscanism during the late nineteenth and early twentieth centuries, see G. Platteau, 'Heilig, gek of revolutionair? Franciscus van Assisi tussen cultus en cult: een internationaal fenomeen vanuit Vlaams perspectief (1882–1940)', Master's thesis, K.U. Leuven (Leuven, 2002). For the success of naturism, see, e.g., E. Peeters, 'Degeneratie en dressuur: natuurgeneeswijze, vege-tarisme en naturisme als ontwerpen voor een moderne samenleving, 1890–1950', *Bijdragen en Mededelingen betreffende de Geschiedenis der Nederlanden* 119 (2004), 329–57.
9. D.W. Ellwood, *Rebuilding Europe: Western Europe, America and Postwar Reconstruction* (London, 1995), 47–49.

10. See, e.g., J. Leseure, *Après la paix. La reconstruction économique (esquisses et réflexions)* (Paris, 1943), 2; A. Leeman, 'Hoe wil de Vlaamse arbeider in de toekomst wonen?', *De Gids op Maatschappelijk Gebied* 38 (1947), 72–84.

11. 'Amerika's reconstructieplannen', radio talk by J. Rens, 24 June 1942 – Brussels, Studie- en Documentatiecentrum Oorlog en Hedendaagse Maatschappij (SOMA) AA 830/274.

12. J. Monnet, *Mémoires* (Paris, 1976) 282.

13. *Ibidem*, 286–87.

14. H. te Velde, *Stijlen van Leiderschap: Persoon en politiek van Thorbecke tot Den Uyl* (Amsterdam, 2002).

15. Quoted in G.S. Wood, 'Democracy and the American Revolution', in J. Dunn (ed.), *Democracy, the Unfinished Journey: 508 BC to AD 1993* (Oxford, 1994), 99.

16. Quoted from the partial reproduction of the report in the *Modern History Sourcebook*. Retrieved 14 December 2006 from: http://www.fordham.edu/halsall/mod/1942beveridge.html

17. 'Le Cinquantenaire du Ministère du Travail', *Revue du Travail* 46 (1945), 320–21.

18. 'Un projet d'accord de solidarité sociale', *Revue du Travail* 46 (1945), 10–21.

19. M. Janssens, 'Opbouwen', *Reconstruction Nationale, Revue Militaire Belge*, special issue, off-series (n.d.[1948]), 136–37.

20. Ellwood, *Rebuilding Europe*, 49.

21. H. Giersch, K.H. Paqué and H. Schmieding, 'Openness, Wage Restraint and Macroeconomic Stability: West Germany's Road to Prosperity, 1949–1958', in R. Dornbusch, W. Nolling and R. Layard (eds), *Postwar Economic Reconstruction and Lessons for the East Today* (Cambridge, 1997), 1–27.

22. K. Schuyt and E. Taverne, *Nederlandse cultuur in Europese context:. 1950, Welvaart in zwart-wit* (The Hague, 2000), 272–74.

23. R. Baudouï, 'Imaginaire culturel et représentations des processus de reconstruction en Europe après 1945', in D. Barjot, R. Baudouï and D. Voldman (eds), *Les Reconstructions en Europe, 1945–1949* (Brussels, 1997), 309–21.

24. J. Diefendorf, *In the Wake of War. The Reconstruction of German Cities after World War II* (New York, 1993), 275.

25. H. Clout, 'The Reconstruction of Upper Normandy: A Tale of Two Cities', *Planning Perspectives* 14 (1999), 187–203.

26. 'Welke huizen gaat men bouwen?', *Wederopbouw* 3 (1946), n.p.

27. Ghobert, 'L'urbanisme et la reconstruction en Ardenne', 203–4.

28. Cf. J. Winter, *Sites of Memory, Sites of Mourning: The Great War in European Culture* (Cambridge, 1995). A good example of this popular refusal to silence memory concerns the reconstruction of the Belgian town of Ypres: see H. Stynen, *De onvoltooid verleden tijd: Een geschiedenis van de monumenten- en landschapszorg in België, 1835–1940* (Brussels, 1998), 253–56.

29. C. Van der Bruggen and L.C. Picalausa, 'Belgian Youth Movements and Problems', in S. Simpson (ed.), *Belgium in Transition, Annals of the American Academy of Political and Social Science*, special issue, 247 (1946), 111–16. For another Belgian example, see M. Coulon, *Jeunesse à la dérive* (Mons, 1945).

30. For Belgium, see in this respect M. Beyen, 'Nostalgie naar een nieuwe tijd: De Tweede Wereldoorlog en de roep van de traditie. België en Nederland, 1940–1945', *Belgisch Tijdschrift voor Filologie en Geschiedenis* 79 (2001), 465–506.

31. H. Righart, '"Ons gezin is ons kleine vaderland": Het zedelijkheidsoffensief van de Katholieke Arbeidersbeweging, 1945–1955', in H. Galesloot and M. Schrevel (eds), *In fatsoen hersteld: Zedelijkheid en wederopbouw na de oorlog* (Amsterdam, 1987), 63–67. In the Belgian Catholic Labour Movement, very similar pleas for a new chastity could be heard: see, e.g., M. Goetstouwers, 'Midden het onchristelijk klimaat van dezen tijd: Het herstel van den mens en den christen in den arbeider', *De Gids op Maatschappelijk Gebied* 39 (1948), 705–20.

32. For this distinction, see M. Beyen, *Oorlog en Verleden: Nationale geschiedenis in België en Nederland, 1938–1947* (Amsterdam, 2002), 261–68.

33. C.H. Woolton, *The Adventure of Reconstruction: Peace, Expansion and Reform* (London, 1945), 5.

34. P. Lagrou, *The Legacy of Nazi Occupation: Patriotic Memory and National Recovery in Western Europe, 1945–1965* (Cambridge, 2006), 59–77.

35. The point is explicitly made in a circular letter by the Belgian Minister of Education, Auguste Buisseret, on 5 February 1946: see *Mededeelingen van het Ministerie van Openbaar Onderwijs* 40 (1946), 22–27.

36. M. Kelly, 'The Reconstruction of Masculinity at the Liberation', in H.R. Kedward and N. Wood (eds), *The Liberation of France: Image and Event* (Oxford and Washington DC, 1995), 117–28.

37. L. Corran, 'La femme au turban: Les femmes tondues', in H.R. Kedward and N. Wood (eds), *The Liberation of France: Image and Event* (Oxford and Washington DC, 1995), 155–80; F. Virgili, *La France 'virile': Des femmes tondues à la Libération* (Paris, 2000), 271–79 shows the European scope of the phenomenon. For Belgium, see M. De Metsenaere and S. Bollen, 'Schandelijke liefde. Sentimentele collaboratie en haar bestraffing in België na de Tweede Wereldoorlog', *Wetenschappelijke Tijdingen* 66 (2007) 228-59, and C. Van Loon, 'De geschorene en de scheerster. De vrouw in de straatrepressie na de Tweede Wereldoorlog', *Bijdragen tot de Eigentijdse geschiedenis* 19 (2008), 45–78.

38. For an example of a study of this for Western Germany, see E. Carter, *How German is She? Postwar West German Reconstruction and the Consuming Woman* (Ann Arbor, 1997).

39. See, e.g., the elaborate inquiry into the social and moral situation of young female labourers in Belgium: 'De toestand van de jonge arbeidsters in het Vlaamse land', *De Gids op maatschappelijk gebied* 38 (1947), 934–48, 1057–67.

40. Zweiniger-Bargielowska, *Austerity in Britain*.

41. Diefendorf, *In the Wake of War*, 75.

42. See A. Kuhn, 'Cinema-going in Britain in the 1930s: Report of a Questionnaire Survey', *Historical Journal of Film, Radio and Television* 19 (1999), 531–43; A. Kuhn, *An Everyday Magic: Cinema and Cultural Memory* (London, 2002).

43. P. MacNeil, '"Put Your Best Face Forward": The Impact of the Second World War on British Dress', *Journal of Design History* 6 (1993), 283–99.

44. M. Taubenberger, '"Ich bin ein befreites Subjekt": Von einer jungen Generation im Nachkriegsdeutschland, die die Freiheit suchte – und den Jazz fand', *Historische Anthropologie* 14 (2006), 268–86.
45. A. Milward, *The Reconstruction of Western Europe, 1945–1951* (London, 1984).

References

Published Sources

Baudouï, R. 1997. 'Imaginaire culturel et représentations des processus de reconstruction en Europe après 1945', in D. Barjot, R. Baudouï and D. Voldman (eds), *Les Reconstructions en Europe, 1945–1949*, Brussels, pp.309–21.

Beyen, M. 2001. 'Nostalgie naar een nieuwe tijd: De Tweede Wereldoorlog en de roep van de traditie. België en Nederland, 1940–1945', *Belgisch Tijdschrift voor Filologie en Geschiedenis* 79: 465–506.

——— 2002. *Oorlog en Verleden: Nationale geschiedenis in België en Nederland, 1938–1947*, Amsterdam.

Blom, J.C.H. 1981. 'Jaren van tucht en ascese: Beschouwingen bij de stemming in herrijzend Nederland', *Bijdragen en Mededelingen betreffende de Geschiedenis der Nederlanden* 96: 300–31.

Carter, E. 1997. *How German is She? Postwar West German Reconstruction and the Consuming Woman*, Ann Arbor.

Clout, H. 1999. 'The Reconstruction of Upper Normandy: A Tale of Two Cities', *Planning Perspectives* 14: 187–203.

Cordt, H. 1947. *Die Wiederaufbau, eine soziale Gemeinschaftsaufgabe*, Aachen.

Corran, L. 1995. 'La femme au turban: Les femmes tondues', in H.R. Kedward and N. Wood (eds), *The Liberation of France: Image and Event*, Oxford and Washington DC, pp.155–80.

Coulon, M. 1945. *Jeunesse à la dérive*, Mons.

De Metsenaere, M., and S. Bollen. 2007. 'Schandelijke liefde. Sentimentele collaboratie en haar bestraffing in België na de Tweede Wereldoorlog', *Wetenschappelijke Tijdingen* 66: 228–59.

De Smet, P. n.d.[1948]. 'La préparation des élites', *Reconstruction Nationale, Revue Militaire Belge*, special issue, off-series: 68–70.

Diefendorf, J. 1993. *In the Wake of War: The Reconstruction of German Cities after World War II*, New York.

Ellwood, D.W. 1995. *Rebuilding Europe: Western Europe, America and Postwar Reconstruction*, London.

Ghobert, J. n.d.[1948]. 'L'urbanisme et la reconstruction en Ardenne', *Reconstruction Nationale, Revue Militaire Belge*, special issue, off-series: 203–4.

Giersch, H., K.H. Paqué and H. Schmieding. 1997. 'Openness, Wage Restraint and Macroeconomic Stability: West Germany's Road to Prosperity, 1949–1958', in R. Dornbusch, W. Nolling and R. Layard (eds), *Postwar Economic Reconstruction and Lessons for the East Today*, Cambridge, pp.1–27.

Janssens, M. n.d.[1948]. 'Opbouwen', *Reconstruction Nationale, Revue Militaire Belge*, special issue, off-series: 136–37.

Kelly, M. 1995. 'The Reconstruction of Masculinity at the Liberation', in H.R. Kedward and N. Wood (eds), *The Liberation of France: Image and Event*, Oxford and Washington DC, pp.117–28.

Kuhn, A. 1999. 'Cinema-going in Britain in the 1930s: Report of a Questionnaire Survey', *Historical Journal of Film, Radio and Television* 19: 531–43.

——— 2002. *An Everyday Magic: Cinema and Cultural Memory*, London.

Lagrou, P. 2006. *The Legacy of Nazi Occupation: Patriotic Memory and National Recovery in Western Europe, 1945–1965*, Cambridge.

Leseure, J. 1943. *Après la paix: La reconstruction économique (esquisses et réflexions)*, Paris.

MacNeil, P. 1993. '"Put Your Best Face Forward." The Impact of the Second World War on British Dress', *Journal of Design History* 6: 283–99.

Milward, A. 1984. *The Reconstruction of Western Europe, 1945–1951*, London.

Monnet, J. 1976. *Mémoires*, Paris.

Peeters, E. 2004. 'Degeneratie en dressuur: natuurgeneeswijze, vegetarisme en naturisme als ontwerpen voor een moderne samenleving, 1890–1950', *Bijdragen en Mededelingen betreffende de Geschiedenis der Nederlanden* 119: 329–57.

Platteau, G. 2002. 'Heilig, gek of revolutionair? Franciscus van Assisi tussen cultus en cult: een internationaal fenomeen vanuit Vlaams perspectief (1882–1940)', Master's thesis, K.U. Leuven, Leuven.

Righart, H. 1987. '"Ons gezin is ons kleine vaderland": Het zedelijkheidsoffensief van de Katholieke Arbeidersbeweging, 1945–1955', in H. Galesloot and M. Schrevel (eds), *In fatsoen hersteld: Zedelijkheid en wederopbouw na de oorlog*, Amsterdam, pp.63–74.

Schuyt, K., and E. Taverne. 2000. *Nederlandse cultuur in Europese context: 1950, Welvaart in zwart-wit*, The Hague.

Stynen, H. 1998. *De onvoltooid verleden tijd: Een geschiedenis van de monumenten- en landschapszorg in België, 1835–1940*, Brussels.

Taubenberger, M. 2006. '"Ich bin ein befreites Subjekt": Von einer jungen Generation im Nachkriegsdeutschland, die die Freiheit suchte – und den Jazz fand', *Historische Anthropologie* 14: 268–86.

Te Velde, H. 2002. *Stijlen van Leiderschap: Persoon en politiek van Thorbecke tot Den Uyl*, Amsterdam.

Van der Bruggen, C., and L.C. Picalausa. 1946. 'Belgian Youth Movements and Problems', in S. Simpson (ed.), *Belgium in Transition, Annals of the American Academy of Political and Social Science*, special issue, 247: 111–16.

Van Loon, C. 2008. 'De geschorene en de scheerster. De vrouw in de straatrepressie na de Tweede Wereldoorlog', *Bijdragen tot de Eigentijdse geschiedenis* 19: 45–78.

Virgili, F. 2000. *La France 'virile': Des femmes tondues à la Libération*, Paris.

Winter, J. 1995. *Sites of Memory, Sites of Mourning: The Great War in European Culture*, Cambridge.

Wood, G.S. 1994. 'Democracy and the American Revolution', in J. Dunn (ed.), *Democracy, the Unfinished Journey: 508 BC to AD 1993*, Oxford, pp.91–105.

Woolton, C.H. 1945. *The Adventure of Reconstruction: Peace, Expansion and Reform*, London.

Zweiniger-Bargielowska, I. 1994. 'Rationing, Austerity and the Conservative Party recovery after 1945', *Historical Journal* 37: 173–97.

——— 2000. *Austerity in Britain: Rationing, Consumption and Controls, 1939–1945*, Oxford.

Periodicals

De Gids op maatschappelijk gebied, 1947–1948.
Mededeelingen van het Ministerie van Openbaar Onderwijs, 1946.
Revue du Travail, 1945.
Wederopbouw, 1946.

Archives

SOMA/B – Studie- en Documentatiecentrum Oorlog en Hedendaagse Maatschappij, Brussels

11

Modern Asceticism and Contemporary Body Culture

Julia Twigg

'Modern asceticism' appears a paradox. By the dominant mythology of modernism, it should not exist. Asceticism is something that the modern world has left behind, together with the Christianity that formerly underpinned it. Here Christianity is regarded as encoding a series of ascetic values, rooted in hostility to sexuality and the body, carried forward in the traditional Catholic valorisation of virginity and chastity. Enlightenment thinkers from Voltaire to Russell have associated asceticism with monkish excess, repressed sexuality and a culture of life denial. Surely modernism is about escaping from all that, and presenting a new secular ideal that views the body and its expression in a positive, healthy form: that is certainly part of the modernist myth. And yet, as the chapters in this book ably show, ascetic impulses did not disappear in the early twentieth century. Modernity did not eradicate their cultural expression. Indeed, far from disappearing, asceticism appears to be part of the modernist project, carried forward at its heart.

One way we can understand this paradox is in terms of the particular historical moment. Modern asceticism is rooted in the rejection of the nineteenth-century bourgeois world. It is about clearing out the clutter of the high Victorian interior – the heavy drapes, the dusty fringes, the elaboration of ornament, the shadowy spaces – and letting the sun shine on a bright, clean, freshly coloured and simplified interior. Air, light, sunshine, cleanliness and purity are the watchwords of the interwar period, and are used in ways that extend beyond their literal relevance. Such impulses were carried through in the presentation of the body, exemplified in the period after the First World War by changes in women's dress, with the adoption of short skirts, cropped hair, minimal underwear, and the espousal of a new boyish, athletic figure, and a suntanned complexion. In the same way, Victorian attitudes to sexuality were to be swept away and replaced by new, 'healthy' ones, informed by Freudian insights, freed from what were seen as repressive codes. One version of this account sees these impulses as the opposite of ascetic, inspired by a new hedonism of the body and associated with the freeing up of sexual constraint. But as earlier chapters in this volume show, these cultural trends also contain more ambivalent elements, seen, for example, in the history of nudism with its repudiation of overt eroticism. Early twentieth-century and interwar asceticism also has links with fascist movements, and through them with a pervasive masculinisation of the body, though these impulses are also present in mainstream democratic regimes. To this end, one can interpret modern asceticism as something located in the particular contingencies of the period – a post-Victorian, secular reaction that carried within it elements of what it reacted against, but whose time is now past.

I want to argue, however, that these ascetic impulses have not disappeared, that we can detect their presence in current cultural phenomena, and indeed that they represent something central to modernism and the high or late modernist world that has succeeded it. In the following sections I will briefly outline three areas of current culture where ascetic impulses can be detected. The first concerns the culture of dieting, and related to it the malignant phenomenon of eating disorders; the second, the growing familiarity with, and mainstreaming of, vegetarian food practices; and the third, the growing stringency in relation to bodily cleanliness in modern culture, and its consequences for the management of sickness and old age. I will then address how we might understand these tendencies, drawing on the work of four key theorists of the body, Norbert Elias, Michel Foucault, Julia Kristeva and Bryan Turner.

Dieting and Eating Disorders

Over the course of the twentieth century, the body ideal for women changed.[1] The generous curves and flowing figures that were prized in the period up until the First World War gave way to a new slim ideal. In parallel with other cultural movements, this can be seen as a revolt against the Victorian era with its heavily upholstered figures, an attempt to free women from the constraints of corsets, petticoats and abundant flesh, substituting a lighter, slimmer, more athletic body, free to engage in sports and other activity. It also represents a retreat from overt fertility and from a body that exemplifies maternity and domesticity. As women increasingly engaged with paid work, so they were required to fit into more masculinised worlds, in which overt fecundity was no longer valued and in which the new demand was for a youthful, boyish, pre-maternal figure. Achieving this, however, requires increased levels of disciplinary activity to control and reduce the abundance of unruly flesh.

The reality of modern bodies is, however, rather different, with a growing incidence of obesity across the Western world.[2] All Western societies display this trend, though with variations in pattern and degree, to the extent that World Health Organisation now terms it a global epidemic.[3] The underlying reasons are complex. At a simple level it arises in the West from modern abundance, and the end of the culture of dearth and famine. But social and cultural changes are also significant. Declining levels of physical activity have resulted from the mechanisation of work and transport, and from the spread of social and physical environments that discourage exercise. Eating patterns have become more fragmented and de-structured, with the growth of fast food, the omnipresence of eating opportunities in the social landscape, and the rise of what Fischler terms the 'empire of snacks',[4] all creating a situation where individuals are constantly presented with opportunities to eat. Food is also increasingly consumed in energy-dense forms that are shaped by the interests of the food industry.[5]

All this has created an obesogenic environment that shifts the onus of responsibility on to the individual, who is increasingly required to exercise conscious control over his or her intake, substituting internal restraint for something that had previously been externally structured through patterns of activity or eating, through social norms, or simply through dearth. Individuals are required to monitor and discipline their bodies by means of activities that draw on traditional ascetic practices, such as conscious abstinence or self denial, but now deployed in pursuit of the new, slim body ideal. Furthermore, it is increasingly not enough for the body to be slim, it must also be lean and toned, and this requires further disciplinary activity in the form of focused exercise, gym attendance and other body work. The emphasis for women has shifted from the external corset of the nineteenth century to the internalised one of musculature and self-restraint. The body is now shaped and disciplined according to a new hard ideal that repudiates soft or flowing flesh, and instead presents a clearly defined and bounded ideal.

In pursuit of this we now have in the West a pervasive culture of dieting, in which being on a diet is normative for most women. Though the figures (at least in the UK) suggest that men are equally, or even slightly more, likely to be overweight, the cultural practices of diets and dieting are strongly feminised; indeed, for this reason some men are reluctant to attend slimming clubs or openly declare they are slimming. This gendered pattern is part of a wider set of disciplinary practices related to the achievement of acceptable forms of femininity. As Wolf and other feminists note, women in the late twentieth and twentieth-first centuries, despite having achieved greater equality in education and employment, are still engaged in extensive disciplinary practices in relation to their bodies, toning, exercising, limiting, constricting, shaving, painting them in pursuit of a body ideal.[6] At the level of the media, these disciplinary practices of femininity are closely policed through the bodies of female celebrities and other women in the public eye who are made subject to the 'fat police' or the 'cellulite patrol', humiliated for failure to achieve normative femininity.

Such practices take on more extreme and malign forms in eating disorders, understood here as a range of conditions centred on bulimia and anorexia nervosa.[7] Attempts have been made to identify the condition historically, in particular associating it with 'fasting girls' in the early nineteenth century, or the practices of medieval saints or holy women. Bynum argues persuasively, however, that medieval practices need to be interpreted within the specific religious context of medieval women's relation to food, the body and the meanings of ingestion and abstinence.[8] Though problems of population selection and changing levels of recognition mean that there are difficulties in obtaining secure figures on current incidence, there is general agreement that numbers have risen significantly in the last thirty years. Eating disorders can thus be seen as a phenomenon of the late twentieth and twentieth-first centuries. Current interpretations of eating disorders recognise that they are complex phenomena that expresses both individual psychopathology and wider cultural themes – an analysis captured in Bordo's characterisation of anorexia: 'psychopathology as a crystallisation of culture'.[9] At one end of the continuum, eating disorders, particularly anorexia, are serious life threatening psychiatric disorders; at the other, they represent practices and meanings that are widespread in the culture, for example in the widespread practice of binging and purging among young women.

Eating disorders have a strongly gendered character, the commonly quoted ratio of female to male being ten to one; and cultural analyses draw heavily on gender as an explanation. Indeed, feminist analyses have long led the field in their interpretation.[10] Eating disorders are here seen as reflecting the paradoxical situation of women in modern culture, representing a working through, at a bodily level, of tensions in relation to women's wider social position. In this they are both a rebellion against contemporary femininity, with their creation of an ugly, pathological body in which the visible signs of femininity have been eradicated, and an exaggerated adherence to aspects of it, in their pursuit of a stripped, ultra slim body on which not an ounce of fat is visible. Some writers, such as Showalter, have drawn parallels between the current epidemic of anorexia and the late-nineteenth century one of hysteria, which similarly combined exaggerated adherence to the norms of femininity, in the form of passivity and weakness, at the same time as rebellion against them, through extremes of behaviour and unfeminine wildness.[11]

In her analysis of anorexia, Bordo explores the ways in which the phenomenon carries forward a deep set of themes found in Western culture.[12] In particular she points to the dualist tradition that has been present in Western culture from the time of the Greeks in which the body is seen as a form of limitation and containment, something that is heavy and that weights us down, and that we aspire to transcend and free ourselves from. Here the body is seen as alien, as something against which the spirit wages a war of denial and mastery. She sees these beliefs as forming a central part of the anorexic's attitude to their body. They are, of course, central to the tradition of Western asceticism. A key theme in the account of anorexia, both in terms of analysis and the sufferer's own narration, is the question of control. Anorexia is about achieving control of the body and self in a context of a personal or social world that feels out of control, in which the body becomes a site for intensive monitoring. To this degree eating disorders have been characterised as 'epidemics of the will', representing exaggerated attempts at self-mastery through acute control of the body; and parallels are sometimes drawn with pathological exercise or gym-use performed by some men.[13]

Anorexia thus displays many of the classic elements of asceticism, involving as it does the close regulation of ingestion, often accompanied by withdrawal from the social world. It centres on the denial of the flesh both in the sense of the fleshly desires of the individual and of literal flesh in the form of the curves of the female body. It is often accompanied by feelings of revulsion. It represents a rejection of sexuality in its pursuit of the pre-pubescent body without menstrual periods. It often calls on purificatory themes through the use of purging, or attempts to create an ethereal, light body through the extreme avoidance of what are seen as heavy, carnal, fat-building foods. As part of this, it is often associated in its early stages with the adoption of a vegetarian diet. Anorexia thus represents a carrying forward into the culture of modernity of many of the classic ideas and practices associated with asceticism.

Vegetarianism

The second set of cultural practices I want to explore relates to vegetarianism, in particular the growth in popularity in the late twentieth century of vegetarian diets, and the mainstreaming of these ideas in the wider retreat from consumption of red meat. In its modern form vegetarianism emerged in the nineteenth century, when it was largely a northern European, post-Protestant phenomenon, and it was particularly strong in Britain, Germany and the United States.[14] National traditions of vegetarianism are slightly different with, for example, vegetarianism in Britain having a stronger focus on animal cruelty, and German vegetarianism putting greater emphasis on health. All vegetarian movements, however, share a constellation of arguments and concerns centred around ethical issues, health concerns, ecological arguments and spiritual aspirations. Resonating through these are a set of values concerning wholeness, nature and purity. Modern vegetarianism is commonly found in conjunction with a range of broadly 'progressivist' movements, some of which have been discussed in earlier chapters. It is recurrently associated with pacifism, feminism and ecology. At a religious level, its associations are with free versions of Christianity, like Quakerism, with ideas of Indian or Eastern spirituality, and with the free-floating 'spirituality' characteristic of late modernity. In the UK, it is recurrently associated with the Left, though in Germany and other continental European traditions its political links are more complex. It also has strong connections with alternative medical traditions.

Modern vegetarianism differs from earlier forms. In the Middle Ages, though vegetarianism as a term did not exist, the diet was implicitly present, encoded in ideas concerning the meaning of meat and abstinence from it. Avoiding red meat, and sometimes all animal products, was part of medieval fasting practice, tied to the cycle of the Church's year and week. It also underpinned hierarchies of holiness in relation to monastic life, with monks adopting stricter versions of this pattern, and with the strictest orders adopting the most austere versions. Underlying these practices were a series of connections made between meat, flesh and carnality, in which the ingestion of meat, especially red meat, was seen to stimulate the passions, particularly those of sexuality and aggression. Some of this was carried over into nineteenth and twentieth-century vegetarianism, but in the context of a very different set of ideas. Modern vegetarianism focuses on this-worldly health and well-being, rather than austerity and denial, oriented towards the hereafter and pleasing to God. Most importantly, modern vegetarianism is strongly concerned with cruelty to animals, something wholly absent from the medieval version. Lastly, it seeks to establish a permanently purified or higher state, rather than one structured by the cycle of fasting and feasting.

Modern vegetarianism encodes a hierarchy in terms of the meanings of foods that derives from, and is shared by, the dominant meat-eating culture. At the top is red meat, followed by white meats such as poultry. This is followed by fish. At the level below are foods like cheese and eggs that derive from animals but are not made of their living substance. Finally, we reach the vegetable foods like fruits and grains that involve no animal element. Within dominant culture, the categories at the top of the hierarchy have the greatest status: they alone have the capacity to form the basis of a high-status meal. Animal products like cheese and eggs can be the basis of a meal, but only a lower-status one such as a light lunch or a snack. In the dominant view, vegetables alone are not sufficient for a full meal. The hierarchy also intersects with cooking: in general within the dominant scheme cooked meals are accorded greater status than uncooked, and the highest categories of food – such as meat – are those that require being cooked. This hierarchy is replicated in vegetarian and quasi-vegetarian practice. Vegetarians eschew meat and fish, but eat animal products like milk and eggs; vegans, however, adopt a stricter set of rules and confine themselves to the bottom category alone. There are also intermediate categories such as 'fishetarians', who avoid meat but eat fish, or people who only avoid red meat. Again their practices reiterate and endorse the structure of the hierarchy. The hierarchy is also reflected, as we noted earlier, in medieval practices of abstinence.

As we have noted, vegetarians eat down the hierarchy, and that is part of why vegetarians' food is traditionally regarded as deficient by the dominant culture. It is seen as lacking, and this condemnation is often carried over into the evaluation of vegetarians themselves. There is a gendered aspect to this, with the condemnation attaching more strongly to men. Meat and men are seen as linked, at both the symbolic and pseudo-physiological levels. Men are presented as 'needing' red meat, and those who eschew it can be seen as failing to achieve dominant masculinity. Vegetarianism is thus a feminised diet; and the practice is indeed biased towards women, particularly younger women, a pattern also reflected in borderline practices such as only avoiding red meat.

Vegetarianism has recurring associations with feminism; and since the late nineteenth century, feminists of both the first and second wave, particularly those who adopted a radical feminist position, have made the connection between the exploitation of animals and of women. Many have presented vegetarianism as part of a wider feminist project of creating a reformed and redeemed version of the world that reflects women-centred values and that eschews the world of violence, cruelty and oppression. At the symbolic level, the diet also encodes female values in that many of the elements that make it up are ones traditionally regarded as female: light, pale, fresh items, as opposed to the dark, heavy ones of meat. Within vegetarian culture this endorses a series of oppositions around: light/heavy, fresh/rotten, alive/dead, clean/unclean, pure/impure. In this, vegetarian food is seen as embodying the positive values of renewal and life, as opposed to the negative ones of decay and death. Vegetarianism is presented as building up a light, purified body, as opposed to the heavy toxin-laden body of the meat eater. This is part of why eating vegetarian food is assumed within dominant culture – but against nutritional science – to involve 'slimming'. The association is also under-pinned by the issue of cooking, with salad similarly perceived as slimming and in some sense connected with women. A vegetarian diet thus resonates with some of the themes we encountered earlier in relation to the culture of slimming. As we shall see in the next section, there are also connections with the clean, purified body of modern hygiene.

Modern vegetarianism thus shares aspects of dominant meat-eating culture in the form of a hierarchy of foods, at the same time as radically disrupting and revaluing them. Vegetarianism is presented positively not in terms of what is given up, but what is gained. It is helped in this by its alliance with other wholefood or dietary reform movements, so that vegetarianism is not confined to avoidance, but associated positively with new ways of eating, centred around wholeness and nature. It presents a distinct way of eating and cooking and not just a removal from the diet of avoided items.

In the late twentieth century, in Britain and North America at least, vegetarian ideas have seeped into the mainstream. The diet is now widely familiar, and vegetarian options are ubiquitous on restaurant menus. Being a vegetarian no longer condemns an individual to a separate existence, as it once did; and with this has gone a softening of social condemnation. Indeed, there is a growing trend across North America and Europe away from the consumption of red meat in general. This partly arises from health concerns, with the predominant advice of nutritionists being to eat less meat, especially red meat, but it also reflects changes in sensibility, a wish to eat in different ways, that have been influenced by ideas from vegetarianism.

Can we still talk of vegetarianism as an ascetic practice? It certainly has strong ascetic elements in its history, exemplified in the retreat from carnality and the pursuit of moral and bodily purity. It previously marked people as set apart, pursuing distinctive and specific practices that cut them off from the mainstream; and in this it underpinned ideas of holy community or a redeemed social order that echoed other forms of ascetic withdrawal. But these practices in modern vegetarianism are now carried forward within a different set of ideas, ones that present the diet not in terms of abstinence, but positively in terms of benefits. Vegetarian food is seen as better, morally and physiologically: fresher, lighter and purer. The redemptive qualities it offers are also generalisable, in that they are not confined to a holy elite, to moral or religious virtuosi, nor are they structured by fast and feast. Modern vegetarianism thus contains aspects of traditional asceticism, but carried forward within a new set of values that emphasises this-worldly well-being and the possibility of a generalisable secular moral redemption.

The Clean Body

The third cultural tendency I want to explore concerns growing standards of cleanliness in relation to the body.[15] In his account of the history of washing, Vigarello traces the shift from a late medieval concern with the cleanliness of just the visible parts of the body, in the form of face and hands, towards the emergence in the early modern period of a wider preoccupation focused on the freshness of linen. Frequent changes of linen both acted to cleanse the body through the removal of sweat and dirt, and enabled the public display of cleanliness through its visible whiteness. By the nineteenth century, the focus had moved to the body as a whole, and to direct forms of washing and bathing. Vigarello, deploying a Foucauldian analysis, interprets this in terms of the steady advance from a concern with only the visible surfaces of the person towards ever more thoroughgoing surveillance of the body underneath.[16]

These cultural trends were reinforced in the nineteenth century by technological developments, in the form of the fixed and plumbed-in bath tub (located in rooms specifically designated for cleansing), of abundant piped hot water, and soaps specifically developed for use on the skin. In the nineteenth century, cleanliness became a class issue, as the poor were increasingly perceived to smell – a social division reinforced by rising standards among the bourgeoisie. The discourse of class division along olfactory lines continued in Britain into the 1930s, only finally disappearing in the postwar era. In the second half of the twentieth century, bathrooms became universal in the Western home. By the early twenty-first century expectations of frequent washing and showering, together with the growing privatisation and individualisation of the body, mean that the ratio of bathrooms to bedrooms in the modern home approaches one to one. There is now a widespread expectation in Europe and North America that people will shower or wash daily, and that they will not smell, or if they do only of soap or perfume.

The retreat from body smell is part of a wider re-evaluation of the senses.[17] With the passage to modernity, the eyes and vision assumed new dominance, becoming the basis for what Jay terms the 'scopic regime of modernity'.[18] The sense that has lost out in this is smell, which has become subordinated to sight. Corbin notes the steady retreat from the eighteenth century from pleasure in strong body odours. At the end of the nineteenth, it was still possible to speak of the *bouquet de corsage*, the attractive smell of perspiration that arose from the body in the ballroom, but by the 1930s, this had become colloquially known as BO, short for body odour. This remained a recurrent preoccupation in women's magazines and adverts in the postwar era, but is rarely mentioned today, mastered as it has been by more frequent washing and more effective deodorants. Once again there is a gendered dimension in this, with 'nice' standards in relation to the body traditionally regarded as an aspect of femininity, something men need not be so concerned with. Smells are still significant in the modern world, however, but they are increasingly artificially produced, omnipresent in soaps, shampoos and cleaning products. Occasionally, protests are raised against this ultra-clean, artificially scented, body ideal, which is presented as antiseptic, asexual and implicitly denying the body in its suppression of odours and its washing away of human secretions, but it remains the cultural norm; and the stringency with which it is applied has, if anything, increased.

This model of the body is, however, threatened by inescapable aspects of life in the form of sickness, decay and death. Öberg suggests that modern sensibilities result in conditions like sickness or incontinence becoming increasingly unacceptable and marginalised, marking sufferers off from the mainstream.[19] Lawton provides an extreme account of this in what she terms 'dirty dying' in the hospice where the disintegration of the body leads to a gradual annihilation of the self.[20] Increasingly, these aspects of life are sequestered in special, hygienic spaces, such as hospitals, hospices and old people's homes. Such institutions, she argues, are there to 'enable certain ideas about living, personhood and the hygienic, sanitised, somatically bounded body to be symbolically enforced and maintained'.[21] In the modern West, identity and selfhood are dependant upon the possession of a physically bounded body. In earlier cultures, she suggests, identity is more relational, and personhood less fixed and individual, more fluid and permeable. With this went a different attitude to the body and its boundaries. Where people are not thought of as having a singular authentic identity mapped on to a singular separate body, substances emitted from the body were not seen as problematic in quite the same way as they are in the contemporary Western paradigm. Unboundedness undermines modern individualistic constructions of the person as stable, bounded and autonomous. This is why body smell is particularly significant. It extends the person's corporeality in ways that intrude and seep into other's spaces. As Classen and colleagues argue, this boundary-transgressing quality acts 'to threaten the abstract and impersonal regime of modernity', running counter to the modern world-view, with its emphasis on the individual privacy of discrete, defined bodies.[22]

Are such tendencies ascetic? It is certainly the case that water and washing have long been associated with purificatory regimes in which the body is cleansed from sins, presented anew. Ascetic practices often draw on ideas of cleansing that is both bodily and spiritual. Aspects of this can be detected in the modern concern with bodily cleanliness, particularly as evinced within the closely related fields of beauty therapy and spa culture, with their deployment of ideas of cleansing, both inner and outer. But these practices occur within a different structure of ideas from that of traditional asceticism. In the case of the beauty sector they are located within discourses of pleasure, of pampering, of body pleasing rather than body denial. They are certainly never ascetic in the old sense of neglectful of the body – ragged, indifferent, dirty like desert hermits. Their focus is profoundly this-worldly. They are also strongly individualistic, centred around the well-being and pleasure of the individual – indeed the focus on the individual is a central part of their message, with their recurrent offer of 'time for you'. The hypercleanliness of modern society thus contains ambivalent elements, balanced as it is on a thin line between the impulse of asceticism and the pursuit of bodily ease.

The Body in High Modernity

The key to these cultural trends, and indeed to modern asceticism itself, is the body. Asceticism is, at its core, bodily, and that is so even where it is extended culturally to other fields such as intellectual pursuits (Chapter 9) or the architectural environment (Chapters 6 and 7). To understand it, therefore, we need to draw on the work of theorists of the body, particularly those who have explored the different ways in which it has been historically and culturally constituted. I want to discuss briefly four of these – Norbert Elias, Michel Foucault, Julia Kristeva and Bryan Turner – and suggest some of the ways in which their work alerts us to important aspects of modern asceticism in terms of refinement, discipline, the rejection of the abject and a shift to a this-worldly orientation.

Norbert Elias, in his celebrated work *The Civilising Process*, traces changes in expectations of conduct accompanying the rising threshold of shame across a range of areas: sexual behaviour, bodily functions, eating habits, table manners and violence. As a result, certain aspects of life become perceived as distasteful, and are moved behind the screens of social life, confined to new private spaces such as the bedroom and, later, bathroom. It produces, in Bourdieu's terms, a new habitus, a second nature of internalised, automatic restraint. These processes are accompanied by an increasing individualisation of the self and the body, and a growing concern with privacy, separation and distinctiveness.[23]

In relation to eating, Elias's account famously traces the arrival in the late Middle Ages of the fork and its impact on table manners, marking a culture of growing refinement and separateness in which eating with your hands or from a common dish becomes increasingly unacceptable. In relation to meat, these shifts are linked to the growth from the eighteenth century onwards of tender-mindedness towards animals. The banning of cruel sports like bear baiting; the rise of legislation around animal cruelty; the concern with slaughter regimes; and, more recently, the growing concern over factory farming: all rest on a growing internalisation of concern for animals that is part of Elias's civilising process. In terms of the presentation of food, it results in a gradual movement away from direct displays of animality, with a retreat from consumption of distinct and visible body parts such as the head, feet or brains, once openly displayed as delicacies. Joints still have their status, in the UK at least, though butcher's shops no longer display whole carcasses in the way that they once did. Modern sensibilities are more squeamish. Meat is now presented, particularly in supermarkets, in trimmed, discrete forms that sanitise its animal origins. The civilising process thus underlies a wider cultural shift in sensibility in favour of vegetarianism and the quasi-vegetarian practices that we noted earlier.

Elias's work is also relevant to changing norms around the body in relation to slimness and cleanliness, the movement towards both of these reflecting his central argument about the growth in personal refinement, and the transition from grossness in behaviour or manner. The clean, showered body of modernity is the reverse of the earlier Rabelaisian, or Breughel-like carnivalesque body, with its gross appetites that rejoiced in strong smells and body fluids, and that relished violence and sexual excess. The slimmed, toned body of the modernist ideal, with its emphasis on control, on limitation and discipline, is similarly a repudiation of these Rabelaisian appetites, part of the internalisation of the civilising process. These insights from Elias enable us to understand a key element in modern asceticism: it is never about the neglect of the body – wearing rags, having dirty, matted hair – as it has been in earlier periods, rather it is a form of asceticism that is about control and discipline, in which refinement of behaviour plays a central part.

Modern asceticism centres on disciplining the body. Here the key theorist is Michel Foucault, who perhaps of all writers has done most to alert us to the significance of the body and its cultural constitution. For Foucault, the body is never natural or given; rather, it is produced culturally, and historically, through the operation of discourses, particularly those of power/knowledge. In his early work, Foucault pursued these processes through the key institutions of the prison, the clinic and the asylum, and their related discourses of penal theory, medicine, psychiatry and sexology.[24] Power and knowledge act here as a unity, a single discursive structure that is all-pervasive and anonymous, its sites diverse and scattered. It is thus not personal, and has no defined centre, operating at a capillary level, located in a web of cultural processes.

Foucault's early work was criticised for its failure to encompass agency, but he attempted to redress this in later work through the concept of techniques of the self.[25] These allowed for a shift away from the earlier preoccupation with power, and its anonymous operation, towards a focus on processes of self-formation. He describes the techniques of the self as processes that 'permit individuals to effect by their own means or with the help of others a certain number of operations on their own bodies and souls, thoughts, conduct, and way of being, so as to transform themselves in order to attain a certain state of happiness, purity, wisdom, perfection, or immortality'. He sees his work as concerned with 'technologies of individual domination, the history of how the individual acts upon himself'.[26] Techniques of the body are thus active forms of self-formation wherein individuals apply disciplinary practices to themselves. This is a departure from the earlier emphasis on power/knowledge and its role in creating docile bodies. By such means individuals can author themselves, cultivate themselves through 'arts of existence' in such a way as to become self-determining agents. The focus on the body remains, but it is the body in interaction with the self. This analysis fits well with the practices outlined above. Diet and dieting are attempts to mould the body into a form that is acceptable to modern taste; they are about the achievement of an ideal, the accomplishment of a programme of personal self development carried forward at the level of the body and offering dreams of happiness, success, popularity and acceptance. Vegetarianism similarly offers a form of self-development, though here carried forward terms of a purer, healthier, more moral life, one that does not rest on the ingestion of cruelty and violence, or other forms of grossness of diet, and that aims to build up a purer, fresher, healthier body that supports a higher mode of being. The increasing concern with bodily hygiene also contains something of this sense of the techniques of the self, with its emphasis on self-cultivation and refinement and the creation of a cleansed, ordered body contained within its individualised boundaries.

The third writer whose work is helpful in thinking about this area is Julia Kristeva with her concept of the 'abject'. Kristeva, a poststructuralist and feminist, draws on psychoanalytic theory, particular that of Melanie Klein, in conjunction with the work of – the very different – Mary Douglas, to develop a concept of the abject. This represents that which is expelled and rejected and is, in consequence, regarded with horror or distaste.[27] Kristeva sees the abject as arising from the breakdown of meaning resulting from the loss of distinction between subject and object, self and other. Her primary example of this is one's reaction to a corpse, but human dirt and other ambiguous categories of matter can also elicit it. Abjection contains a strong threat of contamination or engulfment. In a classic psychoanalytic way, she presents this primal human response as rooted in the person's earliest experiences in relation to the mother and her body, in which the infant both desires the closeness of the maternal body and fears engulfment and the threatened eradication of the self.

Something of these feelings underlies asceticism with its desire for purity, its striving for separation and containment. Modern asceticism often seems to be about establishing control over threats of engulfment or Rabelaisian excess, and establishing order and discipline over the chaos of the body and the self. Her ideas can also help make sense of some of the gendered connections of the phenomenon, since for Kristeva the abject is closely connected with unacceptable forms of bodily femaleness. Women, as we noted, are more linked with the practices of modern asceticism. They are more likely to consciously engage in slimming and to endorse the ultra-slim and toned physique. They are more likely to adopt vegetarianism and quasi-vegetarian diets, and are symbolically connected with these forms of eating with their language of lightness, purity and freshness. These gendered connections are, as we have noted, also carried over in cultural expectations in relation to standards of hygiene and cleanliness. From a psychoanalytic viewpoint, however, such preoccupations also signal their opposite, in the threat of abjection that lies within women's bodies, the instability that arises from their flow and flux, and through which their bodies are less clearly bounded, less individually delineated than men's. As a result they may be seen as requiring more in the way of discipline and control, particularly in a culture that increasingly valorises these qualities, and in which there are rising expectations that bodies be clearly defined and individually delineated.

Lastly, I want to turn to writers whose work has addressed the body in high modernity, in particular Bryan Turner, who has argued that we need to understand the transition to high modernity in terms of a shift in focus from work on the soul to work on the body.[28] In this Turner draws on Weber's celebrated account of the Protestant ethic and the shift it produced from a focus on the specialised virtuosi religion of monasticism and priesthood to the generalised requirement that all should pursue holiness in daily life and in their secular calling. With this went a further shift towards individualism and interiority.[29] In the specifically British context, this was associated from the eighteenth century with the rise of Methodism which, in addition to its spiritual requirements, enjoined a more general sobriety in life and behaviour, exemplified in modest dress, abstemious habits and cleanliness of the person. Indeed, it was Wesley who popularised the phrase 'cleanliness is next to godliness'. In the twentieth century, with the decline in religious belief and practice, these impulses increasingly took on secular, this-worldly forms. There was a shift from work on the soul to work on the body, which became the focus of new moral requirements. Ascetic practices were no longer adopted in order to be pleasing to God, or to show obedience to his commandments, but as part of creating and shaping the body in particular ways through regimes of exercise, diet and body work. Shilling argues that in late modernity the body has become the key project, a focus of new levels of interest; with this shift in focus goes an intensification of individualisation, as people seek this-worldly forms of salvation through their bodies and the control of them.[30]

Asceticism Revisited

Asceticism is about control of the body, and through it, of the self. It rests on restraint and denial, particularly of what have at various historical times been portrayed as fleshly or animal desires. Though it can be pursued to excess, it commonly contains an impulse to moderation, a retreat from excess, particularly where this is associated with loss of control. This is frequently enshrined at a bodily level through moderation in eating and drinking, through the avoidance of stimulating or inflaming substances, through retreat from the expression of anger, aggression or sexuality. It often draws on concepts of purity that aim to extract the individual from the contamination of the world. As such it frequently deploys rituals or practices of purification, like cleansing or washing. Like all human impulses or expressions it is protean in character, capable of being found in conjunction with myriad social forms. It recurs, however, because of its nature as one of what Mary Douglas argues are 'natural symbols'; that is, expressions of social relations, typically rooted in the body, that are capable of bearing varied meanings, and that require to be interpreted in context, but that have certain recurring associations that arise from our common experience of embodiment.[31] In presenting three broad areas of modern cultural practice, I have endeavoured to show how they draw on aspects of traditional asceticism, but in ways that are new, that are consonant with the central values of the modernist project, and indeed reflect central themes within it, in particular in relation to the wider set of disciplinary practices that act to constitute the body in high modernity.

Notes

1. For a history of the slim body, see P.N. Sterns, *Fat History: Bodies and Beauty in the Modern West* (New York, 1997); H.A. Levenstein, *Paradox of Plenty: A Social History of Eating in Modern America* (Berkeley, 2003).

2. For reviews of the extensive data and literature from a UK perspective, see Government Office for Science, *Tackling Obesities*, 2nd edn (London, 2008); and Royal College of Physicians, Royal College of Paediatrics and Faculty of Public Health, *Storing Up Problems: the Medical Case for a Slimmer Nation* (London, 2004).

3. WHO, 'Obesity: Preventing and Managing the Global Epidemic', World Health Organization Technical Report Series 894 (Geneva, 2000).

4. C. Fischler, 'Food Habits, Social Change and the Nature/Culture Dilemma', *Social Science Information* 19 (1980), 937–53.

5. M. Nestle, *Food Politics: How the Food Industry Influences Nutrition and Health* (Berkeley, 2002).

6. See N. Wolf, *The Beauty Myth* (London, 1990).

7. For accounts of eating disorders, see K. Chernin, *Womansize: The Tyranny of Slenderness* (London, 1981); M. MacSween, *Anorexic Bodies: A Feminist and Sociological Perspective on Anorexia Nervosa* (London, 1993); S. Bordo, *Unbearable Weight: Feminism, Western Culture and the Body* (Berkeley, 1993); J. Hepworth, *The Social Construction of Anorexia Nervosa* (London, 1999).

8. C.W. Bynum, *Holy Feast, Holy Fast: The Religious Significance of Food to Medieval Women* (Berkeley, 1987).

9. S. Bordo, 'Anorexia Nervosa: psychopathology as the crystallisation of culture', in *Unbearable Weight*, 139-64.

10. See H. Bruch, *Eating Disorders: Obesity, Anoexia Nervosa and the Person Within* (London, 1974); S. Orbach, *Fat is a Feminist Issue* (London, 1978); M. MacSween, *Anorexic Bodies*.

11. See E. Showalter, *The Female Malady: Women, Madness and English Culture, 1830–1980* (London, 1987).

12. S. Bordo, 'Anorexia Nervosa', in *Unbearable Weight*.

13. S. Benson, 'The Body, Health and Eating Disorders', in K. Woodward (ed.), *Identity and Difference* (London, 1997), 121–82.

14. For vegetarianism, see J. Twigg, 'Vegetarianism and the Meaning of Meat', in A. Murcott (ed.), *The Sociology of Food and Eating: Essays in the Sociological Significance of Food* (Aldershot, 1983), 18–30; N. Fiddes, *Meat: A Natural Symbol* (London, 1991); A. Beardsworth and T. Keil, 'The Vegetarian Option: Varieties, Controversies, Motives and Careers', *Sociological Review* 40 (1992), 253–93; A. Beardsworth and T. Keil, *Sociology on the Menu: An Invitation to the Study of Food and Society* (London, 1997); A.C. Adams, *The Sexual Politics of Meat* (New York, 1990).

15. For accounts of the historical development of cleanliness, see G. Vigarello, *Concepts of Cleanliness: Changing Attitudes in France since the Middle Ages* (Cambridge, 1988); J.P. Goubert, *The Conquest of Water* (Cambridge, 1986); N. Tomes, *The Gospel of Germs: Men, Women and the Microbe in American Life* (Cambridge MA, 1998); J. Twigg, *Bathing: The Body and Community Care* (London, 2000); V. Smith, *Clean: A History of Personal Hygiene and Purity* (Oxford, 2007).

16. See G. Vigarello, *Concepts of Cleanliness*.

17. A. Corbin, *The Foul and the Fragrant: Odour and the French Social Imagination* (Leamington Spa, 1986); C. Classen, *Worlds of Sense: Exploring the Senses in History and Across Cultures* (London, 1993).

18. M. Jay, 'Scopic Regimes of Modernity', in H. Foster (ed.), *Vision and Visuality* (Seattle, 1988), 3–23.

19. P. Öberg, 'The Absent Body: A Social Gerontological Paradox', *Ageing and Society* 16 (1996), 701–19.

20. J. Lawton, 'Contemporary Hospice Care: The Sequestration of the Unbounded Body and "Dirty Dying"', *Sociology of Health and Illness* 20 (1998), 121–43.

21. Ibid., 123.

22. C. Classen, D. Howes and A. Synott, *Aroma: The Cultural History of Smell* (London, 1994), 5.

23. N. Elias, *The Civilizing Process: The History of Manners* (Oxford, 1978); S. Mennell, *All Manners of Food: Eating and Taste in England and France from the Middle Ages to the Present* (Oxford, 1985), elaborates Elias's ideas in relation to food. For Bourdieu's notion of habitus, see P. Bourdieu, *Outline of a Theory of Practice* (Cambridge, 1977).

24. M. Foucault, *Madness and Civilisation: A History of Insanity in the Age of Reason* (London, 1971); M. Foucault, *The Birth of the Clinic: An Archaeology of Medical Perception* (London, 1973); M. Foucault, *Discipline and Punish: The Birth of the Prison* (Harmondsworth, 1977); M. Foucault, *The History of Sexuality: Introduction, Vol. 1* (Harmondsworth, 1979); M. Foucault, *The Uses of Pleasure: The History of Sexuality, Vol. 2* (Harmondsworth, 1987); M. Foucault, *The Care of the Self: The History of Sexuality, Vol. 3* (Harmondsworth, 1988).

25. M. Foucault, 'Technologies of the self', in L.M. Martin, H. Gutman and P.H. Hutton (eds), *Technologies of the Self: A Seminar with Michel Foucault* (London, 1988), 16–49.

26. Ibid., 18.

27. J. Kristeva, *Powers of Horror: An Essay on Abjection* (New York, 1982).

28. For the body in high modernity, see B.S. Turner, *The Body and Society: Explorations in Social Theory*, 2nd edn (Oxford, 1996); M. Featherstone, M. Hepworth and

B.S. Turner (eds), *The Body: Social Process and Cultural Theory* (London, 1991); C. Shilling, *The Body and Social Theory* (London, 1993); S.J. Williams and G. Bendelow, *The Lived Body: Sociological Themes, Embodied Issues* (London, 1998); P.A. Mellor and C. Shilling, *Re-forming the Body: Religion, Community and Modernity* (London, 1997).

29. M. Weber, *The Protestant Ethic.*
30. C. Schilling, *The Body and Social Theory,* 4-8 ff.
31. M. Douglas, *Natural Symbols* (Harmondsworth, 1970).

References

Adams, C.J. 1990. *The Sexual Politics of Meat,* New York.

Beardsworth, A., and T. Keil. 1992. 'The Vegetarian Option: Varieties, Controversies, Motives and Careers', *Sociological Review* 40 (2): 253–93.

——— 1997. *Sociology on the Menu: An Invitation to the Study of Food and Society,* London.

Benson, S. 1997. 'The Body, Health and Eating Disorders', in K. Woodward (ed.), *Identity and Difference,* London, pp.121–82.

Bordo, S. 1993. *Unbearable Weight: Feminism, Western Culture and the Body.* Berkeley.

Bourdieu, P. 1977. *Outline of a Theory of Practice,* Cambridge.

Bruch, H. 1974. *Eating Disorders: Obesity, Anorexia Nervosa and the Person Within,* London.

Bynum, C.W. 1987. *Holy Feast, Holy Fast: The Religious Significance of Food to Medieval Women,* Berkeley.

Chernin, K. 1981. *Womansize: The Tyranny of Slenderness,* London.

Classen, C. 1993. *Worlds of Sense: Exploring the Senses in History and Across Cultures,* London.

Classen, C., D. Howes and A. Synott. 1994. *Aroma: The Cultural History of Smell,* London.

Corbin, A. 1986. *The Foul and the Fragrant: Odour and the French Social Imagination,* Leamington Spa.

Douglas, M. 1970. *Natural Symbols,* Harmondsworth.

Elias, N. 1978. *The Civilizing Process: The History of Manners,* Oxford.

Featherstone, M., M. Hepworth and B.S. Turner (eds). 1991. *The Body: Social Process and Cultural Theory,* London.

Fiddes, N. 1991. *Meat: A Natural Symbol,* London.

Fischler, C. 1980. 'Food Habits, Social Change and the Nature/Culture Dilemma', *Social Science Information* 19(6): 937–53.

Foucault, M. 1971. *Madness and Civilisation: A History of Insanity in the Age of Reason,* London.

——— 1973. *The Birth of the Clinic: An Archaeology of Medical Perception,* London.

——— 1977. *Discipline and Punish: The Birth of the Prison,* Harmondsworth.

——— 1979. *The History of Sexuality, Vol. 1: Introduction,* Harmondsworth.

——— 1987. *The Uses of Pleasure: The History of Sexuality, Vol. 2,* Harmondsworth.

——— 1988. *The Care of the Self: The History of Sexuality, Vol. 3,* Harmondsworth.

——— 1988. 'Technologies of the Self', in L.M. Martin, H. Gutman and P.H. Hutton (eds), *Technologies of the Self: A Seminar with Michel Foucault*, London, pp.16–49.

Goubert, J.P. 1986. *The Conquest of Water*, Cambridge.

Government Office for Science. 2008. *Tackling Obesities*, 2nd edn, London.

Hepworth, J. 1999. *The Social Construction of Anorexia Nervosa*, London.

Jay, M. 1988. 'Scopic Regimes of Modernity', in H. Foster (ed.), *Vision and Visuality*, Seattle, pp.3–23.

Kristeva, J. 1982. *Powers of Horror: An Essay on Abjection*, New York.

Lawton, J. 1998. 'Contemporary Hospice Care: The Sequestration of the Unbounded Body and "Dirty Dying"', *Sociology of Health and Illness* 20(2): 121–43.

Levenstein, H.A. 2003. *Paradox of Plenty: A Social History of Eating in Modern America*, Berkeley.

MacSween, M. 1993. *Anorexic Bodies: A Feminist and Sociological Perspective on Anorexia Nervosa*, London.

Mellor, P.A., and C. Shilling. 1997. *Re-forming the Body: Religion, Community and Modernity*, London.

Mennell, S. 1985. *All Manners of Food: Eating and Taste in England and France from the Middle Ages to the Present*, Oxford.

Nestle, M. 2002. *Food Politics: How the Food Industry Influences Nutrition and Health*, Berkeley.

Öberg, P. 1996. 'The Absent Body: A Social Gerontological Paradox', *Ageing and Society* 16(6): 701–19.

Orbach, S. 1978. *Fat is a Feminist Issue*, London.

Royal College of Physicians, Royal College of Paediatrics and Faculty of Public Health. 2004. *Storing Up Problems: the Medical Case for a Slimmer Nation*, London.

Shilling, C. 1993. *The Body and Social Theory*, London.

Showalter, E. 1987. *The Female Malady: Women, Madness and English Culture, 1830–1980*, London.

Smith, V. 2007. *Clean: A History of Personal Hygiene and Purity*, Oxford.

Sterns, P.N. 1997. *Fat History: Bodies and Beauty in the Modern West*, New York.

Tomes, N. 1998. *The Gospel of Germs: Men, Women and the Microbe in American Life*, Cambridge MA.

Turner, B.S. 1996. *The Body and Society: Explorations in Social Theory*, 2nd edn, Oxford.

Twigg, J. 1983. 'Vegetarianism and the Meaning of Meat', in A. Murcott (ed.), *The Sociology of Food and Eating: Essays in the Sociological Significance of Food*, Aldershot, pp.18–30.

——— 2000. *Bathing: The Body and Community Care*, London.

Vigarello, G. 1988. *Concepts of Cleanliness: Changing Attitudes in France since the Middle Ages*, Cambridge.

Weber, M. [1976]. *The Protestant Ethic and the Spirit of Capitalism*. London.

WHO. 2000. 'Obesity: Preventing and Managing the Global Epidemic', World Health Organization Technical Report Series 894, Geneva.

Williams, S.J., and G. Bendelow. 1998. *The Lived Body: Sociological Themes, Embodied Issues*, London.

Wolf, N. 1990. *The Beauty Myth*, London.

Notes on Contributors

Marnix Beyen teaches contemporary political history at the University of Antwerp. He has published on Dutch and Belgian historiography during the Second World War, intellectual history, political culture, and on thinking in terms of race in science and politics before the Second World War.

Sofie De Caigny received her Ph.D. in history from the University of Leuven and is currently working at the Flemish Architecture Institute. Her scholarly research interests lie in gender studies and architectural history and theory. She has published on the relationship between architectural theory, interior design and living culture during the interwar period in Flanders.

Henk de Smaele teaches contemporary cultural history at the University of Antwerp. His scholarly research interests include gender history, the history of sexuality, political history and the history of political theory.

Lesley Hall is currently working at the Wellcome Library for the History and Understanding of Medicine in London. She has published on various aspects of the history of gender and sexuality in the nineteenth and twentieth centuries, including *Outspoken Women: An Anthology of Women's Writing on Sex, 1870–1969* (2005).

Michael Hau is senior lecturer in history at Monash University. His publications include *The Cult of Health and Beauty in Germany: A Social History, 1890–1930* (2003), and he is currently working on a cultural history of performance in Weimar and Nazi Germany.

Wessel Krul teaches cultural history at the University of Groningen. His research interests lie in the history of art and culture in Europe from the eighteenth to the twentieth century. His publications include an annotated translation of Edmund Burke's *A Philosophical Enquiry into the Origin of our Ideas of the Sublime and Beautiful* (2004).

Evert Peeters received his Ph.D. in history from the University of Leuven, where he is currently working as a postdoctoral research fellow. He has published on *Lebensreform* in the late nineteenth and early twentieth century and on historiography and nationalism in early nineteenth-century Belgium.

Tom Saunders teaches at the Department of History at the University of Victoria. His general area of research is Germany between the wars. His major thematic concerns are culture and society; the interaction between cinema, business, the state, and the press; and the significance of public scandal for the political process. He is the author of *Hollywood in Berlin: American Cinema and Weimar Germany* (1994).

Julia Twigg is professor of social policy and sociology at the University of Kent. Her research interests centre on the body and its management. Her doctoral research was a sociological and historical study of vegetarianism in the UK from 1839 to the present, and she has recently published *The Body in Health and Social Care* (2006).

Klaas van Berkel is professor of post-medieval cultural history at the University of Groningen. His research interests are mainly in the field of international intellectual history, and the history of science and universities in the Netherlands. He is editor of *A History of Science in the Netherlands: Survey, Themes and Reference* (1999).

Leen Van Molle teaches contemporary social history at the University of Leuven. Her main research interests are in rural and gender history. She has recently published work on Belgian women entrepreneurs, the history of co-operative banking, and an overview of recent research on rural history in the North Sea area.

Kaat Wils teaches contemporary cultural history at the University of Leuven. Her research focuses on the gendered history of medicine and the human sciences in the nineteenth and twentieth centuries, and on nineteenth-century positivism and intellectual culture.